Interrogating Cultural Studies

R43381

D1609944

Interrogating Cultural Studies

Theory, Politics and Practice

Edited by
Paul Bowman

Pluto  Press
LONDON • STERLING, VIRGINIA

First published 2003 by Pluto Press
345 Archway Road, London N6 5AA
and 22883 Quicksilver Drive,
Sterling, VA 20166–2012, USA

www.plutobooks.com

British Library Cataloguing in Publication Data
A catalogue record for this book is available from the British Library

ISBN 0 7453 1715 4 hardback
ISBN 0 7453 1714 6 paperback

Library of Congress Cataloging in Publication Data
Interrogating cultural studies : theory, politics, and practice /
  edited by Paul Bowman.
    p. cm.
  Includes bibliographical references and index.
  ISBN 0–7453–1715–4 (hbk) — ISBN 0–7453–1714–6 (pbk)
  1. Culture—Study and teaching. 2. Culture—Study and
teaching—Interviews. I. Bowman, Paul, 1971– .
HM623.I58 2003
306'.071—dc21
                                                         2002010233

306
BoW

10   9   8   7   6   5   4   3   2   1

Designed and produced for Pluto Press by
Chase Publishing Services, Fortescue, Sidmouth EX10 9QG
Typeset from disk by Stanford DTP Services, Towcester
Printed and bound in the European Union
by Antony Rowe, Chippenham and Eastbourne, England

Contents

Acknowledgements

This book would not have happened were it not for my friend, Mark Little, of the University of Northumbria. The idea was born in conversation with him, we discussed ideas and deliberated who to invite, together. I am indebted to him for his support, intellectual stimulation and friendship during its preparation. No less importantly, I am grateful to Anne Beech at Pluto Press, just as I owe thanks to every one of the contributors to this collection, all of whom deemed it worthwhile enough to devote a lot of time and energy to. Thanks also to Alison Rowley, who carried out one of the interviews; and to Diane Elam, Sue Golding, Gary Hall, and Joanna Zylinska, all of whom have helped me to do this in various ways. Margaret Shaw, Head of Media and Cultural Studies at BSUC, worked timetabling wonders to help me out, and Fiona Montgomery, Head of School, provided some financial support for me to carry out a couple of the interviews. Many thanks to Barbara Engh for pointing me in this direction in the first place, years ago. Above all, though, I am indebted to my wife, Alice. Any errors, oversights, deficiencies, or faux pas, either of (inevitable mis)representation in the various introductions, or in the organisation and editing overall are, I hope, entirely my own.

1   Introduction: Interrogating Cultural Studies

Paul Bowman

MISREPRESENTATION, MISCONSTRUAL

Few, if any, entire academic fields have attracted more consistently febrile attention than cultural studies. It has always received criticism, invective, vituperation; often angry, often confused and confusing (mis)representations of what it is, what it does, and why it goes about things the ways it does. It has also, of course, had its fair share of celebration, (over)indulgent congratulation and flattery. These two types of reaction entail each other: if cultural studies has often announced itself as being somehow messianic or at least deeply consequential – 'radical', 'revolutionary', 'emancipatory', and so on – then it is surely inevitable that those who are not involved who often, obliquely or directly, find themselves to be the objects of its cutting critiques, will protest. On reflection, more or less everyone else in the university, every other discipline, has at one or another time been critiqued, criticised, even excoriated, by cultural studies. Those in the 'old' arts and humanities disciplines, those in the sciences, those who are involved in anything even remotely uncritical of things like 'capitalism' and 'patriarchy' have regularly found themselves accused of being not only old fashioned and out of date (hurtful and offensive enough accusations in themselves), but also to be responsible for perpetuating such evils as sexism, racism, elitism, ethnocentrism, Eurocentrism, homophobia, right-wing conservatism, capitalist domination, social exclusion, and so on. When they retort that, actually, no, they do not believe themselves to be evil ministers of all forms of domination, exploitation, and exclusion, a chorus of cultural studies critics unequivocally reply: 'Oh yes you are, you just don't understand the ways in which you are.'[1]

Celebration and condemnation are entailed from the outset. And in many respects, this has become the dominant form of debate around cultural studies, a discourse that has become something like a merry-go-round, or a pantomime (albeit one which may well have profoundly serious consequences). Cultural theorists of the notion of 'performativity', who argue that there is emancipatory potential in everyone's propensity to 'perform' (and hence establish) different social identities, which might thereby transform the socio-political world, could perhaps do worse than to work out a way for cultural studies to step out of the pantomime-like, discursive black hole within which it has become embroiled. Amusing as 'What you're doing is bad!', 'Oh no it isn't!'; 'Oh yes it is!', 'Oh no it isn't!', can be for any young subject, surely one must grow out of it, or grow stale and pathetic. Needless to say, of course, this state of affairs is not simply something internal to cultural studies: it's not exclusively its own fault, it does take two to tango. But if cultural studies is content to blame and decry others (who in turn criticise and deride it) for the lamentable quality of these academic exchanges, then, you could say, it has no one to blame but itself.

This book was conceived with a view to attempting to transform the terms of the debate, and to do so paradoxically by reiterating some extremely traditional questions. My belief is that the historically necessary and once vitally effective 'high polemical moment' of cultural studies has today become less than enabling, and more of an encumbrance. The radical polemics of the past have passed. Of course, what they concern has not been completed, finished, or exhausted. That is not what I'm suggesting. Cultural studies is indeed an incomplete project. However, just because evidence abounds of the continued proliferation of its chosen problematics, that does not mean that its own traditional strategies, or its standard ways of trying to intervene, have not become tired. What demands more attention today is the modality or manner of cultural studies' efforts. The Foucauldian lessons about the need to repeat, in as many contexts and places as possible, that which you want to become laid down as 'true' in the 'hearts and minds' of the many, isn't much justification for this repetition when what is predominantly getting repeated is a fevered and systematically misrepresentative farce. What is repeated, regularly and in dispersion, are not simply the lessons of cultural studies (its intended messages), but rather their 'reception': not what they 'in themselves' articulate, but how they become articulated *as* something within a wider discursive context, for a wider audience.

Of course, we cannot ultimately control how what we say is received, nor how we ourselves are represented. But, of course, we also can. If not 'ultimately', then at least in certain contexts, in certain scenes, at certain times. Perhaps not 'in the heat of the moment', as it were, as in the initial polemical explosion of cultural studies' appearance as part of a larger 'discursive formation' of basically very angry political and cultural movements. But perhaps one can begin to consider what one looks like to your interlocutors, if not when the flames themselves are under control, then at least when one's relationship with the task becomes more structured, more regular. The present moment of cultural studies' familiarity – its familiarity to itself and to its others[2] – by virtue of its very predictability, affords a unique opportunity for reassessment, and hence a new chance for revivification. What does the face cultural studies presents to the world look like and signify, and what reactions will that presence most likely elicit? There have got to be different ways of making something present, presenting ourselves, our case. But of course, I do not wish to simplify things. The polemical force of cultural studies' accusations about the largely unrecognised political aspects inextricably entailed by all forms of pursuits of knowledge, and (perhaps) all forms of cultural practice, was eminently valuable, and must never be devalued or forgotten. The battles should certainly be memorialised, revisited. There is a value in taking the kids to the pantomime, as it were, and in studying it; a need to rake and re-rake through the lessons of this history; for, as John Mowitt has argued, 'what we believe to have happened to us bears concretely on what we are prepared to do with ourselves both now and in the future, [and] the formation of such a memory is inseparable from historical, and ultimately political, practice'.[3]

Today, is cultural studies' responsibility really just a straightforward process of pointing out the deficiencies of its academic others?[4] True, such work has effects. But perhaps they are not so straightforwardly transformative, radical or emancipatory as they are often claimed to be, or as it was once thought they might be. One of the unintended consequences of cultural studies' polemical elaboration might well be its having become the unknowing participant in a repetitive and increasingly normal pantomime, that has been misrecognised or misdiagnosed, believed to be 'crucial' or 'central', but which may well be off the mark. Of course, the repetition of something that appears to be the 'same' will also be different each time it occurs: polemicists will necessarily modify their positions, changes will occur. But one of these changes is also the growing institutionalisation of cultural studies itself. And if it is institutionalised as an acceptable actor in nothing more than a novel academic pantomime, then is this really all it could or should be?

I do not want to become too skewed by the effects of thinking in terms of metaphors and facile analogies of the carnivalesque: the idea of figuring the contemporary scene as a pantomime now threatens to dominate my entire efforts to think cultural studies' relation to the other disciplines and institutions.[5] So, to echo more than one contributor to this collection, the question, first of all, is *how* to conceive of cultural studies: which metaphors have structured its history; which metaphors has it, does it, should it, 'live through', and what effects have these had on what it can see, think, know and be inclined to do? There are many other metaphors, equally suggestive. One can think of cultural studies as the incessant irritant, the annoying little parasite that won't shut up and leave everyone else alone; that speaks out, that shouts too loud, that may well therefore be unknowingly placing itself in more and more jeopardy, actually becoming more threatened to the extent that it threatens or is capable of threatening – in short, more literally endangering its life to the extent that it is institutionalised and apparently 'stable'. This idea is contrary to the way that most people interpret its growing institutionalisation. But perhaps establishing a greater institutional stability for cultural studies actually conceals its fragility, or the increasing likelihood of its demise. So what form should or must its apparently growing 'stability' take?

One idea has always been that its proliferation reduces its ability to be cutting edge, radical or transformative. But what edges need to be cut now anyway? And is it, indeed, as valuable, urgent, radical and transformative as it sometimes claims; or is this its delusion, its ideology? The mainstays of the regulative fictions of cultural studies have always been its (fetishistic?) attachments to the marginal, the abject, and to 'resistance'. Perhaps this is why it fears 'success': as this would call its bluff, blow its cover. Is the 'proper' cultural studies world view nothing more than an expression of its resentment? And, in any eventuality, what is the relation between its regulative fictions and its academico-political potential? Is its growing stability and proliferation helpful or deleterious to its ethico-political aims and intentions? Are its aims and intentions 'realistic'? Need they be? What relation do its conscious intentions have to the consequences or effects its existence and activities have produced, wittingly or unwittingly? Is it friend or foe to the status quo, what actually is that status quo, and does cultural studies risk its own life, or guarantee itself a future, through its actions? What kind of future might it have?

This book poses 'traditional cultural studies questions' on these themes, not simply to clarify what cultural studies is about, has achieved, has not achieved, could do, cannot do, should try to do, etc., but also to convey a sense of its stakes, its urgency. The book is not so much 'what is cultural studies?' as 'why cultural studies?' and 'how cultural studies?' Of course, any answers to any such question imply answers to the others, and open out onto potentially ever more. I wanted to frame things or tether this down, so as to reduce the potentially interminable slippage of one question into another, in terms of the question(s) of *institution*. This is perhaps 'arbitrary' and inessential, but current and currently vital and vitalising nevertheless.

Does a more stabilised cultural studies amount to a neutralisation of its potential or a strengthening? Does it become, as it were, hypocritical: claiming radicality whilst yet policing its own instituted orthodoxy, imposing codes and conventions of propriety, and being an agent of the disciplinary power that it always claimed to challenge? Or does its 'success' both rely on and produce what it has always been accused of: namely, its 'Mickey Mouse' status, its indiscriminate studying of anything (including Mickey Mouse); a strategy chosen or perpetuated conveniently and/or cynically perhaps *just because* it is popular, *and just to keep it popular* (because disciplines need students)? Is it that, actually, it effaces its own pointlessness and political and intellectual ineffectuality, providing spurious token justifications for its own existence by invoking alibis about 'political engagement', 'resistance to domination', 'ethical relations to alterity', etc., which are utterly without substance?

Those who attack cultural studies often present some version of this argument. These representations are too easy to make. Fortunately, though, their sophistry, amphibology and tendentiousness are also incredibly easy to demonstrate. However, what if there is *something* in it? For, actually, very many people involved in cultural studies do indeed see this as a real threat. It is possible to discern, in some places and in some of its manifestations, a drifting away from the traditional, initial and initialising, *injunctions of* cultural studies. In some incarnations, the practice, object and orientation of cultural studies have become the simple celebration of popular culture, subculture, cyberculture, technology, obscurantism, etc., matched by a *depoliticising* of its agenda; as if, while the name remains the same, its initial, formative, 'authentic' or authenticating identity or project has been evacuated, denuded, obscured, or more and more erased. It's as if cultural studies is forgetting or losing the sense, not of what it once was, but of what it was once meant to be(come). Many voices within cultural studies, from old-guard stalwarts to 'new radicals', see some important threads being severed *or* fruitlessly strung out, attachments to crucial lineages and orientations waning *or* growing sclerotic, and the traits of cultural studies mutating (even if that mutation takes the form of a new sedulous refusal to change), such that a commitment to 'its' 'own' 'proper' historical manifestos, remits, and enlivening/frustrating problematics have been abandoned, or have become pretexts for pointless playing.

The sense is one of an increasing abandonment of a particular *kind* of relationship to the enlivening and identity-conferring problematics of cultural studies: the perhaps interminably intractable contradictions, aporias and antagonisms that are thrown up when one not only wants to know the whys and wherefores of culture, history, the ascription of value, the determinants of desire, the constitution of subjectivity, the logic of the economy (and the economy of logic), the problems of truth, knowledge and power, politics, subject-and-structure (the question of agency), but when one unremittingly also pays attention to the implications of acknowledging one's own intractable imbrication within it all. The accusation is of there having been an abandonment of the very *problematic of* cultural studies (in all the senses that the expression 'the *problematic of* cultural studies' can connote).

To the extent that different interlocutors in these debates (if a debate exists, if 'debate' is not a misnomer for what is taking place) might listen to and hear each other, it would in fact be a very valuable thing. The idea of questioning, engaging in dialogues that critique each other and hence forward knowledge, attempt to establish what's right, what's wrong, what's best, and what the consequences of various positions are, is a core part of cultural studies' desire, or myth – its desire to 'intervene', its desire to 'make a difference'. The idea of a productive dispute, a debate across fields, contexts, disciplines and practices, is part of the very dream of cultural studies. But what if no one ever actually receives the intended message of anyone else's critique? Surely, given the multitude of different and perhaps mutually untranslatable languages, language games, the language of one discipline or group cannot hope to be intelligible in the language of another – even, and perhaps *especially*, when they both sound and look the 'same'. Who could possibly be authorised to translate and adjudicate? Obviously, given the unlikelihood of everyone mastering the language games and competencies of all disciplines,[6] a state of 'disagreement'[7] is inevitable. But we don't even need to go that far: what is the likelihood that everyone within cultural studies understands the 'same' things the 'same' way? What does it portend when people use the same words, but understand very different things by them?

This was one of my initial questions. This book was conceived as a very straightforward way to find out what people understand by some of the key terms of cultural studies, to see what the variety of answers to the questions would be, to enable one to begin to work out what this proliferation (consensus or dissensus) enables or scuppers. At the very least, the idea was that everyone so inclined would be able to find in this book a way to get a better sense of what, why and how the discipline is about. I believe that this book does constitute precisely this sort of good way *in*, for those who want or need one; and indeed, by the same token, that it will *offer a good way out* of that dimension of circular, boring and predictable febrile (non-)debate that, perversely, structures so much stupidity into the heart of the dominant debates about the university and the production of knowledge.

(MIS)CONSTRUCTION, (DIS)ORGANISATION: A NOTE ON THE TEXT

This book also seeks to show the lie of a growing myth. This is the tacit assumption that there is an inevitable and necessary distinction between two 'kinds' of academic book. On the one hand, there are 'textbooks' geared towards an introductory readership, designed specifically and only for teaching the things that are well established within a discipline. On the other, there are books that are aimed at, written by, and designed for advanced researchers – more innovative, trailblazing, 'difficult' explorations. The sense is that, for some under-interrogated reason, never the twain shall meet – as if the distinction is inescapably necessary and absolutely inevitable. I conceived of this book, however, with the hypothesis that this distinction and division of disciplinary space need not necessarily be the case for a subject like cultural studies, a subject that otherwise consistently views itself as trailblazing through and through, and not just at its own 'cutting edge' or 'outer margins'. For, as more than one of our contributors argue, there are all sorts of institutional, political and economic reasons why such distinctions ever creep quietly into being in the first place.

Such a trifling issue as this may hardly seem to warrant attention. But the point is that many, if not all, distinctions, features, characteristics, 'commonsensical' intuitions about how things are, and 'obvious' understandings about the way things should be and how everyone 'must' go about doing and thinking things – all those things that might on first glance appear either quite trivial, inevitable, or both – may well be consequences of political, ideological, economic and cultural factors or movements, which will themselves have political, ideological, economic and cultural consequences. So, the very fact that there is a belief in the necessary and inevitable differentiation between introductory and advanced books might well be a symptom and expression of the growing institutionalisation of cultural studies, and a contradiction in (its own) terms. So what are the implications for a practice that always claimed to seek to intervene in cultural and political issues and struggles, when it becomes compartmentalised, standardised, professionalised, domesticated, and divided? (And conquered?)

Such questions as these, questions about the workings and internal affairs of an academic subject, may also appear to be secondary or supplementary to the primary questions of the real, urgent, acute or chronic political and cultural events and phenomena 'out there' that cultural studies has always claimed to be overwhelmingly concerned to understand and intervene in. But again, these secondary questions are actually primary. For, the question of the institutionalisation of anything is always political, and always has real consequences: how is it organised, arranged, elaborated? What goes and what cannot go, for what reasons, and why? What consequences does the form it takes have for what it can and cannot do? What limits does its institutionally accepted form place on what it is and does? For, the *way* in which those who study culture are institutionalised, orientated, motivated, policed and demarcated, determines an awful lot about what they can possibly know about the objects of their attention – and this is both an important academic and political matter.

That is to say, if you are blinkered in a certain way, or unknowingly motivated by certain biases and prejudices, then this cannot but have effects on what you can 'know', what you will be able to 'see', what you will be inclined to 'do'. This is why this book has privileged the apparently secondary matter of cultural studies *itself,* as opposed to any particular thing that cultural studies might choose to study. Now this is *not* a theme that is exclusively either introductory or advanced, either historical or cutting edge, either mainstream or radical for cultural studies. It is its mainstay, stock trade, defining characteristic, even its lifeblood. My contention is that the questions animating this book are both as basic and as advanced, as originary and as contemporary as cultural studies can be. You may not agree. Certainly these assertions imply a certain exclusive (excluding) definition of cultural studies; and accordingly, the exclusion of certain possible definitions and forms of what cultural studies might otherwise possibly be. This might mean I have transgressed cultural studies' own traditional claims about its 'inclusiveness', its 'openness', its own refusal to be defined or pinned down to an object or approach.

But these normal cultural studies claims of openness, inclusivity, and the refusal to be defined, efface their own impossibility. To claim that cultural studies is simply open, inclusive, indefinable, and so on, may be something of its preferred fantasy, one that, if accepted (as if 'simple'), entails refusing to see that openness itself excludes: it excludes closure, or it includes it. It cannot *simply* be open. And the idea of its inclusivity harbours the undecidable problem of whether to exclude or include exclusion, and which way any exclusion or inclusion would be most inclusively done. Also, of course, any refusal to be defined will be done in some definitive kind of way, and is already somewhat definitive, limiting, exclusionary and enclosing.[8]

The simple advocation of these ideals can become a self-aggrandising or self-satisfied and complacent ideology – which would make cultural studies into the very thing it would least like to be. For this would imply its own unknowing complicity with certain forms of cultural, political and historical power. In other words, it would mean that it remained ignorant of the very things it is supposed to know all about. However, on the other hand, the insistence that cultural studies *should* be open, inclusive, indefinable, and so on, can still be advocated, as a *problematic* and hence generative, regulative and critical ideal, which might prove politically and culturally valuable in any number of ways. The very fact that such notions are riven with contradictions, problems, uncertainty and undecidability suggests perhaps the fundamental vitality of cultural studies. So, yes, this book has deliberately staged and set up a closed and exclusive defining sense of cultural studies, positing the presupposition that it could not and would not *be* cultural studies if it were not primarily political (both preoccupied with the political, and itself political, through and through). This was both to find out in what ways this presupposition might be justified and in what ways it has effects. It was also, of course, to find out what cultural studies *means* when it speaks of 'the political'.

This task is important at all levels. Researchers and teachers, whilst finding much that may be familiar in these pages, will also find plenty that will be new, whether in the content or in the conjunction, the juxtapositions. The book consists of brand new statements on common but inexhaustible themes from the unique viewpoints of each of the key thinkers (from within and around cultural studies) gathered together here. Students will find much that is entirely new to them. Some interviews, and some sections of all the interviews, will prove immediately intelligible, some more complex, and some apparently impenetrable. But all weave the familiar and the unfamiliar together in ways that will develop every reader's own thinking and understanding in untold directions. Not all of the contributions are as user-friendly as the student might initially like; not all of them are as complex as the more advanced reader might initially like. But, given the accessibility of the interview form, and given that they are all constructed around the same set of questions, at the very least the similarities and differences will stimulate and engender much, in ways that I cannot pretend to predict.

The interviews can be tackled in any order. The book is polyvocal and intertextual – or hypertextual, if you prefer. But it is hypertextual without imposing actual hyperlinks or other such signposts to guide or control your navigation – for such signposts, while apparently helpful, are ultimately also limiting, as they also work to place a structure, to place limits, on the range of possible connections and meanings that could be produced. Of course, I have arranged the interviews into an order that suggested itself in terms of giving the book a certain form and rhythm. I hope that this does not overcode, over-categorise, irritate or offend. In arranging the book, I conceived of it as being primarily in conversation with itself. I did not look outside these pages, into the archives of historical polemics and movements within and around cultural studies in order to determine some proper order into which they should or could otherwise be placed. Instead, I merely identified some striking ways in which each chapter referred to others. But each refers, relates, to all of the others in some way: every one sheds new light on aspects that may have been occluded or difficult in another, or problematises and complicates aspects that one or another interview might have presented as being certain and straightforward. I arranged them into a kind of conversation that I liked the shape of. I did this to try to guide, a little, but not too much. For, as Thomas Docherty argues in his interview,

> education should be of the nature of the event: the Docherty who is there after reading and thinking about Joyce or Proust or Rilke or Woolf is different from the Docherty who was there before that activity; but the earlier Docherty could never have predicted what the later one might think – that was the point of the exercise of reading in the first place: to think things that were previously undreamt of in my philosophy.

Whether undergraduate or professor (friend or foe; or indeed, even the academic and publishing industry's much fantasised hypothetical 'interested general reader'), this book cannot but be thought-provoking and beneficial to everyone's necessary continued education. Each statement and argument overlaps, complements, contrasts with, or contradicts those of other contributors, so that the reader will acquire a strong sense of both the common ground, community, and the conflicts that constitute the disciplinary space in and around cultural studies, as well as a strong sense of the stakes of cultural studies itself. That is to say, teachers will find it valuable for teaching, students will find it valuable for studying, and researchers will find here a unique research archive in its own right.

These grand sounding claims can be made for very straightforward reasons. It is not just that any text lends itself to a potentially infinite range of readings and readerships, in the way that a text can be made legible, intelligible, interesting and important both to young children and to the world's most eminent philosophers (like *Hamlet* is, for example), or the way in which certain texts have both an immediate force, accessible to almost all, and a subtle complexity that is available upon ever more rigorous reading (like *The Communist Manifesto*). It is rather because, firstly, the book poses the same direct questions to very different thinkers. The questions themselves are basically reiterations of some of the main things that cultural studies academics have pondered for years, questions on the day-to-day issues enlivening cultural studies, questions you might assume could be 'taken as read', for cultural studies. Whilst the questions might now be taken as read, the answers never can be. Hence the need to keep reiterating the questions.

Secondly, because the book takes the form of interviews with figures from different 'fields' within and around cultural studies, each interview elicits responses to these basic questions in terms of the specific expertise, interests and experience of each interviewee. In this way, the book also introduces even more of the field's diversity, and orients and aids the understanding of even the most 'difficult' or 'obscure' argument by virtue of the direct and explicit nature of the questions. Even where a passage might be extremely difficult, the reader should always be able to work through it by recourse and reference to the question that inspired or provoked it. Even though not all of the chapters explicitly contain the questions, they were all inspired by them.[9]

In selecting who to invite to participate in this collection, I was not unduly preoccupied with questions of hierarchy, lineage, affiliation and canonicity. I did not attempt to find the 'best' representatives of 'the proper canon' of cultural studies. That seemed to me to be a very un-cultural studies thing to do, even though, perhaps, the inevitable desire. The paradox is that those trailblazers who first worked (among other things) to deconstruct so many institutions and canons inevitably became institutionally famous and canonical themselves. Also, of course, thereby the best people to ask. But that is to formulate it in a simplistic way: there is no *one* canon, there is no *one* consensus. That's the whole point. And even if there was, my interest and aim was more to do with constructing a sense of the diversity of the field – more specifically, with trying to collect a group of diverse, complementary, contradictory, at times utterly incompatible thinkers, in order to establish what different conceptions of 'the political dimensions of institutionalised cultural studies' currently animate thinking and acting within, across and around cultural studies. In order to try to stir things up a bit, I also invited people whose work is self-consciously defined as other than cultural studies, but which, perhaps for that very reason, is nevertheless important and valuable to it.

Criticising cultural studies is too important to leave to anti-cultural studies polemicists. It is infinitely more important, informative and helpful when it comes from those who know what they are talking about, those who have immersed themselves in it, rather than those who, at the very mention of cultural studies, wrinkle their noses as if having just spotted a brown stain on a hotel towel. As I have indicated, cultural studies is misconstrued and mis-represented at every turn. Most criticisms of it are so febrile and misinformed as to be hilarious, were it not for the fact that every major misconstrual and tendentious misrepresentation may well place the subject in jeopardy. So I did deliberately court critique and polemic, but from those who *know and think*, rather than from those who think they know but believe this without actually ever bothering to read nor taking the time and effort to try to understand the complexity and stakes of it all. So this book is far from a cele-bration or simplification of cultural studies. If anything, it is a sustained complexification staged by inviting some very different scholars to respond, in any way they chose, to these seven questions:

(1) How do you position yourself and your work in relation to the cultural studies project? Or, rather, do you see cultural studies *as* a 'project', and is contemporary cultural studies still the 'same' project or discipline as it once was?

(2) Cultural studies is said to be a political project. What, to your mind, are the politics of cultural studies? Does it have 'a' politics, or is it, rather, political in some other way? Another way to phrase this would be to ask you what are the politics or what is the political significance of your own work? What do you consider to be the 'proper destination' of your work?

(3) What are the *institutions* of cultural studies? That is, what works, methods, orientations, etc., have become instituted as the repositories of 'knowledge', methodology, and ways of going about doing things? This is as much as to say, what do these insti-tutions (or the institution of these authoritative guarantors as 'the proper' or 'the best') forbid, censure/censor, limit and enable? What factors determined or overdetermined their institution?

(4) How does the institutionalisation of cultural studies affect, support or undermine it?

(5) Does cultural studies have any significance outside of the university at all? If so, what forms does this take?

(6) What is, has been, might be, or might have been, the signifi-cance of cultural studies within the university?

(7) Where is cultural studies *going*? This question is obviously tied to that of 'where has it *been*?', which is an interesting and

important question itself; but I wonder where you think it *should* go, or what you think it should now do or try to do: in short, what has cultural studies 'achieved', what has it 'failed' to achieve, and to what extent are these 'failures' inevitable, structural, or is it just that their realisation is only a matter of time or strategy?

NOTES

1. I defer pursuing the question of whether any or all of these accusations are justified or otherwise. Suffice it to say that many have emphasised a different kind of sequence: such as that cultural studies went about its modest business and never really bothered anybody, only to find itself having incurred inordinate amounts of condemnation and opprobrium for no rational reason. Diagnoses abound as to what such heated reactions are symptomatic of. These matters have occupied me for some time (hence, of course, this book); and my own studies of it appear as 'Alarming and Calming. Sacred and Accursed', in S. Herbrechter (ed.), *Cultural Studies and Interdisciplinarity* (Amsterdam and Atlanta: Rodopi, forthcoming); 'Between Responsibility and Irresponsibility', *Strategies*, 2001; and 'Proper Impropriety', *Parallax* 19, 2001.
2. Of course, as Hegel pointed out, 'What is "familiarly known" is not properly known, just for the reason that it is "familiar." ... it is the commonest form of self-deception', quoted in Spivak's Translator's Preface to Jacques Derrida, *Of Grammatology* (Baltimore and London: Johns Hopkins University Press, 1974), p. xiii.
3. John Mowitt, 'Introduction: The Two Texts', in *Text: The Genealogy of an Antidisciplinary Object* (Durham and London: Duke University Press, 1992), p. 2.
4. And, we might well ask, how does this 'hostility' square with cultural studies' much-championed 'ethical' position of 'hospitality' to the other?
5. Nevertheless, it is compelling, particularly as less than ten minutes after writing these words I was interrupted by my wife calling to me to tell me that Terry Eagleton today has a column in the *Guardian*. I went to have a look, and on arrival she laughingly read out a brief letter in the same paper: 'I was going to write about what a tired, blinkered, middle-aged old pantomime dame John Lydon has become ... but I can't be bothered.' The (chance?) coincidence of Eagleton's mainstream success coupled with the growing comicality and/or tediousness of a once allegedly 'radical', 'cutting edge', 'revolutionary', 'dangerous' punk icon *suggests* a peculiar, and not necessarily straightforwardly legible conjunction (if it is one). See the *Guardian*, 18 May 2002.
6. Which is actually the condition of possibility for anything like *proper inter-disciplinarity* – which, of course, actually reveals that 'proper interdisciplinarity' is impossible.
7. As Jacques Rancière has argued, a 'disagreement' occurs not when one person says 'black' and another says 'white', but rather when both say

'black', *but mean different things by it*. See his *Dis-agreement: Politics and Philosophy* (Minneapolis: University of Minnesota Press, 1999).

8. Cultural studies arguably spends more time defining itself, or ruminating on the limitations of self-definitions, than anything else. This may seem comical, but it occurs because a key part of the problematic of cultural studies entails attending to the conceptual and pragmatic consequences of definitions, characterisations, pigeonholing, the role of these processes in all forms of understanding, and the connection between forms of understanding and the forms of practice that they foster and/or preclude.

9. In the case of interviews carried out over email, some contributors directly answered all of the questions, some answered more or less of them, and some took the questions as read in composing a chapter. In the case of interviews carried out face to face, the core questions themselves and the interviewees' responses to them inspired yet more, always related, questions.

Part One:
From Cultural Studies

INTRODUCTION

The first interview, with Catherine Belsey, clearly conveys the dominant narrative of cultural studies' historical formations. It paints a very lucid picture of the inception and development of cultural studies. Like Mieke Bal's contribution, both focus on the problems attendant to the specificity and implications of the methodological orientations of cultural studies, as does Martin McQuillan's – each, though, in very different ways.

Belsey celebrates cultural studies' heroic historical achievements, but berates its institutionalisation, seeing therein its stagnation. She proposes the need for a revivification of cultural studies – a revivification not necessarily entailing the change of name that she suggests (from 'cultural studies' to 'cultural criticism'), although this would help to signify a development of orientation and a more contemporary remit, as appropriate to the tasks required by the times. Mieke Bal proposes something similar: she proposes the distinction between cultural *studies* and cultural *analysis*, because of the rigour and specificity denoted and connoted by 'analysis', as opposed to the nebulousness of 'studies'. This is echoed, although differently, by Martin McQuillan. It is perhaps suggestive about the nature of the present time, or of a current sense within cultural studies, that Belsey, Bal and McQuillan should choose to go somewhat against the once dominant historical refusal to 'pin down what it is' that informed the initial choice of the plural and open, non-specific title 'cultural studies'. But, as all see it, the time has come for serious, sustained and drastic attention to the question of method, and hence the *hows*, *whys* and *whats* of any kind of cultural study.

Belsey explicitly advocates deconstruction and psychoanalysis (so-called 'high theory') as being the best supplements to guide any attempt to understand and engage, in culturally, politically and intellectually important ways; but she disapproves of the complicity of the language of theory in separating cultural studies or cultural criticism from the very culture it studies and critiques. For, she argues, if something *matters*, then it matters *widely*. So cultural critics must at once be informed by (highly theoretical, or rigorously conceived) intellectual perspectives that will therefore be considerably different from everyday or commonsense perspectives, but they must also be alert to the extent to which such theoretical language can separate those who use it from the world they would perhaps most like to reach.

Mieke Bal engages in a similar consideration of the question of the intellectual, theoretical and methodological resources that we bring to our analyses. She is predominantly concerned with the question of visual cultural analysis and the political dimensions of pedagogy: as she argues, we tend to proceed all too *uncritically*, having inherited traditional methods and ways of going about thinking and acting from the very disciplines that we were meant to be transforming. Clearly, part of our implicit contract or obligation as cultural critics or analysts must involve developing a more particular, self-reflexive and refined repository of methodologies, rather than uncritically accepting traditional disciplinary protocols. This pragmatic concern is animated by something of a utopian hope: Bal speaks of the aim of developing and uniting the academy, in order to strengthen and enrich the possibilities and contributions of intellectual cultural work, in academic, political and cultural contexts. McQuillan problematises perhaps *everything* about the two preceding chapters, up to, and including, this book's very formulation, title and orientation. All three propose moving 'from' cultural studies, but, paradoxically, in the name of something like the 'spirit' or 'project of' cultural studies.

2 From Cultural Studies to Cultural Criticism?

Catherine Belsey

(1) How do you position yourself and your work in relation to the cultural studies project? Or, rather, do you see cultural studies *as* a 'project', and is contemporary cultural studies still the 'same' project or discipline as it once was?

I should make clear from the beginning that I address your questions from outside cultural studies itself. I have learnt a great deal from cultural studies, but in the process I have also developed some reservations about what seem to me (still from the outside, and perhaps, therefore, from a position less well informed than it might be) the limits of its focus. Or perhaps 'reservations' is too strong a term. My unease is not about what cultural studies does, and does well, but about the areas it appears to leave out. I reflect on the issues you raise, therefore, out of an interest in developing an alternative – cultural *criticism* – as a new field of study that embraces a wider range of material than most existing departments of cultural studies.

To be more specific about what seems to me the motive for change, or at least modification, the absences in cultural studies as it exists now derive from the degree to which it is still the same project as it once was. Paradoxically, what was once its great strength has now begun to seem like a constraint. The strength was its popularising impulse; that impulse is now in danger of settling down as populism; and, as we in the UK found out in the Thatcher years, populism can too easily turn into conservatism.

(2) Cultural studies is said to be a political project. What, to your mind, are the politics of cultural studies? Does it have 'a' politics, or is it, rather, political in some other way? Another way to phrase this would be to ask you what are the politics or what is the

political significance of your own work? What do you consider to be the 'proper destination' of your work?

Your second question allows me to move into a historical justification of the proposition that cultural studies slides towards populism, and that this is not unequivocally to its advantage. The story of the discipline is already familiar, but it might be worth rehearsing in order to suggest how a popularising and thus liberating drive can settle into a populist limitation.

The early exponents of cultural studies in the 1950s, supremely Raymond Williams and Richard Hoggart, were reacting primarily against English studies as it was then understood, but that reaction was an ambivalent one, because of the uncertain status of the popular at the time. It was clear that English invested heavily in value judgements. Indeed, the main object of the exercise seemed to be grading. There were four great English novelists, F.R. Leavis insisted, paradoxically to a wide audience of schoolteachers and Penguin-readers, as well as academics. And there was also D.H. Lawrence, of course. But just *how* good was Dickens, who was a great popular success in his own day? Well, maybe *Hard Times* would make it into the canon. And Hardy, perhaps the nearest among the candidates for canonisation to a popular novelist? Ah, that was a tricky one. As far as poetry was concerned, Donne was heavily promoted by Leavis himself and by T.S. Eliot, but Milton, in the eyes of the same team, was an altogether bad influence, because he introduced a Latin element into the native rhythms of popular English speech. The value judgements in all this were unremitting, but the attitude to the popular was extraordinarily equivocal: it was judged as positive in relation to past cultures, but treated with deep suspicion when it came to the present.

Eliot himself, meanwhile, was defending the proposition that only high culture could save civilisation as we know it. This was Matthew Arnold's *Culture and Anarchy* all over again, but without the liberal ideal that had made Arnold palatable. The Leavises, F.R. and Queenie, were busy denouncing the evils of contemporary mass culture. American criticism at this time was marginally less deeply immersed in hierarchies of value, and a good deal more attentive to the text. Those of us who couldn't align ourselves with the imprecations of the Leavisites turned to New Criticism for sustenance. What we found there was more intellectual, more surprising, but radically ahistorical – and still grounded in a vocabulary of 'success' and 'failure'. A poem (poems were the main focus) was more or less successful to the degree that it was more or less 'balanced', 'humane', and politically uncommitted. I discovered New Criticism all by myself as an undergraduate (rather late in the day), seduced by the lyrical title of *The Verbal Icon*, and I tried ineffectually to cobble together a way of reading that also took account of some of the old historicism of C.S. Lewis. In a fumbling way, I was trying to relocate the icon in its cultural context.

Lewis was brilliant. My respect for his knowledge has, if anything, deepened with time. And he told stories – of the progressive unfolding of medieval and early modern culture. But he, too, was given to value judgements, and his happy endings usually culminated in the founding of the Anglican Church. E.M.W. Tillyard, who was also interested in cultural history, but who sold to a wider public (and is still in print today), was committed, meanwhile, to demonstrating conclusively that we had all been much happier, and produced much *better* literary works, in England's golden age, when we knew our place in the social order, and gave no thought to social mobility, criticism of the authorities, or, perish the thought, welfare states.

The Second World War, however, had called into question the accepted social hierarchies of the previous generation. As everyone now knows, soldiers had seen their officers at close quarters and under pressure; the public schools no longer seemed to have a monopoly on courage or leadership; on the home front, too, the classes had mixed and mingled as never before. Even the BBC was recognising regional accents. The hierarchies of value that English departments were still fostering in the 1950s, even though they were mainly meritocratic and bourgeois, rather than aristocratic and elite, seemed somehow out of tune with the moment. It was time for change. Raymond Williams and Richard Hoggart, ably supported by the Marxist historian E.P. Thompson, all writing from their background in adult education on the edges of the then tiny and highly selective university system, called attention to the long, distinguished and all-but-buried tradition of popular culture, and addressed their analyses to a wide audience in paperback. Thompson's *The Making of the English Working Class* (1963) famously sold a million copies for Penguin Books after its appearance in paperback in 1968.[1] Hoggart's *The Uses of Literacy*[2] first appeared in 1957, and came out as a Pelican paperback in 1958. Williams published *Culture and Society* in 1958, and *The Long Revolution* in

1961 (paperback 1965).[3] At the beginning of an overdue expansion of higher education, the Birmingham postgraduate Centre for Contemporary Cultural Studies was founded in 1962 with Hoggart as its first head. The first students were admitted in 1964.

The impulse of the new discipline was to attend to working-class culture, which was by no means confined to written texts, but included oral and musical traditions, for example, and (though this was not at all the same thing) to consider the mass culture of the day, the forms of entertainment by which the workers who attended adult education classes, not to mention the students now coming into higher education, were actually surrounded. Mass-market fiction, cinema, popular music, radio to a degree, and in due course television became the material of the fledgling cultural studies. The motive was political: all the early pioneers were committed to one version or another of left-wing politics. The objective was in the first instance the defence of working-class values, and then increasingly the unmasking of the values promoted among the working class by capitalist mass culture. Sociology, with its attention to actual forms of life, as well as political economy and the possibility of social and economic change, was seen as an ally or, indeed, integral to the project: 'cultural materialism' was not an empty phrase.

It was a heroic moment: here was an energy and a commitment that was largely lacking from the conventional academic disciplines at this time, and an openness, at least initially, to the possibility of new methodologies, new approaches, new ways of reading. The work of Roland Barthes on cultural myths and Louis Althusser on ideology was embraced when it became available in English in the early 1970s. The Birmingham Centre flowered under Stuart Hall, and truly radical developments in film theory took place in *Screen* in the course of the decade.

So successful was the new discipline that its effects influenced practically every department of the humanities. Do you mind if I take your Question (6)[4] out of order, and address it here? One by one, History, Art History, Classics and English itself were radicalised in the light of the new developments in cultural studies. This was not, perhaps, a simple case of cause and effect. For example, Christopher Hill's brilliant accounts of the cultural disputes that made possible the English Revolution were probably instrumental in the development of cultural studies, rather than its effects, but cultural studies in turn played a part in legitimating their uptake in otherwise relatively conservative history departments. In the 1980s Stephen

Greenblatt's New Historicism sprang out of American anthropology, not British cultural studies, but it did not seem shocking in the UK because cultural studies had accustomed us to seeing all culture as our province. Feminism also played a major part in the move to recover the work of women who had been hidden from a patriarchal history. But it was thanks to cultural studies that the literary canon was already well and truly on the way to breaking down at the stage when analysts of women's writing astutely took advantage of the fact. If I might be autobiographical for a moment, my own efforts to define a different future for English departments were the direct consequence of an encounter in the heady 1970s with cultural studies in general and film studies in particular. (I have never looked back.)

But – and perhaps this takes us to your Questions (3) and (4)[5] – with the institutionalisation of cultural studies, with courses, and exam papers, and journals, and the pressure to publish and peer assessment of papers and book projects, with introductory guides and anthologies, and all the apparatus of respectability, something was unaccountably lost. I think perhaps it was flexibility. Of course, new fields of enquiry opened up and were mapped. Minority cultures and ethnicities were explored; phobias, racial and sexual, were challenged; and this could only be welcome. But the same was more likely to promise success than novelty. The previous generation judges the work of the new, and more readily endorses what it recognises. Institutionalisation slows down change.

Moreover, true to its populist origins, when theory got hard, cultural studies became increasingly ambivalent towards it. *Screen* lost its theoretical edge after 1980; E.P. Thompson roundly denounced Althusserian Marxism; Terry Eagleton repudiated the French theory that had made him famous. Common sense and 'experience' reasserted themselves, but as Gramsci had long ago made plain, those areas are the last bastions of ideology, not guarantees of truth.

Does it matter? I believe it does. The main theoretical casualties of the populist resistance to theory were psychoanalysis and deconstruction. It's true – I've had the debate so many times – that neither of these knowledges is much use on the picket line; neither is immediately and self-evidently indispensable to a group of workers looking to become a class in itself, or a rape crisis centre eager to shelter and support victims of patriarchy. But cultural studies also has a long-term agenda, and in the long term understanding our culture, the culture that arguably makes us what we are, requires all the skills we can muster. Capitalism would not have lasted so long, or endeared itself to the East as well as the West, if its seductions had been obvious or transparent, or, indeed, if they had been purely economic. Culture does not constitute its subjects as conditioned robots, but as complex, sophisticated, multifarious individuals. Psychoanalysis and deconstruction both offer ways of attending to the textual subtlety of culture, its nuances, hints and evasions, what it does not say, as well as what it does, the things it does its best to conceal, and blurts out inadvertently just the same.

There is at work in every cultural 'text', from a cornflakes packet to a Canaletto, a textual resistance to its own overt project, and this matters to analysts of culture for a number of reasons. First, no position, no set of values or norms is so sedimented, so immovable that it cannot be challenged, and challenged, moreover, from within. The inevitable trace of the other that resides in the selfsame, the return of the repressed meaning(s) in any term or proposition, the radical alterity 'definitively taken away from every process of presentation'[6] all demonstrate an instability that points to the possibility of change. Second, that instability itself represents a pressure point for anyone interested in precipitating change. The politics of meaning is not merely referential. If meanings are constitutive of our hopes and desires, as well as our understanding of the way things are, these meanings themselves are a place of contest. And third, it is in the plurality of these meanings, the perpetual possibility of the return of the alterity that is excluded in order to make them appear both transparent and inevitable, that we can glimpse an alternative to the norms that set out to restrict our hopes and desires to the 'possible', the plausible, the obvious.

What is more, the seductive strategies of cultural texts are not confined to their thematic content, but involve their mode of address to a reader, and the position they offer as the place from which they are most obviously intelligible. Unmasking is not enough, if we are to understand as clearly as we can the processes of inscription of the range of cultural meanings we live by. There is, in other words, a politics of reading, which is not the same as the politics of action, or even the exposure of ideology.

Meanwhile, events began to diminish the initial *difference* of cultural studies, the feature that distinguished it from other disciplines, with the eventual result, as it seems to me, that it no longer makes sense to isolate *popular* culture. In view of the success cultural studies has had in directly or obliquely bringing about the transformation of other humanities disciplines, those disciplines themselves have been induced to acknowledge the contingency, the cultural relativity, of their own canons. In my view, the distinction between high and popular culture in itself presupposes a society divided along lines that, if they ever obtained, certainly do not hold now. There is not in the twenty-first century one culture for the bourgeoisie and another for the working class – if, indeed, there ever really was. The ruling ideology, Marx and Engels knew in 1848, is the ideology of the ruling class. The tabloid press, for instance, has a good deal to say about the Turner Prize, and its views on Martin Creed's lights going on and off, or Tracey Emin's bed, are not so radically different from those of some of the broadsheets. Indeed, ever since Duchamp, Thierry de Duve has argued, the question, 'Is it art?' has been open to anyone to answer.[7] Baz Luhrmann made *Romeo and Juliet* thrilling for a range of adolescents way beyond those doing A-Level English.

Less locally, what does it mean to reflect on the cultural difference of postmodernity without reference to art, architecture and the novel, as well as the internet, *The Simpsons*, Ali G. and the movies of Quentin Tarantino? The citationality of the postmodern assumes a range of reference that is not readily divisible between two different kinds of culture. What does it mean, moreover, to discuss this same issue without a strong sense of the cultural history that permits us to begin to define the difference of the postmodern? And here I name my third anxiety about cultural studies now. Initially history played a significant part in its programme: Raymond Williams might be described as above all a cultural historian; E.P. Thompson made his name writing history. Michel Foucault, who surely transformed the list of questions we address to the past, based his work on the discontinuities of cultural history. Marx himself was perhaps the first figure to invoke history knowingly to denaturalise the present. But looking round for historical work under the aegis of cultural studies now, I have difficulty in finding much that goes further back than the nineteenth century, and even that seems very much a minority interest. (Forgive me if here I do nothing so much as betray my ignorance.)

Having taken all your questions in the wrong order, and conflated (3), (4) and (6) with Question (2), without ever answering (2) directly, let me now, if I may, say something about the politics of cultural studies under the heading of your Question (5)! Does cultural studies have any significance outside the university? I should hope so! The founding fathers (I wish I could invoke some mothers here) would turn in their respective graves if they had supposed cultural studies could confine itself to the academic world. And yet that is increasingly what has happened to all our work. With the much-needed expansion of universities, academic publishing has hived itself off and become profitable. It suits the publishers (we work for practically nothing); and it suits the Research Assessment tribunals, who know at once what counts as research from the logo on the jacket. Does it also suit us? Yes, in a way. We should need to write a good deal more engagingly if we had to enlist a genuinely popular audience.

But in a sense it pushes cultural studies into a blind alley. We are talking mainly to each other. Of course, not everything everyone writes needs to be accessible to everyone else. Imagine imposing such a restriction on physics! I myself have just been defending high theory. But scientists have long since learnt to communicate some of the implications of their work to a wider audience. Have we? Only, I think, to a limited extent. But what we do (I include myself here as a cultural critic, though not as a specialist in cultural studies) matters, in the end, only if it matters *widely*. What we have to offer, in the long term, is an understanding of the relationship between human beings and the culture that shapes their values, aspirations, fantasies, dreams.

We should be offering to exert an influence beyond the classroom, though of course the classroom remains crucial as the place where understanding is developed. The first priority at this moment, therefore, is to modernise the discipline itself.

And so I come to your final question, 'Where is cultural studies going?' And my answer, predictably, after everything I have said so far, is 'Towards cultural criticism.' Or, at least, that is what I hope for.

Cultural criticism, as I understand the term, is the study of meanings wherever they are to be found. It therefore breaks with the limitations of cultural studies, insofar as cultural studies concentrates on the present and the popular. Cultural criticism embraces cultural history, if only in order to throw into relief the character – which is to say, the difference – of the present. And it sees no sense at this historical moment in isolating the culture of a class or group. While attending, of course, to the specificities of production processes, as well as target and actual audiences, cultural criticism would repudiate the idea that one big, overriding difference justifies the separation, when it comes to academic analysis, of mass-market romance, say, from other romance forms, including the 'literary' romances that win prizes.

Cultural criticism also breaks, then, with the isolation of traditional humanities disciplines as this has obtained since the nineteenth century. The study of literature has already made this break: more and more members of English departments are attending to what was once art history, as well as invading relatively new terrains of visual culture: embroidery, woodcuts, book illustration, tomb sculpture. The cultural history of the book and reading practices is fast becoming as central as the study of authors and their writing practices once was. A familiarity with the history of sexuality and colonial conquest is now taken for granted in English departments, and it necessarily follows that the popular is no longer outside the frame. Marjorie Garber links Elvis Presley and Shakespearean comedy in a discussion of the implications of cross-dressing.[8]

Something very similar also goes for art history itself. Attribution and brush strokes still matter, of course, but the ideological implications of the debates between mimetic and conceptual values in art are at least as important now. Genres that were once repudiated, like nineteenth-century narrative painting, have taken on a new importance as the material of cultural history. Visuality itself, the possibility of different ways of seeing, has come to constitute an issue in its own right. Film studies, meanwhile, acknowledges an overlap with art history: Stephen Heath's film theory and Norman Bryson's analysis of paintings draw on one another, while both appeal to Lacanian psychoanalysis. And when it comes to the work of Slavoj Žižek, there are no holds barred. When Žižek slips easily and wittily between Kantian philosophy and demotic jokes, Hegel and Hitchcock, the effect is exhilarating.

In other words, at the level of intellectual enquiry, the walls between the disciplines have already fallen, and the first instances of cultural criticism are in place. We are all increasingly polymathic now. The only thing capable of holding us back is the need to develop appropriate reading skills for such a wide range of 'texts'. But where there's a will, there's a way. Besides, we don't all need all of them at our individual fingertips. At last there is a real motive for co-operation and collective work in the humanities, as there has long been in the sciences. In all fields these reading skills will depend for their subtlety, however, on a familiarity with the insights of theory into the complexity of signifying practice. We cannot afford to neglect whatever psychoanalysis and post-structuralism have to tell us about the waywardness of the signifier, its density and difficulty. There is no cultural criticism without an understanding of signifying practice.

Cardiff University now offers an undergraduate joint degree in Cultural Criticism. There is no attempt, in the time available, at 'coverage', that shibboleth of English in its traditional form. Coverage, as each subject expands into new territories, is already a lost cause for the existing humanities disciplines. In Cultural Criticism the emphasis is on skills; students need to learn to interpret a wide variety of cultural forms: written, visual, oral, past and present. They need, in other words, to engage with a range of semiotic practices. The students put them to work in options focused on specialised areas, from the prehistoric to the post-human. They end the course not with a map of a demarcated field of knowledge, but with an attentiveness to signifying practice that will, ideally, enable them to make (a) sense of whatever cultural world(s) they go on to inhabit in the future.

Cultural criticism as an undergraduate discipline shares with cultural studies an interest in a range of media. What it largely excludes, however, is the overlap with sociology that characterises cultural studies as an academic institution. The primary concern of cultural criticism is signification, the making of meanings, wherever that is to be found. It treats culture, including social behaviour and practices, as of interest in the first instance as the inscription of meanings, given that meanings, as I have tried to suggest, are complex sites of political struggle.

If it is legitimate to end the discussion with a personal comment, I should say that I have never taught with more conviction or more energy than I do in this new degree scheme. The students, aware that they are doing something out of the ordinary, seeing themselves as adventurers, are alert, involved, and ready for more or less anything. Some of this shared energy is no doubt the effect of novelty itself. Probably cultural criticism will be institutionalised in due course, with its own promotion procedures and journals and introductions and anthologies, its own hierarchies and habits.

And then it will be time for another change. If cultural history teaches us anything, it must be that other times demand other practices, and new problems require new solutions. No discipline is for ever. If we are not to be at the mercy of our own institutions, we probably need to take the initiative in defining the direction of change. There is work to do!

NOTES

1. E.P. Thompson, *The Making of The English Working Class* (Harmondsworth: Penguin, 1968).
2. Richard Hoggart, *The Uses of Literacy* (Harmondsworth: Pelican, 1957).
3. Raymond Williams, *Culture and Society* (London: Chatto and Windus, 1958); and Raymond Williams, *The Long Revolution* (Harmondsworth: Penguin Books, 1961).
4. '(6) What is, has been, might be, or might have been, the significance of cultural studies within the university?'
5. '(3) What are the *institutions* of cultural studies? That is, what works, methods, orientations, etc., have become instituted as the repositories of "knowledge", methodology, and ways of going about doing things? This is as much as to say, what do these institutions (or the institution of these authoritative guarantors as "the proper" or "the best") forbid, censure/censor, limit and enable? What factors determined or overdetermined their institution?'; and: '(4) How does the institutionalisation of cultural studies affect, support or undermine it?'
6. Jacques Derrida, *'Différance', 'Speech and Phenomena' and Other Essays on Husserl's Theory of Signs*, trans. David B. Allison (Evanston, IL: Northwestern University Press, 1973), pp. 151, 129–60.
7. Thierry de Duve, *Kant After Duchamp* (Cambridge, MA: MIT Press, 1999).
8. Marjorie Garber, *Vested Interests: Cross Dressing and Cultural Anxiety* (Harmondsworth: Penguin, 1993).

3 From Cultural Studies to Cultural Analysis: 'A Controlled Reflection on the Formation of Method'

Mieke Bal

In the wake of women's studies, cultural studies has, in my view, been responsible for the absolutely indispensable opening up of the disciplinary structure of the humanities. By challenging methodological dogma, and elitist prejudice and value judgement, it has been uniquely instrumental in at least making the academic community aware of the conservative nature of its endeavours, if not everywhere forcing it to change. It has, if nothing else, forced the academy to realise its collusion with an elitist white-male politics of exclusion and its subsequent intellectual closure. Everything about cultural studies that makes me not want to say that cultural studies is what I do must be considered as a footnote to this major acknowledgement.

Inevitably, this new interdiscipline has suffered from the unforeseeable difficulties and hardships that every pioneering activity encounters. In defying disciplinary boundaries, it has had to contend with three problems, all of which jeopardise its ongoing intellectual vigour today. For the sake of clarity, allow me to put these rather strongly and without the required nuance.

First, while one of cultural studies' major innovations has been to pay attention to a different kind of object, as a new field averse to traditional approaches it has not been successful (enough) in developing a methodology to counter the exclusionary methods of the separate disciplines. More often than not, the methods have not changed. While the object – *what* you study – has changed, the method – *how* you do it – has not. But without the admittedly rigid methodologies of the disciplines, how do you keep analysis from floundering into sheer partisanship or being perceived as floundering? This is the major problem of content and practice that faces us today, which in turn creates more problems, especially in teaching situations. It is this problem that is the primary focus of my current work.

Second, cultural studies has involuntarily 'helped' its opponents to deepen rather than to overcome the destructive divide between *les anciens* and *les modernes*, a binary structure as old as Western culture itself. This is unfortunate, for this opposition tends to feed an oedipally based psychosocial mechanism that is unhelpful when it comes to changing predominant power structures. The problem is primarily a social one, but in the current situation, where academic jobs are scarce and hierarchies returning, it entails a tendency to a monolithical appointments policy that, under the name of backlash, threatens everything that has been accomplished. Whereas a book like this cannot change that situation at all, a recognisably responsible practice based on reflection on the problem of method may help to pave the way for a more nuanced academic environment.

Third, the inevitable consequence of the inadequate methodology and the reinforced opposition combined is even more mundane yet just as dangerous. At a time of economic crisis, the interdisciplinarity inherent to cultural studies has given university administrators a tool with which to enforce mergings and cancellations of departments that might turn out to be fatal for the broad grounding cultural studies needs.[1]

These problems of cultural studies have led me to use a term that is partly identical, partly different: Cultural Analysis. Some eight years ago, my colleague Hent de Vries, a Derridean philosopher, and I started a graduate school/research institute under that banner. It has been remarkably successful in attracting students interested in unusual topics who were ill at ease in strictly disciplinary organisations. A great number of dissertations saw the light, some of which were totally brilliant and original.

Why, then, is the idea of 'cultural analysis' helpful in seeking to remedy these three problems? By fundamentally changing the way we 'think' methodology within the different disciplines, it is possible to overcome the three major – indeed, potentially dangerous – drawbacks of cultural studies. Against the first and most important one for my project, concepts will be brought in as an alternative for the idea of *coverage*. Within an interdisciplinary setting, coverage – of the classics, of all periods or 'centuries', of all major theories used within a field – is no longer an option. Nor is 'sloppy scholarship'.

If a different alternative can be articulated, then, the divide, which is the second drawback, can be lessened. The creation of a methodological common ground, all the more urgently needed as the self-evidence of coverage is challenged, is the only unified answer we can give to administrative attacks on staff. By solving the first two, the wind is taken out of the sail of administrators too eager to take advantage of the situation.

The political thrust of this style of cultural analysis is, first, to persuade colleagues and students that there is a way out of these predicaments, and second, to offer ideas to those trying to find their way in the labyrinthine land of a humanities without boundaries. Such a land can only unify through travel, through learning foreign languages, through encounters with others. If Europe can unify, so can the academy, and – I contend – with much less difficulty, sacrifice and impoverishment.

The *analysis* part of the name 'cultural analysis' is what is at stake in the distinction between cultural studies and cultural analysis. In my view the counterpart of the concepts we work with is not the systematic theory from which they are taken, although that theory matters and cannot be neglected. Nor is it the history of the concept in its philosophical or theoretical development. And it is certainly not a 'context', whose status as text, itself in need of analysis, is largely ignored. The counterpart of any given concept is the cultural text or work or 'thing' that constitutes the *object* of analysis. No concept is meaningful for cultural analysis unless it helps us to understand the object better *on its* – the object's – *own terms*. Here, another background, or root, of the current situation in the humanities comes to the fore.

The turn to methodology already mentioned was partly a reaction to the cultivation of the object and its details, in critical movements such as the new, literary hermeneutics in Germany, the *explication de texte* in France, and the New Criticism in the Anglo-Saxon world. The general term *close reading* is still with us, but the practice of it, I am afraid, is not. This loss is due to practical changes, in particular, the reduction of programmes. But it is also due to the loss of innocence that came with the awareness that no text yields meaning outside of the social world and cultural makeup of the reader. Nevertheless, I have often had occasion to regret the loss of analytical skills that accompanied the disenchantment with the illusion that 'the text speaks for itself'. True enough, a text does not speak for itself. We surround it, or *frame* it, before we let it speak at all. But rejecting close reading for that reason has been an unfortunate case of throwing out the baby with the bath water. For, in the tripartite relationship between student, frame, and object, the latter must still have the last word.

Whereas this sustained attention to the object is the mission of *analysis*, it also qualifies the term 'cultural analysis'. I will not define 'culture' in this short comment. It is well known that definitions of culture are inevitably programmatic. If 'culture' is defined as the thoughts and feelings, the moods and values of people, then 'analysis' is bound to a phenomenologically oriented approach that shuns the social that is culture's other. If subjectivity is the focus, then social interaction remains out of its scope. And if it is the mind that comprises the cultural fabric, then all we can analyse is a collection of individualities. These traditional conceptions have been abandoned or adjusted, but they continue to share the impulse to define culture in the abstract and general sense.[2] This is the area of study the social sciences focus on. It would be presumptuous to pronounce on what 'culture' is, except perhaps to say that it can only be envisioned in a plural, changing and mobile existence.

The objects of study of the disciplines that comprise the humanities *belong* to culture but do not, together, constitute it. The qualifier 'cultural' takes the existence and importance of cultures for granted, but it does not predicate the 'analysis' on a particular conception of 'culture'. For, in distinction from, say, cultural anthropology, 'cultural analysis' does not *study* culture. 'Culture' is not its object. The qualifier *cultural* in 'cultural analysis' indicates, instead, a distinction from traditional disciplinary practice within the humanities, namely, that the analysis of the various objects gleaned from the cultural world for closer scrutiny are analysed *in view of* their existence in culture. This means they are not seen as isolated jewels, but as things always-already engaged, as interlocutors, within the larger culture from which they have emerged. It also means that 'analysis' looks to issues of cultural relevance, and aims to articulate how the object contributes to cultural debates. This is where the politics of such an endeavour are rooted. Hence the emphasis on the object's existence in the present that is part of my vision of cultural analysis. It is not the artist or the author but the objects they make and 'give' to the public domain that are the 'speakers' in analytic discussion. For now, I wish to insist on the participation of the object in the production of meaning that 'analysis' constitutes.

The most important consequence of this empowerment of the object is that it pleads for a qualified return to the practice of 'close reading' that has gone out of style. My forthcoming book, *Travelling Concepts in the Humanities: A Rough Guide*, as a whole *is* that plea; it 'argues' it by demonstrating it. This is why all of the chapters of that book – different as they are in the way they explore the possible relations between concept and object and the function they assign to the concepts – are *case studies* rather than systematic explanations of the concept concerned. Most of the other chapters focus on the relationship between a concept and a more recognisable cultural object.

My interest was in developing concepts we could all agree on and use, or at the very least disagree on, in order to make what has become labelled 'theory' accessible to every participant in cultural analysis, both within and outside the academy. Concepts, I found over the years, are the sites of debate, awareness of difference, and tentative exchange. Agreeing doesn't mean agreeing on content, but agreeing on the basic rules of the game: if you use a concept at all, you use it in a particular way, so that you can meaningfully disagree on content. That use doesn't go without saying. Intersubjectivity in this sense remains the most important standard for teaching and writing. Whatever else it does, cultural studies owes it to its principles of anti-elitism, to its firm position against exclusion of everything that is non-canonical and everyone who is not mainstream, to take this standard seriously. In the bargain, between Popper and practice, considering intersubjectivity has made me understand the difference between a word and a concept. The book is the outcome of that understanding.

In its eight chapters, I present a number of cases of different forms of intercourse with and through concepts that can be used to roughly guide specific interdisciplinary endeavours. Do not expect an overview or list of the 'most important' concepts, nor a firm definition of what each concept 'really' means, or a prescription of how it should be used. I find all such attempts to pin down the law of cultural analysis politically suspect. The stakes of the book are both lower and higher: lower, in that I submit just one way to use a concept; higher, in that I aim to demonstrate how the variety of ways in which a concept can be brought to bear on an object makes for an analytical practice that is both open and rigorous, teachable and creative. The idea of *Travelling Concepts* is that hopefully, the case studies offered there will open up venues for differentiated but specific uses of concepts as sites of both methodological openness and reflection, and hence, without the loss of accountability and intersubjective communication that so often accompanies such openness. The cases are showcases of practices; and the kinds of practices at issue – not the specific concepts or their handling – are central to my argument. In each chapter, a different practice comes to the fore. Some form of 'travel' occurs in each.

A word on the place of 'theory' in this practice. Theory is as mobile, subject to change, and embedded in historically and culturally diverse contexts as the objects on which it can be brought to bear. This is why theory – any specific theory surrounded by the protective belt of non-doubt and, hence, given dogmatic status – is in itself unfit to serve as a methodological guideline in analytical practice. Yet, and second, theory is also indispensable. Third, however, it never operates alone; it is not 'loose'. The key question that makes the case for cultural analysis, then, is the following: are theory and close analysis not the *only* testing grounds in a practice that involves both methodology and relevance? My contention is that in practising detailed analysis from a theoretical perspective, one is led to resist sweeping statements and partisanship, as well as reductive classification for the sake of alleged objectivity.

Instead of these fatal ills, which cling to both cultural studies and traditional disciplines alike, a close analysis, informed but not overruled by theory, in which concepts are the primary testing ground, works against confusing methodological tradition with dogma. It would appear that to challenge concepts that seem either obviously right or too dubious to keep using as they are, in order to revise instead of reject them, is a most responsible activity for theorists. Interestingly, concepts that don't seem to budge under the challenge may well be more problematical than those that do. Some concepts are so much taken for granted and have such generalised meaning that they fail to be helpful in actual analytic practice. This is where the issue of analysis comes in.

My favourite example of this is 'narrative'. It is hard to find cultural objects that cannot, in some way or other, be labelled 'narrative'. With the extension of its use, this flexible concept adapts its content to the objects that challenge it. To cite an example from my own practice, visual images are almost always narrative in some way or another. If they don't tell stories, they perform them, between image and viewer. What's the point of such extended uses?

The point is dual. The challenge to narrative, the exploration of narrative's limits and the regions beyond, is illuminating for an understanding of those images that 'fight' narrativity, while also shedding new light on what narrativity can mean. Figurative photography, for example, must stay clear of the stories that take the eye away from the image surface into the far regions of fantasy. Not because there is anything wrong with fantasy, but because we fantasise the represented scene to be real, hence, the photograph to tell the truth, to dictate our construction of the world seen. This referential fallacy attached to narrativity needs undermining indeed. Some artists conduct that battle using *distraction* as their weapon. Attention management is the aesthetic of the post-aesthetic era.

Dispersal of vision and attention undercuts narrative's attempt to organise the world, because to organise is to hierarchise it. But narrative need not be so bossy. There is a kind of narrative that is not objectifying at all. This other kind is mobilised in the work of contemporary painters such as David Reed and Martijn Schuppers, to name two I have worked on recently. In its main frame, such a narrative is process- rather than taxonomy-driven. In its mode, it is conversation rather than reportage. In its thrust it is erotic or otherwise attracting rather than pretending neutrality. Such narrative is what I have called, elsewhere, 'second-person narrative'.[3] Here, fantasy is not mistaken for reality, but played out, with a wink. It is a mode of narrative that foregrounds performativity.[4] Perhaps calling it 'drama' would clarify what is meant. But unlike most dramatic performances, this second-person narrative mode is rigorously a one-to-one relationship. The image; the viewer. Those are the two actors. No audience watches what happens. What happens between them remains unstable and invisible to others. When such narrative is performed in a visual medium, its motor is the capacity to hold the viewer in a process of considerable duration. Figuration isn't needed to do this. And in 'classical narrative', this aspect of narrativity can also be present, and if so, needs analysis. Thus, narrative is redefined, whereas the paintings are more profoundly analysed than any traditional art-historical analysis can do.

The three priorities of methodology I have implied so far – cultural processes over objects, intersubjectivity over objectivity, and concepts over theories – come together in the practice of what I have proposed to call 'cultural analysis'. As a professional theorist, it is my belief that in the field entailing the study of culture, theory can be meaningful only when it is deployed in close interaction with the objects of study to which it pertains, that is, when the objects are considered and treated as 'second persons'. This is where the methodological issues raised around concepts can be arbitrated on a basis that is neither dogmatic nor free-floating. Concepts tested in close, detailed analysis can establish a much-needed intersubjectivity, not only between the analyst and the audience but also between the analyst and the 'object'. It is in order to drive this point home that I suggest reconfiguring and reconceiving 'cultural studies' as 'cultural analysis'. Any academic practice lives by constraints yet also needs freedom to be innovative. Negotiating the two is delicate. The rule I have adhered to and that I hold my students to, and that has been the most productive constraint I have experienced in my own practice, is to never just theorise but always to allow the object 'to speak back'. Making sweeping statements about objects, or citing them as examples, renders them dumb. Detailed analysis – where no quotation can serve as an illustration but where it will always be scrutinised in depth and detail, with a suspension of certainties – resists reduction. Even though, obviously, objects cannot speak, they can be treated with enough respect for their irreducible complexity and unyielding muteness – but not mystery – to allow them to check the thrust of an interpretation, and to divert and complicate it. This holds for objects of culture in the broadest sense, not just for objects that we call art. 'Art' can be reconfigured as 'practice'.

Let me give an example that has been in my thoughts a lot: the interdisciplinary field I have called 'visual poetics'. I contend that thinking about visual poetics fares better if it avoids taking definition and delimitation as its starting point. But, to avoid alienating practitioners of the various disciplines of the humanities, let me add that such a poetics works best if its primary starting point – but not outcome – remains the undeniable boundary that separates visual from linguistic utterances. The attempts to produce inter-media texts prove it, and the existence of essentially mixed-media texts such as cinema and video in no way contradicts this. Moreover, although one cannot deny the visual aspect of textuality in general – the visual act of reading – textuality still cannot be grasped at a glance. Nor is the glance self-evident as a way of apprehending the image. Thus, the objects we analyse enrich both interpretation and theory. This is how theory can change from a rigid master discourse into a live cultural object in its own right.[5] This is how we can learn from the objects that constitute our area of study. And this is why I consider them subjects.[6] Perhaps this is the best indication of the politics of cultural analysis. Doing politics – activism, party politics, or what have you – is not best served in the humanities. But a respect for the objects that are given over to cultural interaction by the people who made them seems to me to be able to serve politics in a profound sense better.

The logical consequence of this combined commitment – to theoretical perspective and concepts on the one hand and to close reading on the other – is a continuous changing of the concepts. This is yet another way in which they travel: not just between disciplines, places and times, but also within their own conceptualisation. Here, they travel, under the guidance of the objects they encounter. Such internal transformation can be demonstrated by the emerging concept of visual poetics, implying both a specification of focalisation and a transformation, along the lines of the interdisciplinary travel between literary and visual analysis, and between concept and object. The term 'visual poetics' is not a concept but an approach in which affiliated concepts such as focalisation, the gaze, and framing accrue, to become a little more than just concepts: in fact, the skeleton of a theory.

In the beginning of their book *What is Philosophy?* Deleuze and Guattari invoke a conceptual persona (*personnage conceptuel*) from Greek philosophy: the teacher. In the face of *that* tradition, I end my comments on the figure of the teacher. What pedagogy – or politics of it – subtends cultural analysis thus conceived?

In philosophy, this figure of the teacher is usually the lover. In her book *What Can She Know? Feminist Epistemology and the Construction of Knowledge*, Lorraine Code takes this tradition and turns it around. For Code, the concept-metaphor that best embodies her ideal is the friend, not the lover. Moreover, the conceptual persona of the friend – the model of friendship – is not embedded in a definition of philosophy but of knowledge. This definition is necessarily one that takes knowledge as provisional. If the authority of the author/artist, as well as that of the teacher, is unfixed, then the place it vacates can be occupied by *theory*. Paul de Man defined theory long ago as 'a controlled reflection on the formation of method'. The teacher, then, no longer holds the authority to dictate the method; her task is only to facilitate a reflection that is ongoing and interactive. Knowledge is knowing that reflection cannot be terminated. Moreover, to use Shoshana Felman's phrase, knowledge is not to learn something *about* but to learn something *from*. Knowledge, not as a substance or content 'out there' waiting to be appropriated but as the 'how-to' aspect, bears on such learning *from* the practice of interdisciplinary cultural analysis.

Within the framework of Felman's description of teaching as facilitating the *condition* of knowledge, Code's apparently small shift from lover to friend is, at least provisionally, a way out of the misfit between traditional humanities and cultural analysis. Friendship is a paradigm for knowledge-production, the traditional task of the humanities, but then production as interminable process, not as preface to a product. Code lists the following features of friendship, as opposed to the lover's passion, as productive analogies for knowledge production:

- such knowledge is not achieved at once, rather it develops
- it is open to interpretation at different levels
- it admits degrees
- it changes
- subject and object positions in the process of knowledge construction are reversible
- it is a never-accomplished constant process
- the 'more-or-lessness' of this knowledge affirms the need to reserve and revise judgement.

This list helps to distinguish between philosophy in the narrow sense, as a discipline or potential inter-discipline, and the humanities as a more general field, 'rhizomically' organised according to a dynamic interdisciplinary *practice*.

Philosophy creates, analyses and offers concepts. Analysis, in pursuing its goal – which is to articulate the 'best' (most effective, reliable, useful?) way to 'do', perform, the pursuit of knowledge – puts them together with potential objects that we wish to get to know. Disciplines 'use' them, 'apply' and deploy them, in interaction with an object, in their pursuit of specialised knowledge. But, in the best of situations, this division of tasks does not imply a rigid division of people or groups of people along the lines of disciplines or departments. For such a division deprives all participants of the key to a genuine practice of *cultural analysis*: a *sensitivity to the provisional nature of concepts*. Without claiming to know it all, each participant learns to move about, travel, between these areas of activity. In our travel among the classical humanities we constantly negotiate these differences. We select one path and bracket others, but eliminate none. This is the basis of interdisciplinary work.

NOTES

1. This danger is real and potentially fatal for the humanities. I have had occasion to witness it while serving on evaluation committees of post-graduate programmes. This danger alone is enough to make us cautious about giving up discipline-based groupings too easily.
2. See Wuthnow *et al.*, *Cultural Analysis: The Work of Peter L. Berger, Mary Douglas, Michel Foucault, and Jürgen Habermas* (Boston: Routledge and Kegan Paul, 1984), an early publication that uses the term 'cultural analysis' for a description of anthropological method.
3. See *Quoting Caravaggio: Contemporary Art, Preposterous History* (Chicago: University of Chicago Press, 1999), chapter 6, where I discuss David Reed's non-figurative paintings. On Schuppers, see my essay 'The Dissolution of the World', in *Martijn Schuppers* (Amsterdam: Cato Publishers, 2002, forth-coming).
4. Performativity, a concept brought into currency by speech act theory, indicates the aspect of utterances that makes these *acts* that *do, perform,* what they say. The concept has been brought to bear on visual art. See my *Travelling Concepts in the Humanities: A Rough Guide* (Toronto: University of Toronto Press, 2002).
5. This is, by now, a well-known consequence of the deconstructionist questioning of artistic 'essence'. It is by no means generally accepted, however, as George Steiner demonstrates. See F. Korsten (Unpublished Dissertation, Amsterdam School for Cultural Analysis, 1998) for a critical analysis of Steiner's position. On the status of theory as cultural text, see Jonathan Culler's contribution to my *The Point of Theory* (eds) Mieke Bal and Inge Boer (Amsterdam: University of Amsterdam Press, 1994).
6. As I have written many times – perhaps most explicitly in the Introduction to *Reading 'Rembrandt': Beyond the Word–Image Opposition* (Cambridge: Cambridge University Press, 1991) – the maker of an object cannot speak for it. The author's intentions, if accessible at all, do not offer direct access to meaning. In the light of what we know about the unconscious, even an alert, intellectual and loquacious artist cannot fully know her own intentions. But nor can the maker or the analyst who claims to speak for the maker speak for the object in another sense, the sense closer to the anthropological tradition. The object is the subject's 'other' and its otherness is irreducible. Of course, in this sense the analyst can never adequately represent the object either: she can neither speak about it nor speak for it.

4　The Projection of Cultural Studies

Martin McQuillan

Before I answer your questions, which in some ways are all the same question, let us begin with a question before the question, namely the title. You wish to question the question, 'interrogating cultural studies'. I am worried by this formulation, particularly in light of some of the answers I will give below. Yes, cultural studies can interrogate, or be interrogating. At least, put another way, cultural studies can do some hard questioning. And equally, hard questions need to be asked of cultural studies. While the question itself might be indicative of an ontological mode of thought this does not invalidate questioning as a way of proceeding which might prompt a general deconstruction of the ontological system. However, 'interrogating' remains a word that I am uncomfortable with. It is a word synonymous with the most violent of practices and brutal of regimes. 'Shining a Light in the Eyes of Cultural Studies and Forcing it to Confess', 'Torturing Cultural Studies', these might be equally suitable titles for you. The history of interrogation in modernity is not a happy one and one that renders the word deeply problematic. Who here are the interrogators? Who is being interrogated as representative of cultural studies? I assume cultural studies is also doing the interrogation, auto-interrogation if you will. What information is sought by this interrogation? Is it a matter of the interrogated telling you what you need to know and that you have ways of making us talk? What methods will you use to break us down and tell you the secrets that will be of use to you? What will the status of these confessions be?

Once I find out the purposes to which my confession is being deployed – perhaps used against me – I may wish to retract my confession. I will claim that it was given under duress, sweated out of me for a publishing deadline before I was ready to make a full statement. I say this, not in order to compare harassed academics –

who always have something to say, and who always like to be asked to have something to say – with victims of political torture, although it would be extraordinarily Eurocentric to imagine that they could not be one and the same thing. Rather, my issue is with the very idea of the interrogation as a structure of questioning. It is in fact not a questioning at all. It is pre-programmed by the interrogator's needs and desires, seeking particular information (not to be confused with knowledge or even enlightenment). It is like hunting for buried treasure or extracting a wisdom tooth. Extracting the tooth does not bring wisdom and those who dig for treasure seldom repair the landscape they have defaced. Interrogation is distinct from dialogue, 'Cultural Studies in Dialogue' might have been a more appropriate title (putting the 'inter' back into interrogation). 'Asking Difficult Questions of Cultural Studies but Letting It off the Hook Under Mitigating Circumstances' might also be a more accurate description. Indeed, this will bring us to the question of the question, to the question of the product of interrogation, namely the confession.

As de Man tells us, every confession fails to confess, i.e., fails to render an accurate account of actions in the name of a higher purpose of truth in order to gain absolution for those actions. Whenever I begin to confess I enter into explanation and with explanation and self-justification I ruin my confession. The confession then, as a text, cannot give satisfaction to the interrogator (might we say inquisitor?). The confessional text cannot close itself and will always let the confessor 'off the hook' even if, from the point of view of confession, this might be a shameful thing. On the one hand, this confession will be used against me, held up as a definitive statement and quoted to me in order to demonstrate 'what I think'. The worry is not that I might not think the same thing in ten years or ten months time, but that the confession is not what *I* think, rather it is a response to questions which tell us more about what you (Paul, my interrogator) think, or, what you think that I think that might be of interest to your own thinking. At this point, I am willing to say what you want to hear so that you will stop shining that damn light in my face and let me sleep. However, when the confession is read back to me it will read like a closed statement, a summation, of my views and opinions on cultural studies. A statement that I will have to live with as it substitutes metonymically for the whole of my writing, now and in the future, a statement caught up in the formal structures of iteration ('interviews' can have that occult power). On the other hand, writing experts can be brought forward to debunk the validity of the confession, demonstrating its inconsistencies, showing how it was forged and forced, releasing me on appeal, letting me off on a technicality. Of course the confession fails to confess but that does not stop it from trying, or stop the interrogators from forcing their confession, extracting the teeth and publishing them in a book entitled 'The Wisdom Teeth of Cultural Studies'.

Paul de Man is an interesting case in point here. He was interrogated by investigating magistrates in Belgium after the Second World War. They chose not to prosecute him. He was interrogated by the Harvard board of Governors after an anonymous denunciation. The board chose to allow him to continue his studies. From this occasion we have a copy of his 'confession' available for inspection. He was of course interrogated and condemned posthumously by the media and the academy. Writing experts came forward to protest against the forging and brutal forcing of a confession from a dead man with no right of appeal. Here we see the sealed and predetermined nature of the interrogation. De Man was accused of heinous crimes based on a single text which patient reading would show to be a forced statement extracted 'in mitigating circumstances'. The monument of de Man defaced as a result of this single text, a victim of the very mode of metonymic substitution he identified. One might equally ask, how many real interrogations and tortures were prompted for others as a result of de Man's irresponsible journalism? It is impossible to know. My point, as you will have gathered, is that I am uncomfortable with the notion of interrogation. Interrogation is not the same as critique or auto-critique. Cultural studies should critique itself but whether it should police itself is an open question at this point.

Let me then divide your questions into two kinds, 'What is cultural studies?' (1 and 7), and 'What are the effects of cultural studies?' (2 to 6), the latter being a corollary of, and easily subsumed within, the former. This may seem reductive but the questions overlap so much that it would be impossible for me to give discrete answers to each.

(1) BECOMING (7)

I am not sure how to answer Question (1) by any means other than autobiography, auto(immunised)biography perhaps. I was for a long time completely unaware that I did cultural studies. Indeed I did not know that I did cultural studies until you (Paul) told me that I did. Let us not ponder for too long on what 'doing' might mean in this context. My PhD was in English Literature, much of the work therein is published in the Muriel Spark book and the book on narrative, both recognisable products of a classic literary training. Although as a graduate student at Glasgow I had made waves, to say the least, by the promotion of theory with other doctoral students in what was then a very traditional, Oxbridge dominated, English department. I took my first job in the, what now seems in retrospect, liberating environment of the Staffordshire University, English Department. To call it 'liberating' would be to risk rewriting history but there was a certain freedom available in 'new university' teaching (this was where the 'deconstruction reading politics' work emerges from) and I owe a profound debt of thanks to my then Head of School, Shaun Richards, who understood that literature had a relationship with both cultural studies and philosophy. Whenever I am pressed on this point – *what do I do?* – I describe myself as a 'literary theorist', a modest claim I hope. On a good day I might go so far as to say that I was interested in philosophy and literature. I would have to be feeling pretentious to call myself a cultural critic, although I sometimes do.

However, when it came time to leave Staffs, for one reason and another, it became clear to me at job interviews that my CV was no longer that of a scholar of English Literature. 'We don't want him, he doesn't do English' was one comment overheard at an interview buffet. Again let's not ponder too long what 'doing' might mean in this context. And so, one day I received a phone call from Paul Bowman (it might have been an email; I can't recall now) advising me to apply for a post in cultural studies at the University of Leeds, at the Centre for Cultural Studies, within the School of Fine Art, History of Art, and Cultural Studies. My first response, as you will recall, was 'I don't do Cultural Studies.' Sooner or later we are going to have to address this problem of 'doing'. Anyway, as the story goes, I was offered the job, I took it, and for one reason or another I became Head of School within 18 months of arriving (something of an inconvenience from the point of view of writing). I am known as the youngest chair of a department in Britain but this has nothing to do with cultural studies and everything to do with institutional accidents. Conversely, one could argue that it has everything to do with cultural studies, to do with the unique nature of cultural studies at Leeds, and with the adventure of becoming-cultural-studies. This will require further explanation.

This résumé gives some indication of the difficulties I have with the idea of being said to do cultural studies. My actual job title is Senior Lecturer in Cultural Theory and Analysis, which may well be a different thing entirely. The issue here is really, what is (are) cultural studies? If cultural studies is such an amorphous and elastic 'discipline' (and so how could it still be a discipline?), or is something of such intolerable dialectising power, to include the work of Richard Hoggart, Raymond Williams, Stuart Hall, Gayatri Spivak, Slavoj Žižek and myself (not that this is a comparison) then any reasonable definition of the boundaries and 'project' of cultural studies is surely impossible. Indeed, if I were to describe what I actually 'do' then I am quite sure that any reasonably broad-minded English Department in the US (although their existence may be mythical) would recognise this as disciplinary English Studies, or even Comparative Literature, despite the fact that I have not been writing recently about novels (which does not preclude me from writing about novels in the future). However, perhaps the point here would be to recognise the becoming-cultural-studies of English. One might equally speak of the becoming-cultural-studies of the humanities in general since the histories of cultural studies are multiple and contradictory: 'English' cultural studies, 'sociological' cultural studies, visual cultural studies, 'media studies' cultural studies, *Kulturwissenschaft*, and so on. Gayatri Spivak speaks of 'Metropolitan Cultural Studies' in comparison to subaltern cultural studies, while for Hillis Miller cultural studies is tied to an array of tele-technology unimagined by Abe Warburg or Raymond Williams.

Perhaps what is required would be a genealogy of cultural studies, certainly a genealogy which questioned (let's not say interrogated) the very idea of the genealogy. I am dissatisfied with the mythic story of cultural studies emerging from the Birmingham School. This story is mythic precisely in the sense that it manages to square a number of contradictions and overdeterminations within a narrative structure similar to that of the story of Oedipus. As the story goes, cultural studies emerges autochthonously from the wilderness of Mosely. It's inaccurate, as Stuart Hall has pointed out several times (although quoting the authority of Hall on the non-unitary nature of cultural studies is as problematic as quoting the authority of Marx to claim that one is not a Marxist). I am not just talking about Williams and the adult education movement as precursors to

Birmingham, or, the fact that Hoggart funded Hall's appointment in the Centre from the fee he took for appearing as Penguin's expert witness in the *Lady Chatterley's Lover* trial (now there's a point of departure for a book entitled *Interrogating Cultural Studies*). Rather, I'm concerned with a confusion between the study of culture and the study of popular cultural forms. The two might not be the same thing, and I would be bold enough to suggest that the latter can on occasion be a much more conservative force than the former.

Raymond Williams provides us with an etymology of 'culture' in *Keywords*. This is a fascinating text in which he tells us that 'culture is one of the two or three most complicated words in the English language'. Of course we know that the roots 'cultura' and 'colore' are related to 'colonus' and 'colony'; thus agriculture and cultivation is linked historically to colonialism. However, the key moment in Williams' definition of this keyword is the figural shift from Humanism on into the eighteenth century in which the metaphorical significance of cultivation is transferred from husbandry to human development in general. Williams identifies a tension between 'cultivation' and 'civilisation' at this time, a difference long since subsumed by cultural studies. This is a pity since the question of civilisation would lead cultural studies, back through Freud, to the problem of the city and, interestingly, to architecture (the architectonics of thought and so on). However, for Williams, it is the influence of the German word *Kultur* and the French word *Cultur* which affects this shift in English. The consequences of this shift are profound for the study of culture. Namely, if we are to appreciate the emergence of 'culture' as an idea in the long history of modernity then cultural studies will need to begin with an 'interrogation' of those texts in which this figural displacement occurs. We begin the MA in Cultural Studies at Leeds with Rousseau's *Discourse on the Origins of Inequality* and move on to Kant's 'An Answer to the Question: What is Enlightenment?' If we were conscientious enough we would stop off at Herder, Hegel and Hobbes as only the minimal indices of this figural diaspora. While some would hold their hands up in horror at this prospect – surely it misses the point of cultural studies as a challenge to dominant cultural formations? – it will have deep ramifications for the sorts of questions you want to ask about the institution. Williams acutely links this linguistic development with the growing hegemony of the Humboldtian university and the emerging colonial discourse of anthropology, finally demonstrating that the idea of 'culture' used so blithely in the twentieth century, and uncritically adopted by cultural studies, comes from this anthropological twist, returning the Enlightenment displacement back to the alternative Latin root of *cultus* and *cult*. Thus cultural studies is implicated in several 'projects' (colonialism, Enlightenment rationality, anthropology, Humanism, the Humboldtian and Arnoldian universities, to name but a few) before we can even speak of its own projection.

It seems quite clear to me that the study of popular cultural forms is distinctly anthropological in this sense. Cultural studies in this mode can be little more than a reversed Leavisitism, constructing alternative canons of culture, praising them for the exercise of differing units of value within equally restricted economies. This sort of thing we might term 'Real Cultural Studies' (soap operas, detective fiction, popular musicology, that sort of thing). I've been to enough cultural studies conferences of this variety to realise that this particular blend of 'the discipline' has really lost its way. It is not enough to read Patricia Cornwell as if she were George Eliot in order to challenge the institutional structures which valorised George Eliot in the first place. Frankly, I'd much rather read Eliot. Cultural Relativism of this sort is really only an inversion of the violent hierarchies which determine an institutional idea of 'value', taking its justification from the logic of market trends rather than disarticulating the notion of value (as if that were possible) within the act of reading itself. I could quote numerous examples of completely inadequate attempts to justify the study of popular forms in this way but I would be straying into your second set of questions. I am not dismissing the study of popular forms, only the means of intelligibility open to those who pursue it. We might note at this point that the whole question of culture as civilisation insofar as it is tied to the idea of the city is also ingrained in the question of economy, and that such an analysis will need to be undertaken in some detail. However, the embarrassment of affiliation with this, for the most part, undertheorised and 'anoraky', version of cultural studies is one of the principal reasons for my reluctance in 'coming out' as 'doing' cultural studies. This, of course, might just be a snobbish embarrassment about members of your family. The anthropology of the popular is not my bag, although the popularity of anthropology might be.

However, if I may return to Williams' *Keywords*, the subtitle of this extraordinary book is 'A vocabulary of culture and society'. This is as much as to say that the word 'culture' comes to totalise the field in which it is only one participant among many (let's leave the complexity of 'society' for another day). De Man would call this a transcendental aberration. Derrida would call it transcendental contraband. So, Williams' definition is an exemplary case of an allegory of reading in which the one thing that cultural studies cannot explain is culture. In this scenario culture is the cause, the object, and the product of cultural studies: pure gold, the value of value, worthy of value because it manages to operate (not that it operates as value, simply that it operates – this is anthropology). Of course, it remains a necessary illusion of cultural studies that it can explain culture and indeed there is no end to the attempts to do so. Recently, Hillis Miller proposed that 'culture names the media part of a global consumerist economy'. Compare this to Hoggart or Williams, let alone Herder and Rousseau. It is not that I disagree with Miller's definition, rather that the definition of culture – as that which simply happens – needs to be so vast that unless one were able, like the proverbial cartographers, to produce a map identical to the land-mass it describes then there will never be a satisfactory definition of culture, or an exhaustion of modes of studying culture, or pathways to these moments of analysis. That is why I view the Birmingham myth with such suspicion and those who would make proprietorial claims for cultural studies as the study of 'popular' or even 'working-class' forms with such scepticism.

I am of course equally suspicious of those who would make claims for the propriety of dominant culture – that goes without saying, this argument has been won long ago. However, my point would be that the universal-anthropological idea of culture as deployed by cultural studies (if there is such a thing, if it is one) may be so all-inclusive as to be practically meaningless and may be the dialectic operation par excellence where the other is transformed into the same. There seems to me a very real danger from this sort of 'popular' cultural studies that in the name of pluralism and 'radical subversion' it is repeating the most reactionary gestures of the archiving fever which founds the Humboldtian university. Namely, the double logic that on the one hand the other is really other to the university and remains outside of it, while on the other hand, the other is not really other so can be brought inside. This, of course, follows a familiar argument from Hegel: if absolute difference is absolutely different from everything including itself, what is absolutely different from absolute difference? The same. Thus difference collapses back into the self-same. Perhaps, this is inevitable but it is not unavoidable. Cultural studies has failed to keep up its vigilance against this and has too quickly been seduced by the ontological imperialism of its own inclusive gesture, which may turn out to be simply an unreflective turn to the dialectic. This would not be surprising given the sorts of 'projects' cultural studies seems to be implicated in. Indeed, it may be something implied by the very idea of a 'project' as such.

However, this only obliquely answers the question 'What is cultural studies (its project and its destination)?' Let me offer you two necessary but not sufficient criteria for cultural studies. Firstly, cultural studies might be the study of the contemporary. I think it was Matthew Arnold who suggests that if we cannot understand the contemporary we have no right to go around making pronounce-ments about the classical world. We might note here that the Birmingham School is actually called the Centre for Contemporary British Cultural Studies. So, Hillis Miller's attempt to understand culture in terms of the tele-technological regime of globalisation is an important contribution to the field. In fact, for Miller, cultural studies is defined by its relation to this digital regime, and the dis-placements which cultural studies can effect in the institution are in part tied to the pressure put upon the Humboldtian university by the demands for a technologised and transnational university 'serving the global economy' (as the mission statement for the University of California reads). However, it could be perfectly possible to study contemporary cultural formations and not 'do' cultural studies. Not only is this what anthropologists do but I would also claim that the endless articles on Foucault and football are not 'doing' cultural studies anymore.

Secondly, cultural studies is a transformative critique of the insti-tution. This would be to pre-empt your second batch of questions, but as your questions indicate it is really the whole point of cultural studies. It is for this reason, however, that I am increasingly of the opinion that cultural studies is now an inappropriate name for what 'ought' to be done under the name of cultural studies. If cultural studies has ossified as just another discipline, with its own methods and objects of knowledge, if it is now as comfortable in the university as English Studies and philosophy, then let us abandon this name as a description of the interminable, transformative critique one would wish to effect in the university. This situation is telling, however. The fate of cultural studies (to become the mainstream approach to the humanities, and the same could be said of 'Theory' here) is indicative of a failure of the very logic of newness.

There is nothing older in the western tradition than the claim for radical newness and breaks with the past. The surest way to ensure that one repeats the errors of the past is to claim to have broken with it. The recuperative powers of revolution are obvious for all to see. This is interesting because it suggests several things. Firstly, that cultural studies will always be enfeebled when it drops the vigilance of theory in favour of claims for what is 'proper' to cultural studies (i.e., the popular). It is not that theory and the popular are not coterminous, rather that the whole point of cultural studies is to open the proper to the scrutiny of the improper. This includes the theoretical limits of cultural studies as well as its object of analysis. Transformative critique must also be auto-critique, which not only asks what is proper to cultural studies but what is proper to the impropriety of questioning the proper. Now, that sort of formulation is just the sort of thing which raises the hackles of real cultural studies folk: all this bloody theory. However, without theory, or let me say without theory as a certain spirit of auto-critique, cultural studies is in constant danger of becoming just another disciplinary endeavour – the term 'Studies' gives the game away here – with a naff object of analysis. The point would be that one cannot 'do' cultural studies simply by borrowing its thematics. Any act of cultural analysis (a term I would now prefer to cultural studies) must be interventionist and transformative, theoretical and inaugural, performative of the idiom in which it operates, and 'material' in its attention to what is resistant (both singular and other) in the object it analyses.

This is to go too quickly and to say a great deal. For example, by 'material' I am referring to de Man's notion of the materiality of the letter rather than a form of historicism. However, what I am talking about here is cultural studies as good reading. If it is not good reading, despite its claims for political importance, cultural studies will simply be recuperated as part of the university archive. The moment of reading for cultural studies 'ought' to be a performative praxis of inaugural responsibility which transforms the tradition it analyses while being faithful to that tradition at the same time, without programming or predicting the future. Now, this is why on the one hand I am keen to return cultural studies to the tradition of cultural critique which arises with modernity, while rigorously questioning that tradition as racist and ontological and all the rest of it. Perhaps we should speak here of a culture of inheritance, of ghosts and of the future readers of teleiopoiesis. The injunction of inheritance, as Derrida notes, is to reaffirm by choosing. We need to ask ourselves what we wish to choose from the inheritance of cultural studies or the western tradition. While, on the other hand, I am equally keen to retain the spirit of cultural studies as a transformative lever able to enact shifts within the powerfully inertial hierarchies of the institution. Good 'reading' (the paleonymic appellation I am proposing here for cultural studies) 'ought' to be able to transform and then reinscribe the conditions of reading in an inaugural founding gesture that is without ground or precedent. I guess such reading would mean the constant reinvention of the institution with every act of reading and the positing anew of the culture while being faithful to it. Where cultural studies is 'going', if I had my way, would be to become departments of Reading or even departments of Reading and Writing, although these 'departments' would soon have to evolve into something else. On our web-site at Leeds we state that the aim of the BA Cultural Studies is to produce good readers, a modest enough claim from which everything else flows, including all the political and institutional claims made for cultural studies. In part, I think this explains my profound alienation from both cultural studies and the academy in general. Namely, that this sort of reading should have no proper place and if this reading is synonymous with the idea of cultural studies then it is improper to call it cultural studies. 'Cultural studies' as a name acts as a trap, seeking to name by the aberrant of nomial effect that which it cannot possibly signify.

Moreover, cultural studies is (are) cultural studies not because it (they) only read popular forms but because it (they) neither preclude any object of analysis nor retreat from any theoretical limits. Which is to say that cultural studies is not exclusively the domain of the popular. It would be perfectly possible to read George Eliot in the inaugural and performative fashion mentioned above and still be 'doing' cultural studies, i.e., still be making a transformative intervention into the present of the institution. The point being that unlike, say, English Studies of a certain sort the protocols of cultural studies do not preclude reading Eliot through, say, Disney. However, reading Disney on its own is not a necessary and sufficient condition for doing cultural studies. This then renders the definition of cultural studies infuriatingly problematic. But cultural studies – or perhaps now we ought to speak of the spirit of cultural studies, the ways in which the ghost of cultural studies haunts the academic castle – if it is to continue its work, may need to abandon its name. As long as the work gets done one might as well call it comparative literature, or, reading and writing, or whatever. The same goes for Theory, call it philosophy, call it thinking, such sobriquets can only have ever been strategic. There can be no systematic pronouncements on cultural studies (and/or theory). Cultural studies will – if it is to be true to itself – always be half inside, half outside the academy, crossing borders from exile to exile. Now, this business of 'crossing borders' (one of Theory's great clichés) is not insignificant to the sort of reading I am proposing here. Just as we cannot do cultural studies if we only borrow its thematics, then similarly reading is not reading if it is merely thematic in orientation. Thematic criticism assumes that everything can be translated into English, and in the case of cultural studies, in which Foucault is from Finchley and Derrida is from Detroit, the universalising idea of culture it promulgates becomes synonymous with the universal language of English. This is a danger. Not only because texts (and thus knowledge) are always inescapably tied to the idiom in which they are written and so much is lost and misappropriated in translation, but because in this way cultural studies may unwittingly be 'serving the global economy' by reducing to the self-same, through translation, everything which is singular and unique. I might add here that we are talking about a certain type of hegemonic English and that we should carefully dis-tinguish between the singular idioms of English(s). However, what this might mean would be that cultural studies may have to apply itself a bit more, it may have to put its head down and do some reading before it can continue to make its more *outré* pronounce-ments on politics, for example – more study, less culture. I am sure that cultural studies (certainly cultural studies in Britain) would view this as something of an inconvenience. Cultural studies, as far as I am aware, in its present form, does not speak French (or anything else for that matter) but Tintin and Zinedine Zidane are not English. If you really wonder where cultural studies 'should' go then I think it needs to redress the imbalance between 'culture' and 'study' which has marked its formation up till now. There needs to be a greater theoretical vigilance to and general wariness against the ways in which cultural studies has all too easily become institutionalised as a discipline. I am not saying that cultural studies should not challenge the pomposity of 'High' culture or see its 'project' as a political intervention of one kind or another, but it really needs to ask how the complacency of these positions have led it to its current recuperation within the institution.

QUESTIONS (2) TO (6)

I am having difficulty here even separating out a response to these two sets of questions. So rather than continually defer my arguments let me turn to the other problematic you wish to address, the institution. Let me speak of two things, then I will stop because there is a danger here of commentary running into bad-tempered opinion, while speaking with the authority of the former. Firstly, let's deal with politics and then with this business of 'outside the university'.

The question of the nature of the political and the form of any 'political intervention' by the academic (let's not make it specific to cultural studies, since it would seem that we all do cultural studies now) is something that has vexed me for sometime. I am just finishing a book on this topic, so the arguments are fresh in my mind and at the same time seem rather obvious and reductive to me. Firstly, the claims of the academic must needs be modest. It is not enough simply to call for change to bring change about. I think there is nothing worse than academics demanding revolution behind the barricades of the Senior Common-Room. This is just bad faith. Equally, academics should offer a more robust defence to activists who accuses them of inactivity, namely, without due reflection how can one be sure that the 'political' task one is engaged in is not serving the most reactionary and established of formulations? We might think here of the ways in which 'anti-capitalism' justifies the disciplinary interventions of capitalism, but examples could be multiplied. Academics have to do what work they can where they can. There is little point in declaring the inevitable victory of the proletariat (or the arrival of the democracy-to-come for that matter) in a specialist theory periodical with a readership of less than a hundred people. Rather, the academic, if s/he is faithful to the spirit of cultural studies as transformative critique, will take whatever opportunities are strategically available to craft an intervention into the institutional and social space. The rather obvious place where this happens is in the seminar room or lecture theatre. Extraordinary things can happen here, and they are extraordinary precisely because they go unrecognised and are unpredictable in their effects. If I teach a student how to think critically, to read with a theoretical vigilance of the powers and discourses which dominate him/her, then this has an immense liberatory potential. Insofar as cultural studies teaches future generations, who in turn teach their own children, then cultural studies has a profound, and as yet unknowable, significance outside of the university. Not that the idea of 'outside the university' is appropriate here, given that in such a socio-economic space all knowledge production has its roots in the university as a technologised, transnational player within globalisation, inextricably linked to both the mediatic and 'political' spheres. There is nothing outside the university any more. Given this, it is beholden on cultural studies and its practitioners as the crafters of a transformative critique of the university to counter the hegemonic potential of this situation. Whether this is done by writing articles or teaching seminars it does not matter (the two cannot be easily separated). What matters is that the messy business of education is done and everything else (the victory of the proletariat, if there are any left, or the democracy to come, if it ever gets here) will follow from this.

Now, that may sound all very vague and at the same time precious. However, let me insert two terms into your questions. Let us replace 'cultural studies' with the words 'race' (or so-called 'post-colonialism') and 'feminism'. Does 'feminism' (if there is such a thing and it is one) have any significance outside of the university at all? What is, has been, might be, or might have been, the significance of post-colonialism within the university? I think these questions answer themselves. It is true that neither feminism nor post-colonialism are historically reducible to cultural studies. Stuart Hall would have a thing or two to say about that. However, we might consider that two of the key expert witnesses in the recent Macpherson inquiry into the investigation surrounding the death of Stephen Lawrence were Stuart Hall and Paul Gilroy (another example of interrogating cultural studies). The Macpherson report concluded that the Metropolitan Police were institutionally racist, and this term has now become a part of common phraseology. Such effects were no doubt unknowable at the time when Hall and Gilroy wrote their monographs and taught their students, but that is the way in which the permeable boundaries of the university and the unpredictable nature of academico-political dissemination work. No doubt, Lord Macpherson's understanding of institutional racism is not as rigorous as Gilroy's but such diffusion is merely an effect of the political as such. In this sense I am not sure that cultural studies' 'failures' are inevitable or structural or even if it is only a matter of time before their realisation. Rather, I think the relation between the production of knowledge in the university and events like the Macpherson report might work in an altogether more complex way. Perhaps, we should stop thinking about cultural studies in terms of

'effects' and begin to attempt the task of understanding its dissemination and corruption (I mean corruption in the sense of how
external influences have moved it from its original white, male,
working-class orientation). For dissemination read the 'projection'
of cultural studies.

Part Two:
Cultural Studies (&) Philosophy

INTRODUCTION

This part represents quite a provocative starting point. The views of these two non-cultural-studies philosophers will prove very helpful for students of cultural studies, whilst representing no less of a challenge to cultural studies. Both Simon Critchley and Chris Norris have authored philosophical studies that have proved very influential within cultural studies, yet they keep their distance, never suggesting that they 'do' cultural studies 'proper'. Nevertheless, they reflect on the discipline from largely affiliative, though critical, perspectives.

As the titles of their contributions indicate, Critchley is more effusive, as he sets out to describe 'Why I Love Cultural Studies'; while Norris is less convinced by, and indeed sees more 'danger' in, what he views as cultural studies' general predilection for social, cultural or historical 'constructivism' and 'relativism'. Accordingly, Norris offers only 'Two Cheers for Cultural Studies', praising its critical work and the advances it has made in terms of furthering what the university should study and how that study should be orientated, but expressing deep-seated reservations about its alleged 'relativism', which, he believes, can lead to revisionism and ethico-political problems with serious cultural impact.

All sorts of important questions will be raised by his spotlighting of this matter: true, cultural studies' critique of all forms of canon, all forms of sedimented tradition, cultural value, prejudice and bias, etc., may well have proved to be a very emancipatory and inclusive movement. But, on the other hand, what does the realisation of cultural relativism, or the relativity of one's preferences and beliefs, entail for the notion of 'truth', for our understanding of 'actual events', and so forth? Many will doubtless take issue with Norris' argument, but nevertheless his criticisms remain challenging: for, in short, what is it that guarantees the difference between the justifications of (what many call) 'postmodern relativism' and, say, the justifications underpinning holocaust denial? The accusation may sound extreme, but Norris implicitly urges us to attend to it.

Simon Critchley relates cultural studies to the aims of continental philosophy, and thinks of both in terms of three key ideas: critique, praxis and emancipation. That is to say, he argues that both cultural studies and continental philosophy are implicitly orientated by some version of a belief in the need for critique of the existing state of affairs with a view to emancipation from whatever conditions of inequality, injustice or exploitation there may be. An interesting corollary of this is his explicit championing of art over popular culture and, indeed, over 'postmodernism' in general, in a manner that is related to but perhaps quite distinct from Norris' position. Whereas Norris reflects at some length on the reasons why certain kinds of art or certain pieces of music might be, as he claims, simply (or complexly) 'better' than others, Critchley simply states that he believes popular culture to be rubbish, and that he prefers art – or events that carry out the kind of transformative power traditionally ascribed to art. In many respects, their positions on the status of art versus popular culture can be read together as challenges to some versions of cultural studies received wisdom. Once again, a gauntlet is thrown, and the task of cultural studies here must be to take it up: As Critchley insists, one of his ultimate intellectual aims is to further people's ability to exercise critically their faculties of discernment and judgement. Norris is implicitly aligned with this position, and, of course, it is perhaps a 'philosophical' injunction that exceeds all disciplinary boundaries, one that is universally necessary, and one that clearly ties many of the avowed aims of cultural studies to a philosophical lineage of which it should remain conscious and in communication with.

5   Why I Love Cultural Studies

Simon Critchley

How do you position yourself and your work in relation to the cultural studies project? Or, rather, do you see cultural studies as a 'project', and is contemporary cultural studies still the 'same' project or discipline as it once was?

I see my work as intimately connected to culture and the study of culture; and by culture I mean the processes by which human beings' identities, lives and institutions are formed. By 'culture' I understand 'formation', or what Hegel would call *Bildung*, which can be translated as 'culture'. And I tend to see that in terms of my own discipline, or through my own discipline, which is philosophy. For me philosophy is and should be a meditation on the meaning of culture – a meditation *on* culture. But often it isn't. So what I see as definitive of philosophy in the continental tradition is a concern with culture and cultural formation, which means that philosophy on this model becomes a historically sensitive, contextually sensitive discipline, which is concerned with giving a critique of actually existing *praxis*, actually existing states of affairs.

So the way that I understand cultural studies should be taken back to the way I understand philosophy: Philosophy on my model turns around three terms, which are critique, praxis and emancipation – namely that philosophy is a critique of existing cultural praxis, with a view to how one might be emancipated from forms of unfree praxis towards more free praxis. So, philosophy is an activity of critique of social praxis which aspires towards emancipation. The point here in relation to something like cultural studies is that philosophy can be a meditation upon cultural meanings and can reveal the contingency of those cultural meanings and practices, and the nature of the hegemonic constructions which impose those cultural meanings and practices.

To give you an example of that: How does Hegel do cultural studies? If we think about a classical philosophical example – Hegel's *Phenomenology of Spirit* – Hegel reads Diderot's *Rameau's Nephew*, and finds in *Rameau's Nephew* – or rather, he *diagnoses* in it – the culture of the Enlightenment. The culture of the Enlightenment for him is defined in terms of a certain splitting or division of the subject: the culture of the Enlightenment is the culture of radical self-alienation, for Hegel, and this is experienced in *wit* and *irony*; in a world where there is no God and nothing is certain the only thing we can do is to be witty.

Now, the point of that example is that Hegel is a philosopher who chooses an exemplary cultural object, a text by Diderot, and a text by Diderot furthermore that is a covert text, which can't be coded as either high or low culture. In many ways, *Rameau's Nephew* is an example of low culture, which is why the text was secret (it wasn't published until the late nineteenth century), and through reading it he gives us a diagnosis of the culture of the Enlightenment, and also shows how we might move beyond that culture. So it corresponds to this model of philosophy as critique of cultural praxis which is linked to emancipation. You can say similar things about somebody like Nietzsche, in the way Nietzsche will meditate upon the meaning of culture, for him that culture being a culture of nihilism (the source of which is Christianity). So part of philosophy is this study of culture.

Another way of thinking about this is that this model of philosophy is and has to be a form of diagnosis of the times – in German, *Zeitdiagnose*. The way Hegel puts this is that philosophy is its time comprehended in thought. And what philosophy does as comprehending its time in thought is to pick out what we might call certain 'cultural pathologies'. This has been the case in philosophy at least since Rousseau, in that a large chunk of philosophy is concerned with diagnosing cultural pathologies. So, for example, Rousseau's Second Discourse – the *Discourse on the Origins of Inequality* – is essentially a critique of culture in terms of identifying certain pathologies, namely the pathology of inequality, the pathology that surrounds property ownership, and so forth. So why I mention this is that I think you can see how the project of continental philosophy is unified around these terms – critique, praxis and emancipation. Which means that philosophy has to be a meditation on culture. If you think of philosophy in those terms you can unify it with the ambitions behind cultural studies in its various guises – from people like Richard Hoggart, Raymond Williams, through to its French variants, through to its more recent varieties. So I see the philosophical project as linked to the project of cultural study. And that has to be linked to a notion of emancipation. But in terms of my own work, that means that what I try to do some of the time is try to pick out specific cultural pathologies in certain exemplary objects. For me in many ways a key question is how one discriminates, how one discriminates cultural objects, how one reads a culture in terms of those objects; and I try to do that in different ways: through popular music, and more recently I've been trying to do that in work in film, on the Coen Brothers, and most recently on Terrence Malik. So in many ways I'd like to be able to imagine a more philosophical form of cultural studies, which would show that philosophy and cultural studies were part of the same family, if not identical twins.

Coming back to what I have just said about this sense of exemplary objects and discrimination: I don't think my position commits me to a form of cultural populism, as is so often claimed about the move towards cultural studies. What interests me is an engaged experience of judgement in relationship to particular objects of study. And, in my rather naïve way, the way I see cultural studies would be in terms of judgement in relationship to particulars. Those particulars could be modernist poems, they could be films, they could be chunks of death metal – it doesn't really matter what. For it is a matter of encouraging *the exercise of judgement*. I have no interest in the high culture/low culture distinction. I simply choose to ignore it. I'd like to encourage discrimination in both registers, between registers, and the kind of work I'd like to see would be work that is informed by choices from all sorts of cultural registers.

It sounds to me like your model of cultural studies would be a subset of philosophy – it sounds like we're going back to Plato here in seeing it as a little part of an overall philosophical project, and for you it's continental philosophy that cultural studies is aligned with. But, you've used certain words – you've spoken of philosophy as a 'meditation' on culture, philosophy as 'critique'. But I think that perhaps the difference between cultural studies and the kind of philosophy that you engage in is that cultural studies tries to be more than critique or meditation – for cultural studies it's all about 'intervention'. Do you see that as a difference between what you do and what cultural studies claims or aims to do, tries to do, or fantasises about?

I don't see a contradiction between what I do and the notion of intervention. I'd like to think of what I do as more of an intervention that would be as activist as the most active cultural studies. I'm just coming to that with a different toolbox, a different set of assumptions, and I try to set those to work in relation to ... well, *all sorts of objects*: I'm happy to talk about anything in that sense if it's interesting or if someone can make it interesting. So meditation is probably something of a misnomer. The vision of philosophy that I have is philosophy as an intervention into culture that would be critical of cultural meanings and productive of new cultural meanings – very much more like the sort of Deleuzean model of philosophy, as the production of new concepts under which we might see things in a different way.

Cultural studies is said to be a political project – it calls itself *a political project. It sounds like you think of the kind of philosophy that you do as being very much related to that. But I think that one accusation against cultural studies is that it doesn't really know anything about politics, that it doesn't really have a politics. What, to your mind, are the politics of cultural studies? Does it have 'one', more than one, or is it, rather, political in a different sense of 'political'? And, secondly, for a cultural studies academic, perhaps as distinct from a philosopher, the question of the 'proper destination' of one's work is strongly felt. That is, a philosopher, perhaps, would be quite happy to be talking to other philosophers, whereas a cultural studies academic wouldn't want just to be talking to other cultural studies academics – in a very literal and direct sense. I think you're talking in a more extended sense ...*

Yes. I'm in a philosophy department, I talk to other philosophers. If all I did was to talk to other philosophers I think I'd slit my wrists and slip into a Roman bath and do away with myself. I mean I'd like to say that philosophy is my institutional home, but I want to address as many people as possible. Pure narcissism I think! So that means, happily, coming from philosophy, you have a sort of grid that you can apply to all sorts of areas. But my work isn't really important in professional philosophy. It's not dismissed, but it's hardly mainstream. My stuff has been picked up much more in political theory, critical and legal theory, international relations, art theory, literary theory – areas like that. So in many ways, my audience is really outside my discipline.

I think that your work is really important to cultural studies, especially when it comes to thinking the politics, the ethics, the philosophical under-pinnings of exactly what one is thinking or what one is trying to say or trying to do. So do you think that cultural studies has a politics that you can specify?

As I understand the question – and this is largely based on my experience of a variety of cultural studies conferences I've been to – then there seems to be a lot of hand-wringing about cultural studies as a political project. My historical understanding, which is pretty shaky, is that cultural studies was a political project in the Birmingham group, in the work of Raymond Williams, in the work of Stuart Hall. That's fairly clear. I think it's equally a political project in the work of Foucault, if we include Foucault in the sphere of cultural studies, and Michel de Certeau (maybe even more so in de Certeau). Whether it was political in the same sense, particularly in the way in which French theory was being translated in the English speaking world, is another question, but certainly I think for them it was a political project, and I think cultural studies still is a political project for the people I read who are working in that area, like Paul Gilroy, for example. I see his work as being continuous with the ambition of cultural studies as a political project.

The question then would be what sort of political project should cultural studies be? And the answer is simple: it should be an eman-cipatory project, and that links back to what I was saying in answer to the first question about the issues of emancipation and the way in which my model of philosophy turns around these three terms of critique, praxis and emancipation. So emancipation for me has become increasingly important. Emancipation has changed. The paradox is that in a world that's more globalised and unified, the meanings of 'emancipation' have become more pluralised. In a sense, it makes more sense to talk about *emancipations*, in the plural. And that's doubtless true: we can't subsume emancipation under some unified goal, as in the classical Marxist picture. But that doesn't mean we should give up the notion of emancipation. Not at all. As Derrida has said, nothing is more outdated than the classical eman-cipatory ideal, and for me *why* you write, why you *do stuff*, is in order to reduce unfreedom. It has to be as naïve as that, I think. Unless your work is animated by that then I don't see why you're doing it other than for forms of professional legitimation, which I think are of no interest at all.

In relation to politics as I conceive of it, the first thing I'd say is that obviously in the history of cultural studies in the 1970s and 1980s the category of hegemony from Gramsci was very important to the work of Stuart Hall and others, and I think it's still important. I understand hegemony as a non-negative category. Hegemony is a description of how political identities are formed. The key term in the theory of hegemony, in Gramsci, but more clearly in the work of Ernesto Laclau, is the notion of *hegemonic articulation*: that identities, cultural meanings, practices, are what they are through processes of articulation which are hegemonic and therefore ultimately political. In a sense, everything becomes political with the category of hegemony, and hegemony is the logic of the political, it's what is at the heart of the political, because that is the way power is organised.

Now, two things can follow from that. I want to relate politics to the category of hegemony, and the category of hegemony can be taken in two ways. On the one hand you can see hegemony as a sort of value-free, neutral analytics of power, in the way that some people would interpret Foucault (I wouldn't interpret Foucault that way, but you *can* interpret Foucault that way). So Foucault is giving us an analytics of the way in which power is organised, through disciplinary practices, or whatever. And when people read Laclau and Mouffe, they tend to see the notion of hegemony in those terms. But – and this would be the second option – I think that at the basis of hegemony is a normative claim, or an ethical claim, that, for example if we think about a book like *Hegemony and Socialist Strategy*,[1] on the one hand we are given a genealogy of the history of Marxism, which is a descriptive analytics of the power structures which produced a certain version of Marxism and how that can be taken apart. But what that leads to in Laclau and Mouffe is a conception of the democratic revolution and radical democracy. And I see that as an implicitly ethical concept.

So, to come back to the question, cultural studies is a political project. The political project turns around the use of the category of hegemony; and hegemony at its core has a normative 'push', a normative force. So for me the key question theoretically is linking or thinking about ethics in relation to politics through this notion of hegemony. For me at the basis of all normative notions is an experience of what I call an ethical demand. And the ethical demand is that by virtue of which we become subjects, and it's on the basis of a certain experience of the ethical subject that we can begin to conceive of a transformative politics.

Now, when I was at Bath Spa University College last year for a big cultural studies conference, one of the things that interested me at the conference was the session on Lévinas and cultural studies. There seems to be a great deal of interest in Lévinas in cultural studies, which I think is interesting, and I'm all in favour of that. What that seems to be speaking to is the question that cultural studies is not *just* a political project, or if it is a political project, at the core of that project has to be some sort of normative claim, some sort of ethical demand, an ethical vision. And it seems that one strand of that within cultural studies is the Lévinasian strand – the Lévinasian-Derridean strand – which is one ethical vision. Another strand would be a sort of Deleuzean strand, which I suppose now would be linked to people like Hardt and Negri – which is also a deeply normative vision of transformative politics, but on the basis of a different ontology.

For me the key category that I'm trying to think about in my own work at the moment is the idea of *commitment*. And I'm trying to breathe life back into the category of commitment. There was, and I suppose there still is, a lot of talk about 'engaged cultural studies'. And in many ways that interests me, that idea of engagement and commitment. For me it's the notion of commitment that can link ethics to politics, and that's work that's underway, it's what I'm teaching at the moment. And teaching is always a laboratory for me.

Which is very interesting, especially insofar as it seems like you see cultural studies as organised predominantly around the concept of hegemony, which I agree with. But then that would imply that, say, the work of Baudrillard or Žižek – or the recent work of Žižek – wouldn't really fall into cultural studies at all (Žižek would probably be quite happy about that!), as I don't think that Žižek agrees with the concept of hegemony in that way ...

I think Žižek is a cultural critic in the highest possible sense of that word. He is someone who is engaged in diagnosis of the times, *Zeitdiagnose*, in the old Frankfurt School sense. And I think when you put Žižek in front of an exemplary cultural object, like David Lynch or, as I remember listening to him talking about *Titanic*, it's extraordinary. What he is unable to think, in my view, is *politics*. That's because he's thinking politics on the basis of the wrong categories, namely psychoanalytic categories. I remain doubtful as to whether Lacanian psychoanalytic categories are going to be able to bring you any understanding of politics, certainly in the way Žižek uses them. I see Žižek as a cultural critic whose theoretical grid is psychoanalytic and philosophical, but not as a political thinker. And I think the weakest aspect of his work is in his political pronouncements, particularly those of the last couple of years, which I think take you to a complete ultra-leftist cul-de-sac.

That too raises very interesting questions, because I once heard Žižek talking on Radio Four, and he was unintelligible *to everyone else on the programme: no one understood what on earth he was talking about. In a sense, he might as well not have been talking at all. So, for cultural studies* and *for Žižek,* or indeed for anyone *within the academy to such an extent, on the level that they talk about politics and they try to do political work in this way, the question is, does that have any significance outside of the university at all?*

Well it does have a significance outside the university, empirically, insofar as a lot of people read Žižek and buy his books. I think that Žižek often picks the soft target of universities to attack: so when he's attacking cultural studies, or when he's attacking multiculturalism, or political correctness, or whatever it is, he's doing it in terms of a university model. I think it's very witty – it's incredibly witty what he does. But I don't think that's the be-all and end-all of politics. So if I'm thinking about politics I want to think about politics in political categories, and I think that there are people that give us those. The person I've worked most closely with and learned most from in that regard is Ernesto Laclau, who has the Marxist tradition under his skin and just understands how politics works. There are problems with Ernesto's work, which we've debated, but what he understands is the *logic* of politics. So, if there is a Žižekian cultural studies, the object of its attack would be these institutions, and in that sense, it's missing the target: it's too easy to attack university academics.

So for cultural studies more generally then, outside of the university, does it have any articulation with political movements, does it have any political 'consequences' … ?

Yes, I hope so. There are various political groups that I've spoken to over the years – I did a talk last year to the Signs of the Times group, when they organised a series of seminars, in London: very well attended, very political, and very sort of cultural studies events, but linked to a political project. So I think you can do that, and I think people are hungry for serious cultural analysis. They're not hungry for a sort of flip, ironical, *knowing* use of theory, which ends up in some sort of relativistic soup. They're not hungry for that, that's *demeaning*. I think there has to be cultural density for intellectual work. Intellectual work has to put its roots down into what's taking place in a culture in order for that work to have any meaning. The paradox is that to have the luxury to do that work it helps if you have a university position, and so in a sense we need institutions, we need frameworks of learning, we need frameworks for study, of the most traditional and rigorous kind. But the echo of that work has to be heard outside of the university, and more importantly it has to listen to what's going on outside. I think that is crucial. In my work, the last two books – the book on continental philosophy and the book on humour that's coming out – I attempted to reach a wider public, which of course is going to be a mixed thing. But there you go. Again, as I said before, professionalisation is the great Satan for me. There does need to be a profession, professions need to be organised, there need to be ways of legitimating intellectual work, but that can't be exhausted by the institutions, otherwise we end up doing cultural studies in an intellectual vacuum, sealed from any contact with the outside world (this is always my worry about a lot of work that goes on in the United States, as it seems much more divorced from actual cultural movements).

I'm just thinking of the terms 'reactive' and 'proactive' – you suggest a lot about listening and paying attention and speaking with the most appropriate potential audience, or trying to construct an audience or a readership. So, do you see cultural studies or your own work as more reactive or proactive, or are these categories simply wrong?

It's both. You try to do work which is *for* an audience *and producing* an audience. That's the fantasy. The hope is that you will do work that will create a constituency. The most successful academics, the most successful intellectuals, like Žižek, say, do that, and there's a constituency for his work. And those of us who are less successful are full of envy for his success!

So, speaking from your position as both inside and outside, with one foot inside and one foot outside of cultural studies, as you are at this particular moment, where do you think cultural studies is going? *This question is obviously tied to that of 'where has it* been?*', which is an interesting and important question itself; but where do you think it* should *go, or what do you think it should now do or try to do? In short, what has cultural studies 'achieved', what has it 'failed' to achieve, and to what extent are these 'failures' inevitable, structural, or is it just that their realisation is only a matter of time or strategy?*

In some of the cultural studies literature I'm familiar with, there's talk of the cultural turn, and there is certainly a cultural turn in the universities and outside of universities, particularly in relationship to subjects like literature, say, which are increasingly difficult to separate from the cultural studies project, simply because of recruitment – universities have to offer media studies, TV, film studies, and so forth. The problem with the cultural turn is that it can risk conspiring with an increasingly globalised and an increasingly homogenised notion of cultural production. I think one of the interesting features about cultural production now is its standardisation, so that not only is *Big Brother* a massive phenomenon in the UK, it's based on a Dutch model and every country in Europe has its own *Big Brother*. It's the same thing with *Pop Idol*, same thing with the *Weakest Link*, the same thing with all of these shows.[2] The specificity of cultural production is broken down through increasing globalisation. And I find that enormously depressing.

I think popular culture for the most part is rubbish. My partner has a poster on her wall which was produced by an art collective in east London, which reads something like 'Don't deceive us with popular culture, what we want is art.' And I am interested in art. I'm interested in things, events, with meaning, power, sublimity. I'm interested in cultural events that can transform one's sense of self. So I'm interested in the things that can have that effect; and that can be anything. It can be a piece of popular music, it can be anything you choose. So the high/low culture distinction doesn't interest me because what interests me is events that can have that power, and insofar as they have that power they are doing what art should do. What I hate is irony. I hate postmodern knowing irony. In fact, I hate postmodernism, and I think postmodernism was a massive diversion of energy away from what we should have been thinking about. And I particularly hate the way in which theory can be used to conspire with irony in a generalised cultural knowingness, so that people have a knowledge of a few things – having read a few books or done a course at university, and will know, as Oscar Wilde said, the price of everything but the value of nothing. I think if cultural studies as an institution could be said to conspire with that, then that's lamentable.

That's strange though, because you speak very highly of Richard Rorty. Is his a different sense of irony? Is there something specific to the way Rorty articulates irony with a political project?

Rorty is a complex case. I do think highly of Rorty, and I think that he is one of the cleverest philosophers of the last 50 years – probably, culturally, *the* most important American philosopher of the last generation. Yet I think his separation of the public and the private domains is implausible, and the way he wants to separate the public from the private is that the public sphere is the liberal sphere, the private sphere is the sphere of irony. So irony becomes a private matter, and it's what people of a certain cultivation do. They can sit at home and read Proust, and listen to Mozart operas, and know that their private tastes do not determine the public meanings of the liberal world. I think that's implausible. If you separate the public from the private in the way Rorty wants to, then you end up in political cynicism, and the paradox is that that's not what Rorty wants. Rorty is a man of the left, in the American sense of the American liberal left, and what he wants is a politics of civic hope, which is actually a leftist project. The theoretical resources he produces – some of them, at least – actually undermine that project. I think it's the right project, but you can get there with other means.

I would like to pursue some other aspects of some of the things that you have been alluding to and mentioning (and using). The first one is that when you talk about emancipation you don't like to specify what that should mean, and you say we should pluralise emancipation. But to refer to Derrida briefly, Derrida argues that pluralisation solves nothing: pluralising merely defers the problem of exactly what it is you are talking about, which ties in I think – well, it does and it doesn't tie in – with the question of policy, or 'what is to be done'. You've answered that directly with reference to the question of commitment and trying to be audible and clear and so on. But with audibility, Derrida argues that audibility is strictly structural, not phenomenal: so audibility and intelligibility have nothing to do with the fact that there is a person speaking; rather it is entirely to do with institutions and language, a kind of politics of language. So if you're working towards a certain kind of audibility, isn't that always already political, and is that the kind of policy, is that the kind of pragmatic activity that you envisage for cultural studies and your own work?

The question of emancipation. Let me try to specify the argument in Derridean terms. I see Derrida's work as fundamentally poised around the question of how one thinks together two contradictory imperatives. On the one hand there is – and it's always 'on the one hand … on the other hand' for Derrida – on the one hand there is an unconditional demand that can't be compromised, that Derrida calls justice (among other things), which I think of as an ethical demand. Then there is the question of how that can be made effective with reference to a specific context – if you like, the pragmatic question. So for Derrida, it's always a question of how one thinks together an unconditional demand with the conditions of a particular context. And what that means is that hegemony, which is the actual taking of a decision on the basis of an unconditional demand in a specific context, is going to be different in different cases. So that's what I mean by pluralisation. Pluralisation simply means that what emancipation is going to mean in a specific context is different from what it's going to mean in another context. So it's context-dependent, but not exhausted by context. There is this trans-contextual demand, which Derrida calls justice, which remains formal, but still operative in any decision. So emancipation has to be pluralised but not compromised, if you like.

In relationship to the politics of audibility – it's a difficult question. And the linking of that to policy and things like that … I am a philosopher by training and by institutional location. The fear that philosophers have is of being unintelligible. Therefore I want to be as intelligible as possible. I suppose what I've learned from analytic philosophy as a student and then subsequently is that philosophy, although engaged in often bizarre theoretical constructions, does speak the language of – or has to speak a language that is at least recognisable by – ordinary people. So, often you'll find that rather sophisticated analytic philosophy will proceed in a very prosaic and matter of fact way. That can become banal, but I kind of like that. It keeps a sense of cultural gravity in one's intellectual activity.

The problem with continental philosophy in the English speaking world is that it often lacks that gravity, so that it often ends up speaking past people's ordinary concerns by adopting this often barely understood jargon. And there are lots of examples of that – friends of mine are guilty of that. So I want to make these intellectual insights speak a plain language that's understood. Again that's a fantasy, because it's a very difficult thing to do. You can always refuse to be understood. Plus there is *a risk of* clarity. I'm often obsessed by an ideal of absolute clarity, with the idea that my work could be intelligible to anybody who could read. And the book on humour I hope is the closest I've got to such a thing – of course that's another fantasy that isn't necessarily going to be successful. The problem is that you end up being compromised by the language that you're forced to use. I mean, you talked about Žižek on Radio Four being unintelligible. When I went on Radio Four I tried to be intelligible. The risk is that you end up becoming banal or that you end up losing any critical distance and your political project fades. That's a risk. And in many ways I haven't sorted that out yet. There are people who've taken different routes, people I respect, who've come out of the same sort of background as me – someone like Keith Ansell-Pearson, who's an old friend of mine, takes quite a different approach to these questions. What was the policy question, in particular?

Well, the policy question in particular basically comes down to my favourite Bill Hicks question: 'Yeah? And? So? What?' That's the question that cultural studies feels like it is (or, if I'm in any way representative of cultural studies, that's the question that I feel like I'm) accused by: I feel like I stand accused in the face of that question – 'Yeah? So that's so clever, but so what?' So I feel challenged by that question. And yet I do not think that cultural studies should be policy making or policy-making studies ...

I think the 'Yeah and so what?' question is the right question. It's a troubling question if you don't understand the nature of what it is that you're doing. I think that philosophy is a humanistic discipline, cultural studies is a humanistic discipline, and humanistic disciplines make remarks that are valid only if they're accepted. So in a sense everything you say about a cultural object *has* to be banal, because it has to be intelligible to the person to whom it's addressed. It's not science. Science can produce a theory on the basis of empirical evidence that has predictive power. That theory could be completely unintelligible to the average man or woman in the street – that doesn't matter. It's a different activity. The humanities are engaged in the production of remarks that in a sense have to be measured against something like a *sensus communis* – something like a community, a community of language speakers, or whatever. What one is trying to do intellectually is to force moments of dissensus into that *sensus communis*. But that means that you have to speak everyday language.

So the 'Yeah and so what?' question is right: we're not in the business of producing a theory that's going to explain the nature of culture. It just ain't like that. What we're doing is producing remarks which can be accepted or rejected or put alongside other remarks, and then it becomes a question of rhetoric and persuasion as to which remarks have the greatest force. Now that's a crucially important question, and too little energy is spent thinking about rhetoric and persuasion. What you want to do with language is to *move* people – like the idea that at certain moments in the House of Commons people would actually cross the floor on the basis of a speech. That's the sense of what you want to do: you want someone to be moved by what you say and to cross the floor. And that depends upon rhetorical power, and that rhetorical power depends upon knowing the conditions of your culture.

Here's a very old-fashioned reactionary thought: when I was a student I remember being in somebody's bedroom in the first year and having an intense conversation with this person (who became a friend); he wanted to be a literary critic. This seemed to be a legitimate ambition – to be a literary critic. And he *could* be a literary critic because in a sense literature, a certain understanding of the canon of literature, in particular modernist literature, had meaning. It's the way people like me made sense of their lives. And I think that this is very much the world that Hoggart and Raymond Williams and the first generation of cultural studies came out of and tried to challenge and deepen. But that's gone. That's simply, more or less, evaporated. What we have now is a situation in which our common currency is a theoretical language, which in a sense is international. The difficulty is making that theoretical language speak to people's everyday concerns. I mean why should it? Why should Foucault, or Lacan, or Judith Butler, or whoever, speak to someone's everyday concerns? So in a sense, one aspect of globalisation is the globalisation of theory, which is interesting. You know there's a globalisation of the theoretical language which people have in common. You can go to a conference in Macedonia or Poland or South America, and people will have a common theoretical language. It could also be linked to the interest in visual art. Visual art has in that sense become an aspect of global culture. Why? Because it's translatable. I don't know where it leads.

Richard Rorty comes to mind straight away, again, when he challenged Laclau, saying, more or less, 'It is you who needs to tell the world why you're so interested in this high theory, and why you think it's so important.' Because all of us who are infected with theoretical interests, we all 'know' why Foucault, for instance, is important. So it does seem like the desire is to be some kind of philosopher-king, preaching the word of Foucault, say, or Hegel, or whoever. But, we can't possibly be, so do you think that we should try to be the 'parasite', to use the Derridean term?

Oh yeah, the gadfly, the parasite, the irritant: that's what the intellectual is and can be. Society is not and should not be run by philosophers.

There's a sense in which the intellectual function has gone or that 'intellectual function' is a misnomer now, because it's now the 'capitalist-corporate-advertising-PR-etc.-function', which used to be the intellectual function. Would you agree with that?

No, I don't.

I mean, that sense might be highly parochial, because it just occurred to me that whenever I listen to one of the French radio stations that you can receive in this country, they always seem to be talking about political issues, it seems. And these are major international radio stations. But then you turn on British radio and it's just ... trivia.

No, it's a good point, but I think that when you're working in a university in a country like Britain then it's very easy to devalue the role of intellectual life because it seems that we are ...

... Because it seems that we are interpellated and subjected as irrelevant?

Yes, we're low-level; we're not even civil servants. We're employees – salaried employees who are there to entertain students. But, what I hang on to, this notion of cultural density or cultural gravity, is that there is a massive hunger amongst people to make meaning of their lives and to criticise the way things are, to imagine other ways things could be. And intellectuals can help us to do that, I think, and can help to give ways to do that. I believe that in many ways this is more pressing than it's ever been. The role of the intellectual is absolutely crucial.

The high theory remark is interesting, though, because in relation to, say, Ernesto Laclau's work, it's the case that Ernesto in English *sounds like* high theory. But Ernesto's theory is highly dependent upon the dynamics of populism in a South American context, obviously in Argentina – of which he has a perfect intuitive understanding. It's just a question of context: it makes sense in Argentina, it doesn't make sense in Virginia in the same way, so that's different horses for different courses. What Rorty does is to banalise everything into the language of the pragmatist. And that's a risk, and it's also a risk in what people like me are up to. You can banalise things too far. A critical discourse has to be recognisable, but it's also got to be slightly strange as well. It's got to be a discourse that produces new concepts, in that Deleuzean sense, and those concepts have to be ones that you both recognise or see and at the same time that change the aspect under which you see phenomena. So it's a delicate business.

But one last thing I want to say about the future of cultural studies, or where cultural studies is going, would be that the world is a dark place and the world has become a darker place since September 11th. As I see it, the real danger of the situation we're in now is the following: September 11th is the moment when globalisation and neo-liberalism part company. What I mean by this is that the vision that sustains a book like Hardt and Negri's *Empire*,[3] let's say, is that the sheer creative energy of the multitude is somehow in tune with, or can be in tune with, the forces of production in a way that will produce emancipation and the overthrow of empire. Hardt and Negri's is probably the best version of Marxism that one can have, I think, because it's resolutely modern. Technology's a good thing, capitalism's a good thing, the destruction of pre-modern ways of life is a good thing. The question is how can the good thing that we call capitalism be prevented from producing the massive inequalities of wealth which it produces? It seems to me that post-September 11th that question is becoming even more acute because neo-liberal globalisation has been replaced by what I call *authoritarian globalisation*, or a *repressive globalisation*, where things have become really reterritorialised on the level of the state.

So let me put it this way: if the Hardt and Negri version is one of a sort of a deterritorialising power within capitalism that can then be said to produce its own inversion through emancipation, then that prospect is increasingly remote. What we've seen since September 11th is the attempt to reterritorialise power along state lines, obviously in the United States but also in Russia and elsewhere. The effects of that, I think, are disastrous. So what does one need in the face of that? I think what one needs in the face of that is *seriousness*. We need intellectual work of utter clarity, that's able to read, pathologise, criticise, and imagine the transformation of the present. And nothing else will do. That's why the category of commitment interests me more and more. But this might change in a few years. In many ways I hope it does. But at this point there's a need for intellectuals in cultural studies and in my own discipline to become utterly serious about what they're doing, about the objects that they choose and why they're choosing them, because it's ... later than you think.

NOTES

1. Ernesto Laclau and Chantal Mouffe, *Hegemony and Socialist Strategy: Towards a Radical Democratic Politics* (London: Verso, 1985).
2. *Big Brother* is a TV show in which contestants share a house (entirely monitored by TV cameras) for a protracted period of time, having no contact with the outside world. Viewers vote out contestants week by week. *Pop Idol* operates in a similar 'audience interactive' way, whereby viewers vote out aspiring pop stars until only one remains, and is hailed the successful 'pop idol'. *The Weakest Link* is a (basically sado-masochistic) 'teamwork' quiz, in which competitors work together to accrue points, and after each round vote out the weakest competitor. [PB]
3. M. Hardt and A. Negri, *Empire* (Cambridge, MA: Harvard University Press, 2001).

6   Two Cheers for Cultural Studies: A Philosopher's View

Chris Norris

How do you position yourself and your work in relation to the cultural studies project? Or, rather, do you see cultural studies as a 'project', and is contemporary cultural studies still the 'same' project or discipline as it once was?

One of my difficulties in answering that question would be the problem I have with certain aspects of the trend toward interdisciplinarity. Of course it's good that people should talk across disciplines, and that they should question some of the more restrictive practices that go on within disciplines. It's good that philosophers should talk to sociologists, sociologists to cultural theorists, cultural theorists to historians, historians to economists and legal theorists, etc. It opens up all sorts of interesting and valuable lines of enquiry. But there's also the risk, I think, that if you push too far towards that breaking down of disciplinary boundaries then you'll lose any sense of focus or intellectual integrity within disciplines.

I suppose that among philosophers (and I count myself as a philosopher, since I teach and work within a philosophy department, and I write mainly about philosophical issues) there's always been a strong desire to maintain the integrity of their own discipline. So you do get some philosophers attacking cultural studies from an assumed position of intellectual superiority. Quite often this produces a very specialised and narrow self-definition, especially within certain branches of analytic philosophy. So, on the one hand, there is a danger of excessive protectionism and defensive resistance to incursions from outside. On the other hand, I think there is a case to be made for maintaining certain criteria of what counts as a genuine or valid philosophical argument. And this goes back a very long way.

Philosophy in a sense is a whole range of questions that are left over when the other disciplines have had their say. If you go right back to the ancient Greeks then you find that this was a time when philosophy recognised no limits to its subject-domain or range of legitimate interests. Aristotle thought of philosophy as a discipline of reflective enquiry which in principle covered every subject under the sun, from the natural sciences to rhetoric, from politics to literary criticism, from logic to ethics, medicine, and cosmology. Then gradually, one by one, the various disciplines split off and established their own standards and their own fields of competence. The natural sciences were among the first to go, and psychology was perhaps the most recent. So philosophy is left with, if you like, the 'big questions', those that specialists in the other disciplines haven't got the time or leisure to investigate: questions of truth, knowledge, meaning, the mind/body problem, freewill *versus* determinism, and so forth. And that's perhaps created a kind of defensiveness within philosophy, a sort of anxious desire to re-establish its own legitimacy as a discipline.

This is even more of a problem with cultural studies. At any rate *my* main problem with it is that cultural studies can seem a rather amorphous discipline, or a whole bunch of disciplines trying to establish a sense of shared identity, a shared range of questions and concerns. It's rather like semiotics, I suppose. I remember the first dawn of excitement about semiotics and the possibility of taking Saussure's structural-linguistic model and extending it to a whole range of other fields in the human, social and even the natural sciences. But I also remember going to conferences where most of the time was spent in discussing just what this new discipline of semiotics was, what its scope and its limits were: territorial questions, if you like, but also questions of method and priority. These sorts of meta-theoretical questions occupied everyone's time. So, on the one hand, you get lots of diverse, distantly connected, vaguely analogous fields of study; on the other, you get these meta-questions, which then become a specialised field of research in themselves. So that's at least a part of the difficulty.

So do you see it in any way as a coherent project? Stuart Hall, for instance, most famously, calls it a 'project'. Do you see cultural studies in any way as a project or not? Is it 'just another' discipline?

It is a project in the sense that it's still comparatively 'young' in terms of having a place in the university curriculum. It's still trying to establish its credentials, and mark out its own area. Part of the difficulty is that, as a young discipline, it has to address high-level theoretical questions about methodology and it also has to do the groundwork, the empirical research. Sometimes the two things can seem wildly disconnected.

One of the claims for the specificity of cultural studies, though, is its claim to be a political project in some way. Do you think that cultural studies has to 'have' a kind of politics? Do you think it 'possesses' one, whether that be left, or even liberal, or whatever? Or is it maybe 'political' in some other sense? And do you tie your own work to a political project, or a project of some kind?

Well, taking the second question first: like a lot of academics I worry periodically about the disconnection (or so it often feels) between my academic work and what I'm doing, so to speak, 'in my own time' – political engagement and protest. There often doesn't seem to be much connection between that and the kind of thing that takes up a lot of my time and intellectual energy in often quite technical areas of philosophical semantics or philosophy of logic or, during the last few years, philosophy of science. So it does seem that these two things are pretty remote and disconnected. But I manage to square it with my conscience by trying to convince myself that all this concern with the realism/anti-realism issue in philosophy of language and logic goes back to a desire to defend realism against various kinds of sceptical, postmodern, or cultural-relativist attack.

I do think there's a politics there, if not always an explicit politics. So I can see a connection between this philosophical work and what I wrote about postmodernism and the Gulf War, that is, the whole debate about Baudrillard's infamous essay 'The Gulf War Has Not Taken Place'. There is a moral and political desire to defend realism against these kinds of sceptical assault, and also a desire to question some of the more facile and philosophically misconceived interpretations of, say, quantum mechanics, which involve a very different kind of anti-realism. Of course you wouldn't write a book about quantum mechanics that was directly inspired by such moral or political motives. Still the connection is not so remote if you think about the way that Lyotard and other postmodernists exploit a whole rhetoric of 'uncertainty', 'undecidability', 'chaotic' phenomena, and so forth, based on a vague understanding of modern (or, as they would have it, 'postmodern') science.

So it sounds like you're saying that work associated with cultural studies, work in postmodernism, for instance, is very politically dodgy. Is that the way you feel?

Yes. But I think 'postmodernism' is one of those blanket terms that covers a multitude of positions, often not very clearly spelled out – not only philosophical positions, but also political positions. There are some postmodernists who would quite honourably defend the idea that any kind of absolutism about truth or knowledge, especially historical truth, is dangerous; that it can be used in a coercive, oppressive way, to enforce dominant and to marginalise dissident views. So I think that the ethical impulse behind their work is often, in that sense, good, or at least ethically defensible. But it very easily leans over into a kind of far-gone cultural relativism, which is not only philosophically misconceived, but also politically disabling. For in the end it prevents you from saying that certain positions, certain historical interpretations, are wrong, that they're based on a partial, misinformed, biased, or ideologically loaded construal of the evidence. So any thinker – say, any feminist – who wishes to assert that the historical record has been falsified or misinterpreted in order to enforce hegemonic values is then in a very difficult position. If historical truth is ultimately up for grabs then no interpretation – no rendering of 'the facts' – can be better (more accurate, less slanted or distorted) than any other. In which case you are in no strong position to protest about versions of history that happen to support some political agenda that you find morally repugnant. So, for instance, feminists who adopt a postmodernist position will find it difficult to argue that history has often been written from at best a gender-blind and at worst a grossly male-centred viewpoint. Or if they do then they can only say that this is a sort of persuasive, rhetorical strategy which tries to get people to consider other stories, other possible interpretations. But they won't be able to claim that their interpretation is better, more truthful, or more historically accurate. This is a pretty standard line of argument against cultural relativism in its various forms. And I do think it has some force.

So you see the concept of historiography as a kind of 'pharmakon' in the Derridean sense – both poison and medicine? So it's almost as if histori-

ography without some rigorous academic protocols is potentially dangerous, politically dangerous: a kind of revisionism?

I think so, yes. There's a bad tendency among some high-brow Sunday paper journalists to use 'postmodernist' as a stock term of abuse. It actually came up a couple of weeks ago in an article in the *Observer* about David Irving, the holocaust denier. The journalist quite rightly excoriated Irvine for suppressing evidence and for offering a massively slanted, not exactly 'misinformed', but utterly mendacious and ideologically driven account of events which minimised the scale and extent of Nazi atrocities. *Suppressio veri* and *suggestio falsi*, to adopt the old legal phraseology. In the last paragraph there was a casual reference to postmodernism – well, post-structuralism, as a matter of fact – saying that of course this type of position, which Irvine takes, gains comfort from the fact that so many academics endorse a sceptical view which would likewise deny the reality of historical events or the existence of objective truths concerning them. When I come across that sort of thing, then it annoys me no end and I want to stick up for the post-structuralists and postmodernists, because they clearly don't want to come out in support of crazed ideologues like Irvine.

On the other hand, their position does lie open to that kind of recruitment. Take for instance Hayden White, who in his early and (I think) his best book, *Metahistory*, puts forward the fairly modest claim that one interesting way to read historical texts is to look at their narrative and rhetorical structures, that is, the relative dominance of certain tropes and figures – you know, the famous four: metaphor, metonymy, synecdoche and irony. But at that stage – way back in 1973 – he wasn't denying the reality of certain historical events, or even (so far as one can tell from his book) the objective truth-value of certain statements concerning them. Rather he was making the interpretative point that those events could be emplotted or described or narrated or explained in different ways. But then in the 1980s he went to a more extreme position which seemed to be saying that history is a textual construct and that there's ultimately no difference between historical narrative, even when it claims to be offering an account of what actually happened, and fictive narrative. That's the kind of conceptual confusion that philosophers are good – or ought to be good – at pointing out: the difference between saying that all history is narrated from a certain point of view, and saying all history is a fictive construct. You can say that history is narrative, in some sense irreducibly narrative: you've got to make sense of historical events, and the way you make sense of them is sure to reflect a certain preferential bias, which no doubt amounts to an ideological viewpoint. But there's a great difference between that and saying that history is a kind of fiction, in which case there must be as many different kinds of fictive emplotment or rhetorical construction as there are different ideologies.

If the Birmingham Centre and especially the work of people like Stuart Hall is something like the founding work, the first, the initiation of the archive, the constitution of the discipline; if that's the institution *of cultural studies (in both senses of 'institution', as in: its* moment *of institution and its* becoming the Institution*), does that have consequences for what cultural studies can do, insofar as that orientation, those methods, those politics, that bias, orients the possibility of work that can be included* as cultural studies? So do you see any limitation? Does it forbid things, does it censor or censure things – both* enable *and* limit things at the same time?*

I think that any discipline, almost by definition, is based on certain exclusions and inclusions. In the case of cultural studies, the strong, original, motivating impulse comes from reasserting the value and the interest of what you might call popular culture over elite culture. The whole early formation of cultural studies, not only in Stuart Hall's work, but in Raymond Williams and Richard Hoggart, comes from a desire to convince people that there are all sorts of really interesting, valuable, academically worthwhile, but also socially important work to be done on so-called popular culture. It was a massive, concerted effort to redefine the notion of culture, to take it away from high, mandarin, elitist, mostly right-wing thinkers and open up a new field of study. There was a politically motivated impulse behind the foundation or the first development of cultural studies, which is still there and which still defines the field to some extent. So there is a natural in-built bias, a natural affinity with popular culture. There is the desire simply to knock down some of the shibboleths of high culture. But, whether it's a limiting bias, I really don't know. It *can* take that form, I suppose.

For instance, to take one case: the whole Bourdieu-inspired approach to cultural studies, which often involves a degree of, not so much resentment toward high culture, but a sort of intra-disciplinary desire to scale the commanding heights. So it is sociology – talk about 'cultural capital' and so forth – which puts the other disciplines in their place, especially philosophy and any version of critical theory that leaves some room for notions of aesthetic value. You could say this about Bourdieu: that really what he's doing, and one thing that cultural theorists are doing on the basis of his work, is to cut the other disciplines down to size by insisting that they are simply products of the drive for cultural hegemony. So Bourdieu's approach to deconstruction, to philosophy generally, but specifically to Derrida (as in the Appendix to his book *Distinction: A Critique of Taste*) is to say that philosophy has set itself up as some kind of master discipline, but in fact can be shown to be the product of certain class interests, certain socio-cultural and high-ground professional motivations. So Bourdieu's approach in the end amounts to just a way of asserting the credentials of a certain sociology of culture at the expense of other disciplines.

In Bourdieu's reading of Kant, for instance (no doubt I'm speaking here as a philosopher, so I'm doing the same thing in a way), his approach to aesthetics is to say that this is a non-discipline which was invented at a certain time, which takes its inspiration from Kant, which sets up certain values of disinterest, detachment, pure aesthetic contemplation, and so forth, without any taint of political or worldly interest. But this is merely a cultural construction which reflects the need of the bourgeoisie to legitimise itself by laying claim to this kind of idealised 'aesthetic' disinterest. And Bourdieu would extend that argument to the modern university system and the whole system of cultural capital, so that (for instance) Derrida's reading of Kant is simply one more example of philosophers trying to colonise a subject area which is entirely of their own creating, simply as a means of establishing their own academic prerogatives. I consider this a very reductive, very biased and prejudicial reading of Derrida, since Derrida is doing all kinds of far more valuable and complicated things, among them a deconstructive (which is *not* to say merely dismissive or downright sceptical) reading of precisely that Kantian aesthetic ideology. One thing he's *not* doing is trying to scratch up a few more points on his own cultural credit account.

I'm not saying that Bourdieu is typical of cultural studies, but I think there is that strain within cultural studies that consists in cutting other disciplines down to size, and trying to explain them simply in terms of certain sociological variables which can then be hooked up to a generalised theory of cultural capital.

It's interesting that you speak of Bourdieu as if he simply is cultural studies. But Bourdieu, in my experience, holds cultural studies in some contempt, almost. So you're affiliating Bourdieu with cultural studies, but maybe it's more the other way around. In terms of all these disputes between academics (between Bourdieu having a pop at philosophy, cultural studies using the work of Bourdieu, but Bourdieu having a pop at cultural studies), and I wonder what you think the significance of cultural studies within the university might be? When you inject something like cultural studies into the institution, what sort of effects might that have? And also – this is a different question, but I'll ask it now, because you've mentioned cultural studies' interest in popular culture: does it have any significance outside of the university?

I'll take the last question first: yes, I think it does. I think it's had a huge influence, and you can see that in the supplements of the Sunday newspapers, the weekly magazines, and radio broadcasts – Radio Three, Radio Four, especially late night on BBC Radio Three in the 'world music' or 'mixing-it' slot. You get these sometimes rather miscellaneous, rather disconnected programmes, but there is a general sense that there are all sorts of things to be investigated outside the usual canon of 'great (western) music' or standard topics for cultural debate. It would take some effort to trace that back to *particular* influences within cultural studies. But I think the sense is that the canon has been, if not destroyed, at least opened up and challenged. This is a very direct result of the sort of work done by people in cultural studies and those who have gone from work in that area to work in the broadcasting media.

In some ways my answer to the first part of your question – that of cultural studies' significance within the university – is that it has had the same sort of influence. To take a personal example: when you get students who are doing joint honours philosophy and cultural theory, different questions tend to come up in seminars. One of them is the question we started off with: by what right or through what sort of intellectual prerogative does philosophy claim the high ground on these big issues of meaning and truth? From there you go on to questions like: why do we count certain things fit topics for philosophical debate and other things not fit topics? This is partly a result of the challenge to the traditional self-image of philosophy mounted by people like Martin Bernal in *Black Athena*, where he says that our whole modern image of philosophy as a discipline comes out of a concerted effort by (mainly) nineteenth-century German philosophers to establish their credentials, to set philosophy up as an academic field, and to establish a privileged link with ancient Greece. This is the position you find in extreme, almost caricatural form in Heidegger – you know, the claim that the *only* languages in which you can do authentic philosophy are ancient Greek and German! So what you get is a very narrow definition of what counts as philosophy, genuine philosophy, or authentic *thinking* as opposed to mere idle, quasi-philosophical chatter.

Then other questions tend to come up in seminars, such as: why is it that certain cultures or traditions are thought to have produced genuine 'philosophy' whereas others are standardly denied that claim? For instance, most philosophers recognise that there has been great Arabic philosophy, Indian philosophy and Jewish philosophy, but not African philosophy. I read an article the other day in which the writer (Don Howard) told how he saw a flier for an undergraduate degree scheme in Native American Philosophy; and he confessed that his first reaction was 'this is an oxymoron, a contradiction in terms: how can there be Native American philosophy? They might have creation myths, they might have poetry, oral tradition, legends, all sorts of other things, but not, surely, philosophy.' But then he realised that this was a sheer prejudice on his part. For why do we allow that, say, the sub-continent of India has a philosophical tradition, whereas Africa doesn't? You can go back to Hegel and see some quite startling, quite appalling passages in his lectures on the philosophy of history, where he says that Africa is this dark-age, closed continent that hasn't yet achieved self-consciousness, perhaps even consciousness! And there are passages in Kant – in Kant's 'anthropological' writings, as distinct from his critical philosophy – where he says some equally outrageous things about the native inability of other cultures (or races) to achieve even the earliest stage of conscious let alone 'philosophical' awareness.

You know, we think of the Indian cultural tradition as having a distinct philosophical component, partly because the Vedanta were influential on Schopenhauer and others, so they found their way into European philosophy and its elective self-definition. Likewise there's sufficient cultural closeness between, say, Graeco-Christian, Judaic and at least some branches of Islamic thought for us to count the latter in as genuine contributions to the ongoing philosophic dialogue. But of course it was through Islamic culture that the texts of the ancient Greeks were transmitted to us. There's a fairly selective filtering process that very often goes on here.

So my general point is that one major influence of cultural studies is to alert people to the possibility that their minds have been closed in all sorts of quite drastic ways. But I'd want to make a distinction between that sort of salutary recognition that the canon needs to be opened up, that the self-image of philosophy needs to be questioned, and the kind of cultural relativism which says that philosophy is just a kind of writing and that there is no difference between philosophy, literary criticism, cultural anthropology, or whatever else you care to name – in other words, the Rorty position. Rorty's spent a long time now, 20 years or near enough, saying that philosophy doesn't really exist as a discipline, or that, insofar as it does, then it's just a matter of professional self-definition or *amour-propre*. He says, let's read philosophical texts as if they were poems, let's value them for their metaphors, their narrative interest, their creative brilliance, and so forth. But you don't have to go that far, you don't have to push right through with the 'strong' textualist argument and reject the whole idea of disciplinary standards, in order to recognise that in some ways philosophy has often defined itself in a narrowly prejudicial way.

The point I'm making with the Native American example, or the point that Don Howard was making about it, was that he was quite shocked at his own prejudice, shocked as to why that phrase 'Native American Philosophy' struck him as a contradiction in terms. So he asked himself, can we possibly be justified in making that sort of distinction? And I think the answer is that we shouldn't be making it in anything like such an arrogant manner – or with anything like the kind of false *a priori* certitude – that Kant and Hegel brought to the question when so little was known about other cultural (including philosophical) traditions. After all the ancient Greeks – or the freer, more speculative thinkers among them – were already aware of this, of the fact that other people had different gods, different ideas, different ethical values. Still I would want to say that there are certain questions – for instance, questions about historical truth and the difference between historical narrative and fictional narrative – that *are* philosophical questions, which of course doesn't mean that only philosophers can discuss them.

But what I'm still resisting is the Rorty-style dissolution of *all* disciplinary boundaries. Rorty thinks that the best thing anyone can do for any discipline is shake it up periodically: devise new metaphors, new modes of description, a new turn in the 'cultural conversation', as he would say. That's what keeps things moving along. This is fair enough, but he also seems to be saying something more extreme. For example, you might do a study of the revolution in physics at the turn of the century and the advent of quantum mechanics from a cultural-historical point of view, and that could be very useful. It might tell you all sorts of interesting things about historical conditions, socio-political pressures, and perhaps the way that the orthodox (Copenhagen) interpretation of quantum mechanics was influenced by factors like these. There has been quite a lot of work done in this area and I have written about it myself. Still I would want to say that the truth or falsehood of the orthodox quantum theory is a strictly scientific matter – one for the physicists to sort out, maybe with some help from philosophers of science – and has absolutely nothing to do with those historical, cultural, or ideological factors. But I think Rorty wants to push the argument much further than that. He wants to take a strong descriptivist position which says that language goes 'all the way down', that there is no distinguishing 'reality' from the ways we describe it, whether at the microphysical level (as with quantum mechanics) or at the macrophysical level. He wants to shake everything up, including the criteria for what counts as an interesting description relative to a certain context of enquiry.

Of course he may be doing this partly to flutter the dovecote, to provoke scandalised responses from stodgy old realists and hidebound disciplinarians like me. And I'm not equating cultural studies with, say, the strong programme in the sociology of knowledge. But I do think there's often a marked affinity between the two things. The strong programme goes quite a long way toward the Rorty position, in the sense that it makes no distinction, at least from a sociological standpoint, between successful scientific theories, or so-called progressive episodes in scientific history, and failed episodes, dead-ends, discredited theories, disproven conjectures, or those that have fallen by the wayside. Thus it works on the principle of 'parity of esteem' whereby you have to subject both kinds of theory to the same kind of sociological investigation. This approach is currently quite widespread among sociologists of science and cultural theorists of a similar inclination. It seems to me that this bias goes deep and has produced a regular distorting effect in various applications of the 'strong'-sociological approach. So during the past five or six years I've spent a lot of time looking at examples of it, and arguing that this kind of cultural relativism, or social constructivism, is philosophically misconceived, and can have, for the reasons I was discussing earlier, quite harmful political effects.

You imply that you haven't kept up with cultural studies. Does that mean that you lost interest in it for some reason, and was that something to do with its direction, or its orientation?

Well, it's partly for the boring practical reason that I spend a lot of time reading what I have to teach, which sometimes – if I'm lucky – fits in with some project of on-going research. It's partly that. But my main involvement in cultural studies is through an MA course we launched about ten years ago in Cardiff, called 'Music, Culture, and Politics'. It was started by a colleague of mine in the history department, Rob Stradling, along with myself, a couple of colleagues in philosophy, and people in the music department; and it was very much a cultural studies approach. It was premised on the idea (which I didn't share, but was more than happy to debate) that there was no such thing as musical value, or 'good' music, or a canon of acknowledged great works apart from the way the canon has been constructed through various sorts of hegemonic interest. So it soon turned into a lively discussion – very good for the students, I should say – as to whether some music is better than other music, and according to just what criteria, or whether all judgements of value or taste are sheerly cultural constructions. Rob Stradling had co-authored a book (with Meirion Hughes) on the English Musical Renaissance, which set out to 'deconstruct' the idea that there had been this great blossoming of musical creativity in England during the early years of the twentieth century, starting with Elgar and Vaughan Williams. Again, it was a social constructivist approach, which said that this so-called musical renaissance was planned, devised, programmed, 'orchestrated', if you like, through various well-placed institutions, like the BBC and the Promenade Concerts and the big music festivals. So we shouldn't be taken in by the idea of Elgar's emerging as the new-found voice of English musical genius after four centuries – since the death of Purcell – during which England had been justly described as *das Land ohne Musik*.

I suppose I had been sympathetic to that sort of idea until around the late 1980s. I edited a book called *Music and the Politics of Culture* which was a collection of essays putting pretty much that case, along with other theoretical perspectives (post-structuralist, postmodernist, Frankfurt School, etc.) which fitted the approach well enough. Then

I became disenchanted with it, and would now want to argue, *not* that there is self-evidently 'great' music, so that you just stamp your foot and insist 'This is a great piece, whatever you think!', but at least that one can go a lot further in offering reasons or justificatory arguments in matters of musical evaluation. Of course these are never definitive or knock-down arguments – you can never hope to 'win' in a dispute about musical value, or literary value, for that matter, simply because aesthetic criteria are always open to debate. Kant is a useful guide here, as so often, when he says that aesthetic judgements don't involve determinate concepts (which may be either true or false, right or wrong) but rather involve the subjective – more precisely, the intersubjective – exercise of judgement. But the fact that such responses can be intersubjective (that is to say, make appeal to certain shared evaluative criteria) means that we can go a lot further in defending our judgement of a piece of music than just saying 'I like it' or 'I think it's good.' You can even do old-fashioned things like thematic analysis or the study of long-range tonal development and you can explain *why* you think it's good. So quite a lot of the discussion in these seminars over the last ten years has involved that kind of debate: whether aesthetic value is ultimately a cultural construction relative to a set of ideological priorities, or whether it's something that *can* be discussed, not so much in 'objective' but at least in intersubjectively debatable terms.

I think music's a particularly good example, because people have such fierce passions about it and very often are willing to defend their judgements as far as they can. In Literary Studies I have the impression that it has all gone a bit off-the-boil because a lot of these debates have been worked over for so long – you know, the debate about the canon, about whether it still exists in any form, or how best to open up or explode the canon. To some extent they've become stale. But they've hit musicology and music theory much more recently, so they're still fiercely disputed.

With this question of the musical canon you can go some way in agreeing with the argument that the canon as we have it – the standard concert promoter's idea of the great canon of western music – is to some extent an historical construct. In fact you can be much more specific than that: you can say that it's largely the product of a certain Austro-German idea of musical development, which began with Bach and continued through Haydn, Mozart, Beethoven, and then, according to taste, Schubert, Schumann, either Wagner or Brahms, Bruckner, Mahler, Schönberg, and so forth. It is very much centred on that Viennese classicist idea not only of what constitutes musical history, but also of what constitutes a great musical work of art. You get the same metaphors involved, metaphors of growth, organic form, evolving structure, preordained development, etc.

This connects with the whole Bourdieu question about aesthetic taste, cultural privilege, and so forth; his idea that really what you're doing when you profess a liking for this or that composer or artist, or decide which picture to hang on your wall, is an assertion of class status or aspiring class status. So some people will have Picassos on their wall, they'll listen to Stravinsky, read T.S. Eliot, or whatever, and that will be a way of signalling their superior taste, and hence of their most definitely *not* belonging to the class of those who have chocolate-box pictures on their wall, or read 'cheap' fiction, or listen to – I don't know, maybe Val Doonican. Of course, again, there is some truth in this as a matter of sociological observation, or of why some people ('arty' types) make a show of their high-class cultural preferences. But it is still a crassly reductive approach and one that itself betrays a kind of professional-cultural one-upmanship: it is a way of asserting the superior insights of sociology over the claims of aesthetics, or indeed of other disciplines like philosophy and literary criticism.

That's why aesthetics is so important. You get a range of positions on this, among them the extreme dismissive attitude of someone like Bourdieu, or of Tony Bennett, who may have changed his mind in the interim but who wrote an essay 20 years back saying that aesthetics is 'a completely useless kind of knowledge': in other words, just a hegemonic construct which has no genuine content or object of study but which merely serves to justify certain bourgeois class-privileges, cultural prejudices, and so forth. (This is Tony Bennett the cultural theorist, by the way, not the one who left his heart in San Francisco.) Then there is Terry Eagleton's more nuanced position, which is that aesthetics is a crucial field of engagement, and partly for just that reason: that it encodes or articulates so many issues about politics, culture, and so forth, that you mustn't let it go, you mustn't surrender it to the mandarins and watchdogs of bourgeois 'taste'. At the opposite extreme you'd have a sort of neo-Kantian position, which would be that aesthetic judgement is autonomous, that aesthetic values are timeless and aspire to inter-subjective universality, and moreover that the exercise of judgement in this mode has crucial implications for ethics, or the exercise of Kantian 'practical reason'.

Nowadays you won't find many people subscribing to this line of argument, at least not many people in critical theory or cultural studies! More of them will be apt to take something like the Bourdieu or Tony Bennett line. So there's a degree of scepticism, sometimes amounting to flat hostility, about most present-day discussions of aesthetics. Also there is the fact that Kantian talk of 'autonomy' tends to be endorsed most strongly by right-wing ideologues like Roger Scruton who are anxious to keep art safe from the barbarians, by which they mean Marxists, feminists, cultural materialists, canon-revisionists, and other politically-motivated types. I think Kant was right, in a sense. I don't think he was right that you can distinguish a purely aesthetic realm of experience and judgement which has nothing to do with politics or so-called extraneous interests. But at least he was onto something – something of real importance – which emerges very clearly in Derrida's work on Kant. Derrida has a reading of the *Critique of Judgement* which is, as you'd expect, very sceptical about Kant's idea of aesthetic autonomy or of pure, disinterested aesthetic contemplation. But at the same time he makes the point that one thing Kant was attempting to do was secure the *possibility* of disinterested judgement as a way of resisting the power of (say) governments or coercive agencies of various sorts to impose their agenda on the conduct of free intellectual enquiry.

So Derrida would say that the big question raised by the Third Critique is the question of how the so-called 'pure' disciplines relate to the 'applied' disciplines. Thus it might be pure maths and applied maths, or theoretical physics and applied physics, or what we think of as the paradigm-cases of 'applied' knowledge like business or management-studies and what we think of as the paradigm-'pure' subjects, like philosophy or art-history. Derrida would want to question those distinctions, he'd want to bring out their various internal tensions and complications. But he wouldn't want to go the full postmodernist hog and say that the very idea of disinterest (whether in aesthetics or in various kinds of university research) is just an ideological alibi or a kind of self-serving fiction. So, very briefly, that is the difference between postmodernism and decon-struction. Postmodernism amounts to a generalised scepticism (or cynicism) about the whole idea of disinterested, truth-seeking enquiry; whereas deconstruction is a critical probing and analysis of the presuppositions behind it.

This takes us back to music, where 'postmodernist' is the label often attached to certain kinds of currently popular minimalist works, such as those of Michael Nyman and Philip Glass, or those of the 'holy minimalists', John Tavener and Arvo Pärt. I think that a lot of it is simply bad music and that critics who don't say so – perhaps for fear of being called elitist – are letting themselves and their readers down. Again, I'd want to go farther than just saying 'I don't like it', because that's no argument at all. I think that this music (or most of it) is repetitive, predictable, mind-numbingly banal and dreary. Also I think this is where the connection between aesthetics and ethics comes in: such music is a kind of insult to the listener. It assumes that the listener is incapable of following long-range tonal developments or of recognising thematic transformations and key changes, and all the other things that give value and interest to the experience of music.

So I always feel sort of insulted when I listen to it – partly because people who've read the uncritical critics and who think of it as 'serious' music could be listening to other, much better music, that's to say, music that is far more inventive, mind-stretching, more musically rewarding. I think that Kant's basically right about this, although that's not quite the way he framed the argument. Questions of aesthetic judgement do connect in complicated ways with questions of ethics. In that respect I suppose I'm a kind of, not exactly unreconstructed first-generation Frankfurt theorist, but someone who agrees with Adorno when he talks about regressive listening and the fetishistic fixation on 'big tunes' taken out of context: what you get on Classic FM, if you like, where the bleeding chunks of popular favourites are repeated over and over again. It is evidence of a degraded musical culture and degraded habits of musical response.

I hope I'm not being elitist about this. Perhaps it comes across as a kind of elitism. But it's more the sense that music really is important, and that questions of musical judgement, and even of aesthetic theory applied to music, are also really important. I would go along with Adorno and say that you can do a kind of cultural-political physiognomy of 'the way we live now' by listening to the kind of music that is most heavily promoted, the way it is performed, broadcast, or experienced in various social contexts. I would say that Adorno is right that there is such a thing as regressive listening, and that it does take the form of a kind of incapacity or unwillingness to listen thoughtfully and attentively to music. This is not a puritanical claim, even if it sometimes sounds that way in Adorno; you know, the idea that if music is any good then it has got to be difficult, hold out against easy (pleasurable) consumption, resist the blandishments of the 'culture industry', refuse to yield up its secrets without immense effort on the listener's part. Still it can do some of this – not fall back into all the old clichés and routine patterns of development – without having to be gulped down like a spoonful of nasty medicine.

Insofar as 'postmodernism' means anything at all when it's applied to writing about music, it often comes down to an inert relativism which says that any music is as good as any other, since there are no criteria beyond those that are products of cultural background, class privilege, and so forth. Now, you can resist that idea without falling back on some kind of high mandarin traditionalist defence of the canon – whatever 'the canon' is. So one good thing that cultural studies has done is to raise that question: what is canonical judgement? But again, if it goes too far ... – for instance, the whole attack on 'organic form' in music criticism: it's almost an article of faith among new musicologists that the notion of organic form is a purely ideological construct, one that was invented in the early to mid-nineteenth century in order to uphold the hegemonic claims of a certain musical tradition, along with certain 'bourgeois' canons of taste and discrimination. So 'organic form' is not something *there* in the music but something foisted or projected onto it through the efforts of ideologically-motivated critics, commentators, and analysts. But that's simply not true, or at any rate *not simply* true. One can say with a sense of startled discovery that the notion of sonata form was something that was discovered long after the works that supposedly embody sonata form were composed. But this just means that the composers had a kind of instinctual grasp of it, didn't need to theorise about it, whereas it took the critics and the analysts a bit longer to catch up. It doesn't mean that 'sonata form' is nothing more than a cultural or ideological construct. So there's a kind of counter-cultural attack on the notions of organic form, unity, development, thematic continuity, and so forth – all those classical values. It is healthy in a way, because there are all kinds of other musical forms, all kinds of complex forms that just don't fit into that sometimes (at its worst) procrustean way of thinking about music. But if the counter-movement becomes an iron-cast orthodoxy in its own right then it becomes as bad as the old dogmatic ways of imposing those notions.

What of the relationship between this kind of cultural criticism, the 'difficult' language it uses, and the 'outside world', as it were?

Well that's the old problem of jargon, isn't it? All disciplines develop their own kind of jargon. If you take 'jargon' as a neutral, non-pejorative term, then it can sometimes be very useful. It's a way of saying briefly and precisely what would otherwise require a lengthy paraphrase and would probably come across as very fuzzy. Some kinds of jargon are almost indispensable. That would include, in cultural studies, words like 'hegemony', which we've used several times. It's a very convenient term: there is no equivalent, no simpler everyday equivalent to it. It says precisely what it is required to say. There's a whole background of complex theoretical ideas that have gone into the working definition of 'hegemony'. So when critics, mostly right-wing commentators, attack cultural theorists for using words like hegemony, I think they are completely off the track. There's a place in cultural studies, as in any other discipline, for a certain kind of jargon, or technical language, which is not just an insider trick for baffling all the outsiders. It's a useful way of communicating. Insofar as critics or commentators attack cultural studies' jargon simply because they don't understand it, or because they feel excluded from the fold, then I think they've got it wrong.

One reason why these mostly right-wing commentators (people like the ex-chief-wrecker of schools, Chris Woodhead), are able to score points off cultural studies, and against what they see as Mickey Mouse disciplines, in what they contemptuously call the 'new universities', is that there seems to be a blatant mismatch between the subject-matter of cultural studies – popular culture of various kinds – and the technical 'jargon' that has developed within those disciplines. It strikes them as an absurd disparity between the heavyweight theoretical apparatus brought to bear (which they don't understand, usually, because they haven't bothered to read it) and what they consider the trivial topics to which it is applied. So they can rely on getting a laugh among *Daily Telegraph* readers, or *Times* readers, simply by listing course titles and descriptions of syllabus content. Roger Scruton is very fond of doing this sort of thing and it just shows that he hasn't grasped a basic principle of philosophy, that is, the distinction between first-order (object) languages and higher-order theoretical or formal languages. This was a leading principle of structuralist thought and of course came in for some sceptical treatment by post-structuralists and postmodernists like Lyotard who made a big point of supposedly doing away with any kind of meta-linguistic or 'meta-narrative' approach. But really the distinction is there, even if not explicitly announced, as soon as you start to theorise about texts, discourses, cultural practices, or whatever.

It seems to me that philosophy – analytic philosophy – is currently on the receiving end of a lot of similar treatment. It takes a different form, but if you look at the responses when Quine died last year, there were some very disrespectful, even mocking obituaries. There was one in the *Guardian*, I recall, which said that philosophy was once a really important, central, humanistic discipline, but now you had a 'great' philosopher like Quine who occupied himself entirely with writing about technical issues in philosophy of language and logic, and whose jargon was incomprehensible even to the well-educated layperson. This struck the writer (Peter Preston) as a sad reflection on the way that philosophy had become not just out of touch with the wider public but also more trivial – more footling and obsessive – through its over-concern with these technical issues. But this is like saying that mathematicians fail in their public responsibility when they spend years on some fantastically complicated proof rather than writing elementary maths primers, or that physicists ought to be writing Teach Yourself books on basic physics rather than trying to come up with some new theoretical advance. These comparisons may seem a bit remote from the situation in cultural studies but even there I don't think it is a cause for too much agonised self-questioning if people like Scruton and Woodhead weigh in with the usual know-nothing line of attack.

Another point I'd like to make here – again with reference to my own teaching – is that some of the best students are in fact strongly drawn to just the kind of technical work in philosophy of language and logic that can look pretty off-putting to anyone outside the discipline. A bit of recent history might be relevant here. There was a time (about twelve years ago) when Philosophy in British universities was in a really bad state, with declining student numbers and lots of departmental closures all over the country. The Cardiff department almost closed, and in fact only survived by joining up with English and Communications as a part of a larger (hence economically viable) unit. And then there was a concerted campaign by philosophers to convince the government, parents, employers, and other interested parties that philosophy was a really important, vital, intellectually (and even economically) productive discipline. Without philosophy you wouldn't have had modern symbolic logic, without symbolic logic you wouldn't have had the computer revolution, etc. And of course, besides that, it had a crucial role to play in educating students to be more reflective, more critical, more competent in matters of social and moral concern. That campaign was very successful, so we now have as many students as we can possibly cope with. But I detect signs of a growing counter-reaction in the press, where you find people saying things like 'What are they for, these philosophers? They only engage in such trivial, tedious, irrelevant debates, stuff about whether atoms really exist, whether translation is really possible, whether knowledge can be defined as "justified true belief"', and so forth. So although the charge is rather different from that aimed against cultural studies – not so much the accusation of triviality and absurdly pretentious theoretical jargon, more the accusation of over-specialism and remoteness from 'real' human concerns – it's still the same kind of backlash.

Again, this is exactly what Derrida's talking about when he says that *from a certain point of view* it may be unrealistic or sheerly utopian to think of philosophy – the Philosophy Faculty – as being the place in the university where questions are raised in a spirit of disinterested, truth-seeking enquiry. From an administrative, profit-led, 'realistic' standpoint this may seem an absurdly quixotic conception, and perhaps a good reason for closing more departments down. All the same, Derrida thinks, it's important to conserve that idea of philosophical disinterest – at least as a kind of Kantian regulative Idea – because otherwise there will be no place for criticism, for resistance to state pressure, commercial incentives, or other kinds of 'outside' influence. Not that this ideal could ever be achieved in practice, any more than the study of pure mathematics could ever be pursued in *total* isolation from its possible applied uses, or any more than work in theoretical physics could ever claim *total* non-responsibility for the sorts of applied technological advance to which it gives rise.

You've discussed these connections between philosophy and cultural studies, aesthetics, music, art and science. The traditional idea is that cultural studies was kind of born out of literary analysis, post-colonialism, postmodernism and popular culture. What kind of connections do you see there? What kind of relations?

Well there's a bit of personal history here. The relevant point would be that my first degree was a very traditional London University literature-based English degree, with almost no literary theory. A very canonical approach: 'Beowulf to Virginia Woolf', as the old joke had it. Then as a postgraduate I went to University College, London. Frank Kermode was there, running a graduate seminar, and we read a great range of mainly French or French-influenced theoretical texts: Barthes and Derrida especially, but also a lot of new fiction and other, 'classic' literary works which came out (I think through Kermode's gentle prompting) as *nouveaux romans* before their time. I was very much thrown in at the deep end, and was very excited about all this, and remember thinking: 'Why didn't I read all these things much earlier?' That was when I began to question all sorts of received ideas about literary meaning and value, and it did seem extremely progressive, in a political sense, not just in a vaguely cultural and academic sense, especially the reading of Derrida, which made an immense and lasting impression. That was how I first became interested in philosophy – via literary theory. I did a lot of belated catching up. I read philosophy backwards, so to speak, from Derrida to all the philosophers Derrida had written about: Austin, Husserl, Nietzsche, Hegel, Kant, Descartes, right the way back to Aristotle and Plato. So it was a curious kind of reverse philosophical education.

Anyway, to return to your point about literary theory: I certainly thought those ideas were radical, not just in the 'infantile leftist' sense of turning everything upside-down, but in the sense of being socially and politically progressive. And then, about ten years later, I began to have some doubts about that, partly because I thought that post-structuralism had turned, *via* postmodernism, into a kind of blanket scepticism about truth, knowledge, and reason. Partly on that account and partly because I came to have doubts about that whole late-1960s *Tel Quel* conjuncture – semiotics with a certain reading of Freud *via* Lacan and a certain reading of Marx *via* Althusser, and the idea of the plural text, or the limit text, as Barthes would call it, as a potentially radicalising, progressive, or even revolutionary force. You know, the 'semioclastic' idea (I think this term came from Barthes) that by transforming our language, or our forms of signifying practice, or our modes of discursive or narrative representation, we could somehow transform the world. This came to seem a rather upside-down way of putting it – a sort of reversal of Marx's theses on Feuerbach.

It was also partly the feeling that Frank Kermode identified when he reviewed some of my books and registered a steadily increasing sense of disillusionment with literary theory. What started out as a way of reading texts in imaginative, interesting, productive new ways had now turned into a kind of orthodoxy, where theorists showed little interest in novels or poems, but used them mainly as pegs on which to hang some clanking theoretical argument. So I suppose he feels partly responsible for having introduced all these new ideas which have now turned into something he doesn't recognise or want to acknowledge. Insofar as personal histories are relevant to this, it's been one of partial disenchantment on my part. But also, what I thought of then as philosophy of language – having approached all these things *via* fairly recent, sceptically inclined French ideas – later came to strike me as philosophically deficient and open to all sorts of potentially harmful misapplication. Again I would make an exception of Derrida but, then, he is an exception to just about every generalised statement you could make about the way that philosophy has gone during the past half-century. So really it is a matter of belated education on my part!

Literary theory was once really marginal. Literary criticism was considered marginal, but literary theory was a kind of meta-reflection on the principles of literary criticism. What happened in the mid-1970s – putting it crudely – was that this once marginal discipline then suddenly became very central, and you could see this happening year by year across various disciplines. It first began to have an influence in cultural studies, then in sociology, then in anthropology (or Geertz-style ethnography), then in legal studies, then in musicology – and the list could go on. In 1986, when I was teaching at Berkeley, I had a graduate seminar on deconstruction where students from the Law School used to come along and write essays that were full of references to Derrida, or to articles in the law journals that cited Derrida in every second footnote. Again, it's good to see these interdisciplinary overtures, but not so good when the result of that sort of discipline-hopping is to turn everything into a kind of literary text.

Stanley Fish would be one example of an all-purpose rhetorician whose ideas come out of literary theory but who has since turned his hand to legal studies and a whole bunch of other topics which he treats in just the same way. So he thinks that all theorists are sadly in the grip of one or the other delusion: 'positive foundationalist theory-hope' which leads them to suppose that they can reinforce their case with some knock-down principled argument, or 'negative anti-foundationalist theory-hope' which leads them to suppose (just as vainly) that they can knock down someone else's argument by subjecting it to this or that form of sceptical critique. So on the one hand you have earnest-minded hermeneutic thinkers like E.D. Hirsch, in his book *Validity in Interpretation*, bringing up Husserl and other big philosophical guns to make his case stick, and on the other you have various Marxists, psychoanalytic critics, feminists, deconstructionists, *et al.*, finding 'theoretical' reasons to think that texts don't say what they mean or mean what they say. But all this stuff is beside the point, Fish argues, since what texts mean *just is* what they mean according to the prevalent norms within this or that existing 'interpretive community'. So Hirsch's arguments make sense to people of a similar persuasion, while the Marxists, feminists and deconstructionists will also find a receptive readership only if there are already enough people around who share their language-game, discourse, technical jargon, or whatever. It is not only truth that drops out completely from Fish's neo-pragmatist view of things but also any notion of learning something new or seeing the error of one's past ideas. In which case we might as well pack up reading, thinking, or debating these issues. Thus, as Fish says, the most fitting response from any reader of his work would be a postcard with the message 'You're right!' and then complete silence.

Anyway, back to the personal narrative. I experienced a growing unease with the colonisation of other disciplines by a certain kind of literary theory, which tended toward the sceptical postmodern position that everything is ultimately a textual construct. So to the extent that I've been focusing on issues in philosophical semantics, and in epistemology and philosophy of science, it's perhaps been a roundabout way of trying to resolve questions that were raised most directly in the book I wrote about the Gulf War, *Uncritical Theory*. That was written in the white heat of indignation, mostly on coach trips up to London for anti-war demonstrations. It started off as a polemical response to Baudrillard's two articles on the Gulf War, and then it turned into a book, which took in all sorts of other issues. But the general point behind it is that unless you have a sufficiently strong, philosophically defensible conception of truth then your arguments will be prone to some Fish-type sceptical or other sort of cultural-relativist rejoinder, with ethically and politically dubious results. Fish says that 'theory' has no consequences, nor indeed his own kind of anti-theory, since this whole debate is just a matter of rhetorical preaching to the converted. I think he is mistaken about this and that getting things right or wrong 'in theory' has all sorts of consequences for the way we read, think, and conduct our lives.

Part Three:
For Cultural Studies

INTRODUCTION

In this part we find strong arguments *for* cultural studies: compelling accounts of its successes, achievements and political force. The two interviews comprising it are very different in terms of tone and apparent positioning, but surprisingly aligned nevertheless. Adrian Rifkin in a sense 'universalises' the singular position he finds himself in – so he speaks, apparently, only of himself and his own work, but in such a way as to cast important illumination on what you might call the universal intellectual or academic condition. On the other hand, Griselda Pollock provides an account of cultural studies' importance in general.

Rifkin offers an autobiographical account of his relationship with cultural studies. But, significantly, his autobiographical account explicitly acknowledges – as his title, 'Inventing Recollection' adverts – that memory, however straightforwardly true it may seem, cannot be divorced from both a theoretical component and the dimension of invention. Because something like a theory, and the element of invention, performance, construction, or creation, are *always* at work, Rifkin advocates the need for 'metacritical' and 'hyper-theoretical' work, precisely so one will *not* be laden down with myths of simple truth: he offers an argument about the necessity of distancing oneself from one's own work, in order to deliberately muddy the waters, waters which often appear to be simple 'truth', but are rather, as he argues, 'phantasms' – fantasies, myths, desires, presuppositions. This method of engaging so thoroughly with one's own work, with one's own relation to the objects one studies, is both a distancing from *and* a massively intense involvement that refuses to shy away from any of the complexities of academic work: the question of one's own relationship to the object, of one's own relationship to history, in history, to time and place, to wider methodological fields and the preconceptions one brings to the object of study. He elaborates the importance and effects of such an approach through discussions of such diverse objects of analysis as class politics, art, the university institution, the historical institutionalisation of cultural studies, Levi's jeans adverts, and *Teletubbies*.

Both of the following chapters are very enthusiastic about cultural studies, its achievements and its importance. As both argue in different ways, the emergence of cultural studies constituted, as Pollock puts it, a 'whole new culture of study ... not based on the authority of the university but on the collective desire to understand new currents that were accessed through the close study of articles, lectures and some key books'. For Pollock, perhaps the single most important force of (and also against) cultural studies is feminism. Feminism is important for cultural studies, for political life, and for cultural transformation, because it 'interrupts' things at every turn. She sees feminism as a crucial supplement to cultural studies, just as cultural studies is interminably engaged with and supplementary to feminist projects. Both feminism and cultural studies, while one cannot reduce them to the 'same' project, overlap, inform, frustrate, strengthen and further each other's own projects. Conceived of as independent or as combined, both feminism and cultural studies are part and parcel of larger movements and formations, which Pollock insists are eminently valuable and consequential.

7   Inventing Recollection

Adrian Rifkin

(1) How do you position yourself and your work in relation to the cultural studies project? Or, rather, do you see cultural studies *as* a 'project', and is contemporary cultural studies still the 'same' project or discipline as it once was?

In terms of the possible ways of thinking about that, one of the best ways I can think of starting would be completely autobiographical: it would be to give you an image of myself lying in my bath in my house in Southsea, Hampshire, just after the middle of the 1970s, reading essays by students, who were either on the historical studies course at Portsmouth Polytechnic, or who were doing a mixture of historical studies and cultural studies; and being struck by, and thinking about, some of the key words they were using in their essays, which were the kinds of words that students weren't using in essays even a very few years before I started teaching, in 1970.

Now, what had happened between 1970 and 1975 in Portsmouth was that the first cultural studies BA anywhere had come into existence. It came about through the work of a group of staff (partly including myself, though I was mainly on the edges of it) who came from the kinds of background that were themselves part of the formative myth of cultural studies, as some kind of epistemic break with previous modes of disciplinary formation; but also a group of staff working very closely with Stuart Hall, who came down and helped design the courses and who was himself the first external examiner of the course. Now, the kinds of words which students had used in their essays in the 1970s were words like 'articulate' and 'mediate'. And very recently in a seminar at Leeds at the CentreCATH,[1] at which Stuart and I were both present, we remembered that moment: someone asked the question 'Is this a matter of articulation?' and Stuart said 'It once was.'

That brought back to me the experience of reading these under-graduate essays which orientated themselves around particular words; certain words which took a kind of distance from the materials they examined and suggested that these materials could be put together in a way which was not a question of sequence and not a question of historical temporality, but a question of the way in which ideas, the logic of ideas, and the material conditions of the society, could be mediated through each other via something which we might call 'articulation' or a series of articulations. I think that what was emerging in those essays via the kinds of staff and the histories of those people within theory – within communist theory, within the socialist movement, within historical theoretical processes like the emergence of 'the linguistic turn' for example, within the ways in which Marxism had been modified and taken on psychoanalysis through the work of Althusser – was something which was I suppose both 'metacritical' (taking a step back from the cultural materials and historical materials with which they were engaged, and seeing them as part of a cultural process) on the one hand, and, on the other, part of a political project to move things forward. So there was a project, which was to move forward the relation between disciplinary methodologies and each other in terms of their mutual criticism on the one hand, and to move forward the role of university thinking, in terms of its hold on society, its critique of society, on the other. So if you started reading the use of the word 'articulation' as symptomatic of what was going on, you could say that what those essays symptomatised was a desire – in their discourse, that is: in the particularity of their discourse – a desire for theory to be both productive and effective, to both produce new forms of knowledge and to articulate those forms in such a way that they were genuinely critical.

Now, when I say that the staff came from a very specific variety of backgrounds which are part of the mythology of cultural studies, I mean those classic E.P. Thompson or Hoggart type trajectories, of the disillusion of 1956, the disillusion of 1968, the swing away from Stalinism, the adoption as a critique of Stalinism of one of the two possibilities, which Thompson clearly took up, which was that of a traditional English cultural studies-ism; which is already there with William Morris, and to which to a certain extent I'm thoroughly sympathetic, and always have been, in the sense that I've always thought that William Morris was a great and original contributor to something we'd call cultural studies, particularly in some of his late essays, particularly in his sometimes rather despised economic and moral essays. I'm sympathetic to that position of Thompson's. So that would be one extreme, but the other extreme would be the high Althusserianism of 'interpellation' and of 'the interpellated subject', and of the essays in *Lenin and Philosophy*, for example. Which was a kind of other reaction to the *massism* and inevitable political optimism of the discredited communist movements.

And the staff who came from those kinds of background could be described in theoretical terms, but they could also be described in sociological terms, they could also be described as disgruntled Oxbridge historians, as disgruntled old-university students of literature or as disgruntled sociologists. So I think the element of disgruntlement with one's own formation was also very much a part of that project, of giving a real material educational form to one's disgruntlement with one's own immediate education – and most of these people were quite young then, so it really was their immediate education: it was an education received in the 1960s. And certainly in my case, in terms of my own relation to art history, it meant that the project, which I saw as being the crucial one of the development of a new art history, was very much along the same lines as what was happening in cultural studies. So that relationship to the project, insofar as there was a project, and to this moment of a transition of a number of young academics into the new structures of mass education of the early 1970s, I think was kind of crucial, and I think that I still in certain respects belong to that.

I think it's useful to mention a few of the names of people who participated in that moment, where Portsmouth was actually surprisingly important. They were people like Robbie Gray with his hyper-Gramscian history of the working class in Edinburgh; or John Oakley, a literary historian who paid very careful attention to the most difficult and unlovable aspects of English literature in the nineteenth century, like Bulwer-Lytton, who wrote the *Last Days of Pompeii*, which again he saw as being part of the formation of a hegemonic structure of English knowledge which could be thought through in terms of a Gramscian and Althusserian philosophy. And later on, that particular teaching team came to include some of the first generation of Stuart Hall's students, such as Frank Mort, for example, who came to work at Portsmouth in the 1980s. So in fact it provided a very hospitable space for some of the first people who were trained in cultural studies in Birmingham at the time, and in the ways in which it began to develop under Stuart Hall's directorship.

So that was a crucial moment. And during the mid-1970s, oddly, I missed out on it, because I was engaged in much more 'street active' politics, far left politics, the politics of anti-racism, and so on. I paid very little attention to theoretical developments, which I came back to thinking about after they'd really got going. One stayed in touch with the work of these students, and again I think that's very important – it was the first generation of undergraduates in this area, who really mapped out with us what a syllabus would mean. Again, I think this is terribly important, as it relates to what happens when things become 'theory', or 'institutional' … . Well, here I'm thinking about your Questions (4) and (5):

(4) How does the institutionalisation of cultural studies affect, support or undermine it?

(5) Does cultural studies have any significance outside of the university at all? If so, what forms does this take?

This is to do with institutions and with the broad structure of what we mean by an 'institution', say in a Foucauldian sense. So, when things turn into series of Readers like *The New Accents* or *The Fontana Modern Masters*, which were part of the vehicles through which cultural studies itself came to be articulated, you then begin to see a project as a set of theoretical possibilities, as theoretical suppositions, as a set of publishable analyses of those theoretical suppositions and possibilities, which then become an institution of publishing. So the history of *New Accents* or the history of *Fontana Modern Masters* would be very interesting to look at: if one wanted to follow a kind of Bourdieuian approach to the academic establishment, one could look at those. It's very easy to forget that the formation of cultural studies was in fact a very real fight for syllabuses. And not just a fight for syllabuses *within* institutions, but a real fight to establish those syllabuses in the face of institutions which didn't understand them at all. I don't mean the institutions we were working in – the polytechnics – but I mean the universities, who largely had no idea of what cultural studies was or what was going on in Birmingham, but who at the same time were given power over the polytechnics, in terms of validating and examining our courses, to allow them to come into being.[2]

So at the same time as we were trying to formulate the syllabuses in cultural studies, or the syllabuses in new forms of social historical studies, we had to educate those in power above us to authorise us to do these things. The struggle for a syllabus and the production of the new kinds of student through that syllabus would then make that syllabus work, which is something that is coterminous with the production of the kinds of text which would then further make that set of investigations possible. So if you think of cultural studies BAs lurching into being more or less at the same kind of time that Benjamin's *Baudelaire* is just being published by New Left Books, and certainly not yet widely read; and in which more or less no one has read the *Passagenwerk*; if you think of those courses lurching into being round about the time that Foucault is giving his inaugural lecture at the College de France, 'L'ordre du discours' (which I think – and I imagine a writer like David Macey would agree with this – is probably what actually puts him on the map and gives him the institutional power for his works to become diffused in the way that they were); if you think of cultural studies coming into being at a time when Derrida has already – in 1967, in fact – made his fundamental critique of Saussure, in his interview with Julia Kristeva, later published in *Positions*, but years before that interview's actually going to be published and read by most of the people involved; you can see (and I think this is very characteristic of the early 1970s and the development of education in the polytechnics, where the new things were primarily happening, with a few exceptions in universities), if you look at that configuration, that there is a kind of dialectic of trying to do something that can't be done until something else has come into being, or been figured in its sphere, and that it's quite impossible to put the theoretical field before the project, or the project before the theoretical field – there's a kind of very complex process of formation, very experimental at that early stage, and that it already involves a whole number of debates that you're implying in your questions about 'where does cultural studies belong?' For instance, is it the eruption of the Real in the worn-out world of education as represented by the universities? An eruption of the Real which can be represented within the polytechnics, for example, within the kind of courses we had in Portsmouth? Is it the eruption of the Real into a university like Birmingham University? Not just from the kind of hyper-Althusserian theoreticians or hyper-Gramscian young theoreticians who evolved around the figure of Stuart Hall, but by the people who came in from the community and wanted something out of cultural studies which they could take back to their communities. Already that 'phantasm' of cultural studies as *being useful*, and the argument *against* it being useful were already in place. In the 1970s, as the Stencil Papers went around from Birmingham, and all the series of papers began to come out as published editions, on the one hand one was admiring the theoretical élan of what was going on in Birmingham, in what was actually essentially an MA reading group, and on the other hand one was hearing the most terrible stories of people who were theatre workers or community workers or school teachers looking for something to take back to the classroom, back to the street, to the community, actually finding *no place at all* in that high theoretical production of the centre.

So there was already a kind of very real division about *what* the project was, *which* way it should be going, whether it was to have an influence on the outside world, and whether or not indeed you could *determine* what those influences in the outside world were going to be. You know: did you want to have a more self-conscious, more articulate, better produced community theatre, which would be able to reflect on the histories of concepts like 'community' through a kind of post-Hoggartian model, but one which was more informed by 'real' political understandings, say, taken from Gramsci; or did you want to have an ever-more intense re-reading of previous political histories and modern cultural-political formations like those of feminism, for example, through an intensified and increasingly complex reading of Foucault and Barthes or eventually Derrida, as they become available? And would the influence of cultural studies precisely be in bringing together a level of high abstraction with a new understanding of who is the modern social subject – whether it's the feminist social subject or a queer social subject or whatever?

So all these discussions between academic feminism and street feminism and academic cultural studies and street activity, were running around by the mid-1970s or late 1970s – Sheila Rowbotham's *Women's Consciousness, Man's World* and Griselda Pollock's 'Feminism, Femininity and the Hayward Annual' were epiphanic texts, while poor Guy Hocquenghem's *Homosexual Desire* was hardly read at all. But, at the same time, cultural studies was making an unexpected impact. That is, it was having an influence in the 'real world' through the ways in which the people one was educating were simply getting ordinary jobs. If you were working across the edges of fine art, design and cultural studies, like I was, it became terribly obvious that you were sending people out to the design industries who were educated in terribly sophisticated theory, or what in those days was terribly sophisticated theory. So the way in which one can read together the question of the 'project' of cultural studies and the 'effect' of cultural studies, albeit in an ironic form, would be to, for example, look at the way in which advertising was changing in the 1980s.

Now, for me, one very crucial example of that was the Nick Kamen Levi's advertisement, and also the emergence of certain kinds of populist discourses, populist theoretical discourses, on 'the subject' and 'the sexed subject' in a magazine like *The Face*. I remember, when the Nick Kamen Levi's advert came out there was immense theoretical debate, and colleagues and friends of mine were writing on advertisements and writing on the new figure of the male, and writing on the idea of a figure of the male that could be the object of the female gaze, and this radical transformation of the figure of the male, without thinking that that might *not* be a broad social movement as such, as much as an ironic reworking of cultural studies through the functioning of the advertising industry itself. When you look back now, you can see that the company who produced those Levi's advertisements in a sense knew *exactly* what they were doing. It wasn't some kind of grassroots diffusion of new models of sexual subjectivity beginning to force its way through and having an effect on an industry, but an industry well equipped with people from all sides – from art and design education, cultural studies education – an industry which was becoming staffed by people who had an ironic and commercial understanding of the problematics and projects with which cultural studies had been dealing now for ten to fifteen years.

So if you say 'Does cultural studies have an effect in the outside world?', then the answer is, yes, enormous, inevitably. You know, some of the most complex of cultural studies' formulations around sex and gender can be formulated at the everydayness of the advertising industry through this process of the transference of educational skills into those kinds of industry. I think the most stunning recent example of that is *Teletubbies*. When I saw my first episode of *Teletubbies* it rang a bell. So, not realising it was on at ten in the morning I got up at seven for weeks running to watch it – *just to watch it!* It seemed to me the most truly adult programme that the BBC had ever managed to produce in all the time I'd known it. And after watching a few episodes I phoned up someone, an ex-student, and said 'You know who wrote this stuff, don't you?' And he said 'Yes! It's so-and-so, so-and-so, and so-and-so!' And they were all people one had taught or had been friends of people one had taught or whatever. I recognised the style of those 1970s essays coming back as *Teletubbies*! Now, that for me is an effect of cultural studies in the larger world. One of the great achievements of cultural studies, if you like, is *Teletubbies*, as much as it is the vast field of texts and textualities that we've managed to produce. You might also say that the Levi's adverts were a similar kind of effect. I think that once we'd realised that, we kind of drew back from paying excessive critical attention to the Levi's ads, even. You know, we'd thought they were going to become a really big thing and then we realised that, 'Hey, no, no: this is just talking about ourselves! It's not quite what we thought it was, it really is us, and our involvement in it is narcissistic rather than critical.'

Some more of the broader achievements of cultural studies, where it does operate, or does flow out into a kind of popular discourse, is in the work of Judith Williamson, for example. Not so much in her work on decoding advertisements as in her film criticism. Also the writing of someone like Rosalind Coward in the *Guardian*, taken together with *Female Desire*, for example, constitutes a real breakthrough in terms of a relationship between what one could call a formal educational structure, on the one hand, and a much, much broader field of popular culture or newspaper culture, on the other. I don't think there's really anything else like them. They're something which makes you think of someone like Benjamin or Kracauer writing for *FrankfurterZeitung* in the 1920s. It's that quality of discourse: so original and to do with the meat of production of modern and contemporary cultures. It brings all those insights which are filtered through from Barthes, Benjamin and Adorno into that order of discourse and does so more effectively than Žižek has ever done. For me, those are historically irreplaceable moments and I don't think, in a way, there have been subsequent developments of theorising the popular or the banal, or using the banal to theorise the theoretical, to rethink the theoretical, which are better than those.

One of the reasons they are so good is because they are still embedded in the political project of cultural studies, because they are embedded shamelessly in demystification – but demystification when confronted with an extremely complicated world of popular tastes and consumer industries. So the demystification constantly confounds itself with the writer's own pleasure in that world. If in a sense cultural studies has tended to move back to re-mystification now, away from a hard-line demystification, what one sees in the writing of people like Williamson and Coward are a kind of real borderline, the real impossibility of walking the borderline between the two without teetering and falling, and playing around with the two extremes of demystification *and* dealing with one's own pleasure in the material. Incidentally, I think that if one looks out into the broader field of popular theatre one sees there both antecedents for and things that flow from cultural studies.

In the mid-1970s I spent most of my time working on the far left-wing politics. A lot of the research I did was into political and economic questions, and was written up in the form of articles in far left newspapers. I think that's interesting because very often it's assumed that people who are good at political theory, or cultural studies, or good in an academic sense, know how to comment on the world. And yet at the same time I think there's nothing more disastrous than some of the schemata worked out by eminent practitioners of cultural studies and critical theory, in terms of the way in which capitalism has actually developed. It's interesting to think, for example, in terms of theorists who have used the concept of 'late capitalism', and continued using the concept of late capitalism, roughly drawn from a Mandelian periodisation of capitalism, up to and even after the point at which the Berlin Wall came down. But, if you want to be properly Marxist about your perspectives, you could already have seen that world capitalism, once there was not going to be universal socialism, was still at a relatively early stage of development. I don't think that anyone who ever used the phrase 'late capitalism' ever critically withdrew from it. You find then that despite immense theoretical sophistication, a number of important theorists' comments about the world are sometimes naïve, or even crass. So what I find fascinating about the highly detailed, very utopian work I ended up doing between 1972–73 and 1977–78, was that looking back now I can see that in a very naïve way, but one that was more sophisticated than I recognised, I was unpicking some of the political and economic trends which are coming home to develop right now.

For instance, I remember spending months during the miners' strikes during the 1970s, doing a lot of work on pension funds, and writing up little articles denouncing the manipulation of pension funds by the state and by the employers in the mining industry, for the tiny circulation of an ultra-left-wing daily. And it's really weird now to think that *precisely that* is what is being announced in the broadest possible terms in the crisis in the pensions industry today, and in the way in which the outfall of those manipulations is being exaggerated by the wretched Blairite project of stakeholder pensions, and so on and so on. So one was doing that rather naïve but very detailed analysis of particular institutions, particular economic relations – for example I remember doing a long and very complex analysis of the Lomé Agreement, which, if I could dig out all of that stuff, would today make one smile wryly about the concept of the post-colonial. You see, there's a way in which the concept of the post-colonial, as inscribed in the Lomé Agreement, was something quite, quite different, in fact as a kind of perpetual economic slavery for the third world, and something quite, quite different from the kind of crazy optimisms which were written into the concept of the cultural post-colonial. It was definitely post-colonial because the Lomé Agreement was a settlement of that particular process of countries achieving their independence – or rather, of maintaining western economic hegemony over African and other countries, through the appearance of a free and equal trade agreement.

So there are things which we didn't put together, which maybe historically now could be brought together. One would see that that kind of far left criticism, far from being naïve, had a solidity about it, but which was not appropriate to what cultural studies was actually doing. So when I came back to wondering about what it was that cultural studies was really doing, in a very material, very theoretical, very archival and thorough way, what I found had happened during my 'time out', was that *Screen* had happened.

Between those years 'Visual Pleasure and Narrative Cinema' had come out, Stephen Heath's big essay, 'Difference', had come out, or what they used to call Stephen Heath's 'masterly analysis' of *A Touch of Evil*. So all sorts of things had begun to change. I came back to looking at those things increasingly between 1977 and 1979, and wondering where I was up to, and I remember thinking, 'Jesus! All this has happened, how on earth is one going to catch up?' So I started busily trying to read (not so much the articles as the footnotes!), to see what it was they were talking about. Then I got a shock, because I realised that a lot of the materials which they were using, like Baudry's 'Cinematic Apparatus', or Derrida, or stuff of Kristeva, or whatever, was in fact stuff that I'd been reading in the 1960s; because by some kind of weird mishap, certainly not of my own intending, I'd started reading *Tel Quel* in 1967. So it was a peculiar moment of realising that I'd actually *missed out on my own education*, and that I'd done all this reading in the 1960s without vaguely understanding its significance, or vaguely understanding the uses to which it could be put.

This brings us back to what I was saying earlier: that's the weird problem of talking about things which were set up in the early 1970s, *before that which made them possible had happened*. It's like everything happened back to front: You had cultural studies before you had available everything which made it really possible. So if you take the starting point of 1971–72 again, as when things began to take off, there was *nothing*, or nothing which had been digested and processed and become *institution* in the broader theoretical sense. Then this unfolds in a massive way in the late 1970s and 1980s and becomes articulated into formulae about *how and what it 'is' that cultural studies 'is'*. (This still nonetheless leaves out a lot, like the work of Henri Lefebvre, and so on; a lot of which is now coming back in a big way.)

Anyway, so the question then, if you want to take the question of 'Did *my* work have a project?', or as you put it:

> (2) Cultural studies is said to be a political project. What, to your mind, are the politics of cultural studies? Does it have 'a' politics, or is it, rather, political in some other way? Another way to phrase this would be to ask you what are the politics or what is the political significance of your own work? What do you consider to be the 'proper destination' of your work?

I think in a way that I thought that the direct political project was valuable, but that it was also going nowhere. I felt very strongly that it was immensely valuable, because a number of things that we did in those far-left organisations, for example, in specific, very material ways, was to hold the fascist movement at bay. One did that by argument and one did it actually by hitting people too. You know, thumping them, or standing in their way, or having fights with the police, like the big anti-National Front Lewisham demonstration in 1978, which was a kind of police riot. I think that by making those things physically very high-profile, despite the reservations of the old Communist Party who said that this was the most terrible thing to do, the left did an enormous job in holding certain forms of fascist activity and certain forms of racist activity at bay, and making them look dangerous, making them look unpopular, giving them publicity which they really didn't want. And that includes the famous beating up of Eysenck at the LSE in the 1970s, at which I was present, and which I think was actually not a bad thing to have done, because it took away the kind of humanistic discourse of 'after all, these people are only old scholars', and 'they're nice old men', and 'they're just interested in the truth' and all that 'blah, blah, blah' – you know, just like Adolph Rosenberg was, of course!

So that project in a sense wasn't going anywhere. One could see that. Or, to put it differently: in order *not* to see that one had to be doing a lot of heavy condensation and displacement and self-concealment, by about 1978–79, when you started looking at the next phase of the negative fall-out of international communist politics in China or in Albania, or wherever. You had to be a fool *to not see* that you can't live through those metaphors *yet again*, as people did in the 1930s and 1960s – that, if you like, the death of the metaphors of the 1970s, which Kristeva talks about very eloquently (I think her essay on Chinese women is very much concerned with this kind of problem) – the death of those metaphors means that those processes of direct political action are *not going* somewhere in the global sense which one wanted; and they're not doing an awful lot for the university either. This is so even though they may be essential to continue at a local level in terms of cultural activity, if that's what you want to do and that's what you're committed to.

So when I did come back into doing direct historical or cultural studies type research, I wanted it to be *hyper-theoretical*. I don't think at first I wanted it to be that, but I wanted it to be hyper-theoretical in the sense that it would deal, at that stage (but it's changed immensely since then), with the historical archive, in an ultra-critical anti-narrative sense; that it would take back the kind of critical methods learnt from Barthes, or the critical methods beginning to be learnt from Benjamin, or, particularly, the kind of critical methods learnt from Hayden White or Stephen Bann's critique of historical methodology, to a traditional working-class history in which we in a sense have participated in the failure. So when I started doing the stuff on the Paris Commune it was precisely, in one way, to show how – in what we used to call 'base' and 'superstructure' – the 'superstructural' part, the figural part, takes over from the material and economic part; to show that it's not a question of a dialectic of base and superstructure, but it's a case of the two never meeting in a form in which you can talk about satisfactory forms of historical narrative or satisfactory forms of historical outcome. That was the point, in late 1978, when I met Jacques Rancière.

Rancière's work of that period enabled me to precipitate and consolidate the kind of ideas which I was beginning to develop myself. I was not thinking in terms of 'the relative autonomy of the super- structure', or in terms of the way in which forms of figuration then levered out, utopianly or dystopianly, or whatever; so that, for example, the political cartoons of the Paris Commune (which is what I was then working on) become a register *not* of a kind of treasury of socialist history and its tragedies and its ups and downs, but a site on which we can historically represent the impossibility of reading things in that 'clean way' – that way in which one can construct satisfactory historical teleologies leading up to oneself and one's own desires. So it is a way of taking oneself out of condensation and displacement and daydreaming about one's politics through cultural materials, and thinking of history not so much pessimistically, but in a way in which, if you like, the hyper-metacritical position has to win out over the archive in the end. You have to precipitate situations in which the metacritical wins out over the potential of the 'satisfactory' or 'whole narrative' coming out of the archive.

One really instructive thing for me was when in 1978–79, I did a draft translation of Jacques Rancière's piece, 'Les bons temps aux barrières' from *Révoltes Logiques*, for the journal *History Workshop*, and waited six or eight months before anyone communicated with me at all about what had happened to it. I finally found out, just by chance, that it had been thrown out because the editorial board was so split over it. The old guard had said it was an insult to the working class, and that if it was published they would resign, and the new guard hadn't really wanted them to do that because, after all, *History Workshop* was built on the myth of the old guard, and 'blah, blah, blah'. And so, basically, it wasn't going to be published. Now, that was very instructive for me because it made me realise the extent to which Rancière was right about the way in which we live our historical mythologies, in which people delude themselves about their desire for themselves as if the other were them – i.e., this otherness of the working class and the bourgeoisie to each other as being a point of non-meeting and non-touching – of fantasising around categories, the desire for the possession of which, such as *being* an artist or *being* a poet, is more disruptive than the battles on the barricades themselves. Put very crudely, this is the burden of those early articles of Rancière: that, if what the worker desires is to be a poet, rather than to be on the barricade, in a sense that desire presupposes a dissolution of the whole social relations upon which the concept of the poet itself has become constructed – if you like it's a kind of Kantian category. So this bringing of a kind of neo-Kantianism into the political field, which Rancière achieved I think, was one of an immense metacritical potential, and a potential to disrupt the ways in which studies can settle down into their own genre of becoming themselves, and becoming consolidated. I think that this has largely happened with cultural studies. But that suited me because I came from a very art background: you know, I *believed in* the avant-garde.

The reason I liked the Chinese Great Proletarian Cultural Revolution was because it was so like the European avant-garde, not because it was Chinese and Other, but because it looked like a means of continuing in political form the self-renewing potential of the avant-garde which was represented through artists as different as, say, Rodchenko on the one hand and Duchamp on the other. It was a terribly modernist reading: a self-critical, self-disrupting avant-garde that would constantly break up the boundaries of the old in order to establish a new which will always in itself necessarily be difficult to understand. Now that's also present in Adorno's concept of 'true art' and of the negativity of true art and the kind of late-Adornian concepts of what can work in art: of what's bad about Stravinsky and what's good about Schönberg for example: that point of negation, that point of denial, and that point of reconstruction of something *in its difficulty*, in challenging the process of signification out of which it's come. So that kind of avant-gardism was something which I was educated in, in my early days of teaching in art school, and which seemed amply justified through the kind of theoretical manoeuvres which Rancière was developing. To a certain extent I do see his subsequent history as being precisely that of the development of an almost affective and theoretical avant-gardism, which has successfully continued to challenge theoretical formations from then up to now and in his ongoing work.

So my own resolution of that in his main work was partly through the work on the Paris Commune, but particularly in a piece which I did for one of the very last issues of *Révoltes Logiques*, which concerned the schools of design in England in the 1830s and 1840s and the Great Exhibition of 1851. It was directly taken out of the set of social frameworks which were proposed in the early writing of Rancière and worked through in terms of seeing if one could refigure these concepts of class otherness (which Rancière had derived from France and from French philosophy, from his reflections on

Althusser, and his reading of French history); seeing if one could think them through in terms of English historical formations to escape from the kind of sophisticated Gramscian art history which was being practised (by people I very much admired, but with whom I had certain differences: like Gareth Stedman-Jones and Robbie Gray). I think of the piece on the Great Exhibitions, which was published in the second issue of the *Journal of Design History*, as being a very cultural studies piece. But maybe, looking back, it was actually a postmodern Rancièrean cultural studies piece, and a reading of the archive which is also an absolute critical defiance of any quantitative reading of the archive.

When Rancière's *Nights of Labour* came out – or, was finally read – in America (maybe before it was translated – I think some people were reading it in French despite its complexity), there was an immense reaction against it, particularly with the Yale social historians. There was a very well known debate and argument between Rancière and William Sewell, whereby Sewell (if I crudely summarise his argument) said, 'Look here: it may be true what you're saying' about workers wanting to become poets and break from these structural constraints of their being workers, in which they were constantly being locked by the bourgeois intellectuals like George Sand, who wanted them to be workers. So Sewell said, 'OK, you're right, but it was only 14% of the working class – or between 11% and 14% of the working class' – which completely misses the point of the philosophical critique! And, funnily enough, when I went to Yale ten years later to give a lecture on the great popular entertainer Maurice Chevalier, which was the next phase of my work, and which was still to do with this question of the metacritical phantasm of the working class, someone in the audience got up and started shouting at me after the talk, shouting, arguing vociferously against this point and that point and the other point. And it had all come straight out of that argument with Rancière in the late 1970s. It was *exactly* the same terms, *exactly* the same points of reference, *exactly* the same statistics, and exactly the same I 'couldn't say this about the working class', I 'couldn't say that about the working class'! I knew exactly what was going on, but I hadn't expected someone to have sussed out that much about where I was coming from, seeing that all I was doing was going to the art history department to give a talk on Chevalier.

The weird thing was, and this is again where you realise that these things are institutionally very hidebound, was that the critique peaked with saying that you *can't say* – that *if* you're going to talk about Chevalier you *have* to say this, that and the other. And that was actually what I *had* said. So it wasn't even as if we had disagreed anyway! This is all very anecdotal, but it's interesting to see the way those things were embodied.

So my own take on what was to become cultural studies again got distanced, but this time not by direct politics, or coming back and realising that I already knew some of the stuff that was happening, as with the *Tel Quel* stuff, which I then had to completely re-read. But again it got very much diverted by this relationship with *Révoltes Logiques*, and the break-up of *Révoltes Logiques* – the differences between Rancière and Cottereau, and the differences between Rancière and Farge, and so on. To a certain extent I held up a lot of work in order to resolve my own position within that.

But the resolution of it wasn't going to come from English cultural studies. It was really going to come through a rethinking of a trajectory of cultural studies which English cultural studies had managed to miss out. If you look at English cultural studies the way, say, Griselda Pollock presents it, there was this kind of Barthes and Althusser against Sartre, which constitutes the anti-humanist project of, which is also embedded in, its other, which is the communitarianism of Birmingham. You can see that kind of schema which we used to map out together on cultural studies in Leeds, and which sort of (and this isn't a criticism, because it is a viable model: so this is a distance, not a criticism) missed out on Adorno, on the one hand, and on the other it radically missed out on the theorising of the social which came from Lefebvre. Because, however much Lefebvre was anti-structuralist, it is terribly important, *textually*, for the way in which one can think about people like Foucault, and also for the way in which we can map a broader environment for writers like Adorno. If you start playing with your configuration, putting figures who have been neglected into a position of prominence, not because you want them to be recognised because they were 'great', but because you want to see how things look if you put them in a certain position, where their texts take on a certain value; if you put Lefebvre in, with all his disagreements with high structuralism, with all his disagreements with Saussure, with all his disagreements with Althusser, or whatever, you end up with a much more complex text of what the possibilities of cultural studies are. This is something that Kristin Ross has done to wonderful effect.

That's one way of ending up with a more complex text of what the possibilities of cultural studies are. And you can then map those through Rancière in a way which Rancière himself might not agree with, but which nonetheless achieves this function of allowing oneself a freedom of action which is less constrained by the formulation of cultural studies as it had become formulated through the discussions of *New Accents*, from some of the *Modern Masters*, etc., and at that moment also, the burst of the critique of all that through the paradigm of postmodernism. So one could be less preoccupied with the replacement of one paradigm by the other – the modern by the postmodern, the structuralist by the post-structuralist – and more concerned with the textualisation of the whole field, so that, instead of ending up saying 'Oh my god! Isn't it a problem! Lyotard looks surprisingly like Adorno, so what are we going to do?', or instead of throwing up one's hands and saying 'Given *différance* and that unpronounced "a", let's all forget about grand narratives', or whatever – I'm parodying a bit here – one can kind of not be too bothered by those questions of whether it is or it isn't a grand narrative, and what is and what isn't the political outcome. One can be more concerned with the processes of radicalisation of one's thinking. Now that may lead one into a kind of hyper-theoreticism. But I think that's fine – provided it's moving between, or it operates through reconstructing the field of its own textuality, not by summarising things into different or impossible relations, or antinomic relations, or successions of modern or postmodern, or whatever. And again, coming back to Rancière, those are problems with which he's been sublimely unconcerned, to his immense advantage as a philosopher.

(7) Where is cultural studies *going*? ...

Well, I'm supposed to be in visual culture now anyway, so, I am Professor of Visual Culture and Media, heaven help me! For someone who never watches television it's hopeless really! Although I suppose being just about glued to my computer and the internet could just about count as media. That just about saves me slightly. I never actually properly thought about the question of visual culture. Well I could say that in England one of the other integuments of what became cultural studies as visual culture was a journal like *Block*, which we all wrote for. And I've said elsewhere that one of the things that you did when you wrote an article for *Block*, and this is where life and theory come together, was you got dressed to write an article for *Block*. You went out and bought a new outfit before writing an article for *Block*. One would never sit down in one's carpet slippers and dressing gown to write an article for it, you would get into cutting-edge clothing and all wear it when the edition came out. *When* it came out, which always took months.

All the work I've done has always been a way of putting off something which I should already have done. So *Street Noises* was a way of putting off the Ingres book (*Ingres Then, and Now*), which I'd been putting off for 20 years, in order to study certain nineteenth-century phonemes and their survival in the twentieth century, which were if you like phonemes of class struggles in the nineteenth century turned into mass cultures of the twentieth century. So it was a rethinking of tiny fragments of the nineteenth in terms of broad patterns of the twentieth, which then brought me back to the possibility of doing the Ingres book as a set of phonemes dragged anachronistically back from the twentieth century into the nineteenth century. So they were quite arbitrarily chosen fragments of Lévi-Strauss on the one hand and gay pornography on the other, sort of lurched back into nineteenth-century painting as a way of estranging it, making it look odd, or reconfiguring its archive. So the things make each other possible in quite unexpected ways, rather than being projects which get completed when they're completed. And the Ingres book was a way of putting off doing the 'Gay Poetics' book, which I've now got to get done.

But one of the things that horrifies me, which is something which the work of PhD students of your generation creates, is that one can *never* catch up with the reading. Now, because I read in a certain way, and because I read and re-read things a lot, and because I rarely get through a whole book because I get very stuck on little paragraphs and details, and work out how they can be used and where they can be put and in what way they precipitate crises in my own writing if I introduce them into it; one of the things that horrifies me about my own place in carrying on doing this kind of work – which is not a prescription for where it could go, but it may provide parables about where it could go – is that I can't actually *find* anything to say *and* keep up with the field. Therefore one has to adopt some kind of strategy of consciously *not* keeping up with the field. You have to think about the *way* in which you don't keep up with the field. I mean, I was hoping to get into the library before you came round to conduct this interview, to look at the last two years of *Cultural Studies* and *New Formations*, to actually see what has been written in cultural studies before commenting on where it should be going!

But one of the ways in which one can deal with the question of mastery is by looking at the grounds on which one can master the complexity of one's own discourse rather than mastering the field in order to insert one's own discourse into it. One might say that belongs to a larger structure of dealing with oneself which has become, since Carolyn Steadman's *Landscape For A Good Woman*, more and more a crucial part of cultural studies, although I don't think many of us are going to do anything as good as that, or as good as some other work was: work which was at once paradigmatic, enabling, eloquent and categorically wonderful.

So one of the ways in which I'm working now is by very deliberately recuperating the things I'd put aside in order to do contemporary work. I think the work of someone like Derrida, among others, with the concept of 'haunting', makes this much more possible. One of the ways of doing that is to think through the way in which one's construction as a postmodern subject, or as a modern subject for that matter – say as a modern, radical, gay subject – doesn't belong to oneself, but belongs to complex overlappings and histories and formations of, for example, rhetorical possibilities which produce you as a subject in the enunciation, quite separately from your intentions or alongside your intentions, or in a kind of complex dialectic with your intentions, in such a way not that you vanish in the enunciation, in the way that Benveniste talks about, but in the way in which you produce yourself as other in the enunciation.

Now, this is a kind of complicated idea which I'm working on and working through. Fairly crudely put, what it means is, say, taking something like the currently fashionable concern with 'time', and thinking about, on the one hand, the way in which concepts of time have historically haunted the western imagination since Saint Augustine, and his discussion of the concept of time in the eleventh chapter of the *Confessions*, that very famous discussion which Ricoeur talks about so well in *Time and Narrative*. It's not about simply re-reading that kind of text, but reading it precisely in terms of the way in which we can now think of it as a text which articulates the subject. So, what becomes interesting in that text is not just the proper philosophical concept of time, or the way in which that concept of time underlies so many problematics and aporetics of modern historical narratives (this concept of this infinitely expansive but never-actually-there-presence, or however you want to put it, in relation to Saint Augustine); the way in which for example in Augustine's address to God, the *frustrated* way in which he breaks out into hymns of praise to God, at certain regular points in his philosophical discussions. The way in which that notion of apostrophising is a rhetorical form of the subject that wishes to wring itself into being through the kind of work it's doing.

I've just written a piece in queer theory for a journal called *Umbr(a)*, which I hope will be out soon, in which I've tried to talk about the way in which queer theory apostrophises both Echo and Narcissus as if both were itself; that Echo and Narcissus are two complementary parts of a single myth; both constitute the queer subject in looking at itself in past historical material, and in repeating itself as that which echoes out of past historical material, or the current-day material. It's not a question of reading against the grain or inverting or doing the kind of homographesis that Lee Edelman importantly suggested, but it's something which can be described in quite different historical and mythological terms. Though one can think in terms of historical tropes like apostrophe, which is that of addressing; or prosopopeia, which is that of making the dead speak; one can think of it in terms of a rhetorical term like anaphora, which is that of repetition and the sounding of repetition which links one back to the myth of Echo and Narcissus and seeing and hearing; and the ways in which in that sense the production of a subject through discourse is problematic in the sense that it gives the subject a past but no future; so that the unwilling or aporetic condition of the way in which an area like queer studies has developed is that while it produces a kind of infinite progeny of the queer in the past, the future which it is liable to produce is entropic. That is, it achieves the infinite differentiation, which in fact is fundamentally like complete sameness. And this aporia is produced by not paying attention to the rhetorical forms which seize us, and working with those as a kind of metacritical distancing of ourselves from our own project.

So what I'm concerned with theoretically at the moment is how *not* to belong to one's own project, how to distance oneself from one's own project, and how in a sense to treat one's own project as historical text. Now, I use the word 'historical' there in the sense of having 'deep structure' in the Foucauldian sense of text. I suppose that the writing I get the most out of in doing this – and this is going to sound very odd – is reading much of the recent work of Kristeva. It's not Derrida at all actually – and I was going to say something about some of Derrida's recent writings here. But what I can say is that they leave me feeling very tired. They leave me feeling that you're taken here and you're taken there through a set of infinitely flexible, supple and subtle methodological suppositions which work in a way which might be, if we want to use the rhetorical trope I just mentioned, anaphoric – that they produce themselves as an echoing of the same methods through the multiple differences produced. Quite often when I read some of Derrida's recent stuff I feel kind of fatigued, and feel like I've gone nowhere, and that I haven't done anything. But in a kind of practical way with Kristeva when she's writing about Colette, or Arendt, or Sartre, or Barthes, there's a way in which her own discourse (and these are, of course, spoken seminars which are being published) lies alongside the text, reworks its own history through an understanding of the text, thinks the text through the theoretical suppositions that she already has at her disposition, and things grow around each other while leaving each other relatively intact. So nothing in fact in the end is destroyed, deconstructed, or set aside. Rather, everything in a certain way is left in place. But left in increasingly complex place in terms of the textual interpenetrations, the complex textual formations, the processes of listening to the text, listening to yourself listening to the text, and producing a text which is your own text out of that process.

What I want – and get – out of it goes also for quite a lot of Lacan, for my reading of Lacan, whom I have to say I read as a novelist. I don't read him as a theoretician, because I'm not equipped to read him as a theoretician. I'm not a psychoanalyst, and haven't got the kind of formation that someone like Mark Cousins or Parveen Adams has. So, however much I admire the work, I don't have that formation, and I read him like a kind of late twentieth-century Proust, in a way. But at the same time, he sometimes comes up with quite striking paragraphs or formations of ideas – particularly some bits in the fourth and fifth *Seminars*: 'The Formation of the Unconscious', and the 'Relation d'Objet' – where some paragraphs are overwhelmingly effective in their figurality, as being a figure of the appearance of language, or a figure of the formation of the unconscious, within one paragraph, that one can put alongside other figurations and then trace connections between them as a kind of visual map.

That's what I would say is my enterprise in visual culture. It's a kind of, not a diagramaticising (that's too simple) but a topological analysis of quite tiny elements of theory against quite tiny or sometimes quite extensive figures taken from other forms of culture, and (in the Kristevan terms) a *listening to the dynamics* in such a way as not to say 'this one has authority over that' or 'this one is the subject of that one' or 'the material for that one', but in such a way as to listen to the figural densities of the dynamics of the texts which I am setting alongside each other. So the method is one of parataxis. It essentially works with very tiny units of theory, such as a paragraph of Lacan, say, on the formation of the unconscious, a paragraph of Kristeva, on the double disabusal of the young girl with the phallus, in terms of which she talks about the feminine, therefore the concept of the feminine in Kristeva; and the allowing of the configurations of these materials to lie alongside materials so that one begins to make unexpected kinds of readings of or *listenings to* those materials.

Now this means creating new kinds of objects of attention. In terms of the cultural-historical narrative, I call it *anahistorical*. This is a historical equivalent of anamorphic – it's a kind of historical object pulled out of shape by its framings, which might be Lacan and Saint Augustine. But equally, those framings pulled out of shape by the object, and a reading of the suppositions which we bring to it. So what I've been doing recently is working on an artist who isn't Caravaggio. A Neapolitan artist called Mattia Preti. Some of his paintings look like Caravaggio's and have been mistaken for Caravaggio's, although he lived a whole generation after, and was in fact born more or less when Caravaggio died. But, nonetheless, sometimes their paintings get muddled up. And Preti has none of the kind of virtues that Caravaggio does for a queer art historian. You can't do what Jarman did with Caravaggio: he's not the 'street guy', he's not gay. There's no evidence that would make him desirable for a queer art history. But his images aren't that different, which presents a challenge to you for who you think you are as a gay or queer art historian, in looking at an image which you desire, in the way I talk about this in the Narcissus/Echo term, to be *like yourself*, or in which you like to hear yourself.

So Preti functions quite wonderfully in that respect, because one can get the paintings to nestle amongst the set of theoretical or textual propositions about *what is the time in this*, for example, the time of a martyrdom, the time of a martyr *waiting* for martyrdom, not actually *being* martyred but *waiting* for martyrdom. What is the gender structure, if you like, in terms of the articulation of both a power in the represented figure and a power in the pictorial effect construction of the image as an overlapping text of the represented figure? And what are the relations of that nexus one is then developing to the sets of desires one has set up for oneself, conventional desires one has set up for oneself, as, say, the modern, queer, cultural theoretician? And what, for example, are a series of rhetorical procedures which are implicit in a series of cultural enunciations of which the Lacan, the Kristeva, the painting, the queer theories themselves are all a part, in terms of locating the way in which these different elements belong to themselves and belong to enunciation in a broader sense?

So what I'm concerned with is that – that series of parataxes, and that series of what I call essentially, in the broadest possible way, psychoanalytic readings of the relationship between them; which seems to me to be eminently social, because it's eminently about how we live now and how we think now and how we work now. But it's not designed for the street. I mean, it's not designed to make people in Trafalgar Square get up in a great rage and say 'Hey, we're sick of Caravaggio!' and 'Why hasn't the National Gallery got any Mattia Preti's? We demand Mattia Preti's for the National Gallery!' That's not the purpose.

So that's where I'm going, without suggesting that everyone else has to do it. But it's not half bad to think that the critique of grand narratives has not resulted in a reduction of the production of grand schemas. In fact, the idea of cultural studies having to go somewhere or having 'a' project may in certain crucial respects have far too much to do with the continual hanging over of grand schemas. Fragmentary, paratactical manoeuvres of the kind I'm proposing may be one way of advancing the critical edge of the discipline within its theoretical university, and maybe within a broader field of critical formation, in terms of ways of writing art criticism, and ways of thinking about material in a broader world. Now that said, I don't think that I want in certain respects while doing that kind of work to split off the 'politics' politics from the materials I'm using from the effect that they have if you assume those politics weren't there.

So in that sense of the present conjunction, and according to the theoretical principles I'm trying to develop, I see it as terribly important, politically, *not* to immerse oneself uncritically in theoretical fields from which one then has to extricate oneself, on the grounds that there are objectionable political tendencies, or objectionable political effects, in the broader world of the politics of the balance of power between people's religions, destinies, or whatever.

So that would be a point where a kind of Maoist concept of the politics of a text comes into flat contradiction with my absolute belief in the textuality of texts.

NOTES

1. The AHRB Centre for Cultural Analysis Theory and History, University of Leeds.
2. This was through the CNAA, Council for National Academic Awards, a body that eventually accumulated immense academic wisdom – only to be destroyed and dispersed by the invention of HEFCE.

8   Becoming Cultural Studies: The Daydream of the Political

Griselda Pollock[1]

How do you position yourself and your work in relation to the cultural studies project? Indeed what do you understand as 'the cultural studies project', and is contemporary cultural studies still the same 'project' or discipline as it once was?

I very much like the idea of naming cultural studies a project. I have recently returned from a conference in the United States where I became aware of the great danger of territorial wars in the academy. The Germanic university on which so much of the modern university system is based requires the very clear definition of disciplinary boundaries. In the last 30 years we have witnessed curious developments of new kinds of academic enterprise that are marked by the nomenclature 'studies': these mark the entry of hitherto excluded voices or areas into the domain of research and pedagogy, but at a risk of reinscribing the ghettoisation that the claim for a seat at the table of research was intended to revise.

Cultural studies was, along with women's studies, one of the first such challenges to the conventional map of intellectual life within the academy. My version of its origins always lay in the uncertainties and discomforts of the New Left that found a visible formation in a series of small journals in the late 1950s. This movement, as Tom Steele has shown, had its intellectual and political roots also in the movement for extending education through so-called adult education or extension classes at the margins of the established universities. Only slowly and by a strange set of still to be determined conjunctions did this strand find itself established at a university and the leading model for an initiative that had a far more romantic origin. The British New Left heritage was deeply historical and rooted in a historical sense of both literature and social process.

There is, for me, a clear tension between the varied developments that collectively created the possibility of cultural studies as a university-based enterprise that could exist beyond one originating centre. Thus Birmingham clearly grew out of the inhospitability of English and Sociology, in different ways, to a pressure to reconsider the missing dimension of Marxism: ideology and the superstructures. Possibilities for such a reconsideration grew clearly out of Althusserianism, the translations of Gramsci's *Prison Notebooks*, and above all the impact of the translation into English of Marx's *Grundrisse*. If you look at the early papers of the Centre for Contemporary Cultural Studies (CCCS) in Birmingham, especially those written by Stuart Hall, this working through of hitherto inaccessible Marxist writings was central to the retooling that was taking place.

The huge intellectual shifts that seemed to coalesce in France in the years around 1966 became available to British intellectuals through the translations of a number of young researchers who had worked in France in the period just prior to 1968. Thus the drip of structuralism and the immediate overtaking of it by various post-structuralist diversifications created a completely new territory that was only graspable as an interrelating complex called 'Theory'. Thereby, a theoretical moment of enormous richness, creativity and intensity broke out of the bounds of philosophy, anthropology, linguistics, psychoanalysis, and so on, to create what still seems to me an unprecedented field of transdisciplinary collaborations and exchange. Overnight we were transformed into students who would be reading Lacan one evening, Foucault another and Marx another. We should not underestimate the sociology of this moment, a moment of extra-university initiatives in the form of reading groups, study groups, and the necessary medium of exchange: the small magazine. A whole new culture of study emerged not based on the authority of the university but on the collective desire to understand new currents that were accessed through the close study of articles, lectures and some key books.

These studies were, however, rooted in a reflexive sense of the possibility of reading the everyday and the contemporary with tools honed in both anthropological studies of other peoples' ways of life, and in the specialist studies of western societies' highly specified divisions of labour and intellectual life: history, English and popular culture. So there was a third element to the deep impact of newly discovered and revivified Marxism, to a radical and expanded exchange across linguistics, anthropology, philosophy and psychoanalysis, that was the engagement with contemporary cultural forms and processes that seemed to have exhausted traditional modes of analysis and therefore necessitated a wholly new armoury: semiotics, ideology critique, discourse, representation.

The most obvious differences that would give to cultural studies as a project some precarious sense of identity, sufficient for groups other than Birmingham, and its journals and working papers, to take up the title and found other centres lay, therefore, in being able to name different objects of study from those specified by traditional disciplines. In Art History the object of study is the art work and its creator. A Social History of Art could specify the production and consumption of art, but cultural studies would not focus on art. The process of the production of meaning and its circulation, as well as its effects and its failures, required that a whole series of sites of meaning production be put into novel relations: terms such as 'intertextuality', 'discursive formation', 'regimes of representation', and so on, marked a semiotic economy not entirely indifferent to specific modes of signification but certainly liberated entirely from canonical and aesthetically mystified notions of art. If terms such as visuality, spectatorship, and signification marked a new process, objects of study again ignored disciplines and their objects. Class, the body, sexuality, discipline, pleasure, and, of course, difference marked a new kind of enterprise that perceived continuities or, in Foucault's terms, regularities, that traversed many sites of enunciation whose specificity gave illusions of differences that were phenomenal and not structural.

This liberation was critical for posing cultural studies as the site of an intellectual critique ready to take on the social transformations that were its own conditions of production: late capitalism and its postmodern turn, the realisation of the society of the spectacle, etc.

Cultural studies could have gone and has gone in several different directions: and I cannot pretend to grasp their full impact. There remains a strong legacy of a Williamsist culture and society model that retains its love of literary modes coupled with a deep and socialist sense of history. There is the Foucauldian model that has become in some ways hegemonic. Foucault's writings on the panopticon, disciplinary society and sexuality have become the major motors of a whole array of writings on visual culture, museumology, and visual representation that operate at the crossroads of the cultural studies project, and for scholars still working within revised departments of art history now renamed as visual culture.

What happened at the University of Leeds was shaped by both its strong Marxist tradition that led to a certain scepticism about the seductiveness of the Foucauldian model. Instead students were offered a much deeper history and longer genealogy of the ideas and problematics that had historically surfaced in such a dramatic and important way in the 1970s. Yet as with all intellectual and political moments of overdetermination, each element had a genealogical track that would prevent certain issues from becoming merely the coins and notes of a new cultural studies currency. Cultural history vied with cultural theory creating special tensions and offering a history of cultural theorisations that linked post-war initiatives with older, nineteenth-century critiques of capitalism (Marx, Morris, Ruskin), and with Adorno and the Frankfurt School. The reason I stress this is the double axis of theory and history is once again enshrined in the new Centre for Cultural Analysis, Theory and History (Centre CATH): the three words spell out the terms of the cultural studies project expanded to bring into dialogue and contest the areas touched and even formed by the possibility of cultural studies as a project. Now at Leeds we have degrees in cultural studies at all three levels. Cultural studies co-exists with Fine Art, Art History, Material Culture, Museum Studies, Architecture and with two new forces: Jewish Studies, which could well be called Jewish cultural studies, and Feminist Studies in the Visual Arts.

The relations between feminism and cultural studies have always been anguished ones. The tensions within the Birmingham groups were palpable in the history of their publications in which women shouted back at the men from their book covers and black women shouted back at white women to listen. Cultural studies was founded to explore issues that would, when once given space, tear it apart in productive but scarifying ways. Issues of cultural difference, and race, could be found places through programmes on the nation. Feminism itself interrupts cultural studies at every turn even though there is a strongly developed subterrain called Feminist Cultural Studies which has largely focused on popular culture, film studies, the body, fashion and sexuality.

I have remained vigorously involved in our programme in cultural studies, co-teaching its core modules for many years, directing the centre, and latterly teaching its Marxism and its psychoanalysis: or rather offering modules that deal with theories of the subject. Clearly this enables me to speak of issues of sexual difference, of the sexuated subject and the sexualising of the process of subjectivity. Theoretical developments have led me to appreciate the historical and, I would suggest, *strategic* dissonance of artistic practices as sites of cultural production and redefinition that ideologically cultural studies finds hard to accommodate. Literature and film, as well as other forms of cultural practice, such as music, video, fashion, etc., seem at home here: but the visual arts do not. This remains a challenge. Otherwise cultural studies will become what it has become in the United States: a much devalued and uncritical indulgence in the pleasures of commodity culture that refuses the critical edge that 'high theory', the legacy of Marxism and some Frankfurt School aesthetics provided.

Cultural studies is not a discipline pure and simple. It remains a vital project for me because it was formed in a turn to theory that was itself the political claim of critical intellectuals to the means of analysis of their conditions of commodification and exploitation. We are now developing a BA in cultural studies – and a radical challenge that is: the new undergraduate degree reflects the pre-occupations that formed the experiment that is our MA programme: what are we studying, how are we studying it, what resources do we need, what terms of analysis can we now develop to uncover structural processes in social relations and representation; how do we situate both the new objects of study and the new terms of analysis in histories, histories of the social, the text, the sign, ideology, racism, subjectivity and the massive struggles against normative heterosex-ist notions of sexuality? In this, feminism is both a historic topic, and feminist cultural theory a major theoretical resource.

You conclude that cultural studies remains a vital project for you because of its roots in what you describe as 'the political claim of critical intellec-tuals to the means of analysis of their conditions of commodification and exploitation'. I am wondering how this analysis is enacted in practical terms within cultural studies established in the university, an institution that increasingly is a site of the commodification of intellectual activity? How can cultural studies maintain the particular value it has for you as a political project in this situation? For cultural studies is said to be a 'political' project. What, to your mind, are the politics of cultural studies? Does it have 'a' politics, or is it, rather, 'political'? Another way to phrase this would be to ask you what are the politics or what is the political sig-nificance of your own work, as you see it? What do you consider to be the 'proper destination' of your work?

There are three levels at which I can answer this question. Firstly, cultural studies emerged at a moment at which the concept of the political was itself in crisis. In some ways, I understand the formations out of which cultural studies developed to be entirely political. We have to situate the British development in relation not only to specific texts and writers such as Williams, Hoggart and Thompson, but in relation to the transformations that produced and were embodied in the New Left, and especially in the group around *New Left Review*. This project was a response to the inadequacies of Marxism for the analysis of post-war capitalist economies and the political settlements that were shaping the West in its new definition in contrast to the East.

On both sides of the East/West divide there were claims that politics was over, that the political struggle was finished. Both sides declared the achievement of a political/economic system that had solved the major socio-economic problems of poverty and social exclusion. The Daniel Bell argument about the end of ideology, as much as the post-Stalinist apologists of Soviet communism saw the future in terms of technicians who would effectively tweak the remaining mechanical problems of society, rendering all politics redundant. Zygmunt Bauman wrote a fabulous essay in *New Society* in the 1980s precisely about the foreclosure of the political in post-war societies, in which the long-fought struggle for participatory citizenship was being eroded and dismantled absolutely cynically by specialist bodies such as the Brunswick Group, that included representatives from all major parties as well as the interests of the multinationals who planned how to depoliticise issues such as employment, armaments and disarmament, and an array of other potential areas where dissident social groups tried to protest the management of the social system by the notion of non-elected specialists and social technicians. Bauman further saw that the concept of 'the citizen' was being eroded and redefined as 'the consumer'. Access to social participation depended on the credit card, and anyone without a credit rating was being infantilised and 'managed' through the administrative interventions of those in social services. Thus the poor were being hived off as a site of politicisation to become what Blair now defines as the socially excluded who need 'help'. This stands in stark contrast to the potency of disadvantage and immiseration in traditional socialist politics. With Macmillan's 'You never had it so good' message and the apparent increase in material consumption, the classic formations of class politics were altered, losing their obvious forms.

In response to this changing shape of post-war society, the political rallying points of poverty and disenfranchisement lost their centrality. A generation of engaged Marxist and socialist thinkers emerged for whom it became necessary to expand and reframe a Marxist legacy that had been politically devastated by 1956, the Hungarian Uprising and further revelations of Stalinist atrocities that emerged thereafter. I see the theoretical strands out of which cultural studies emerged developing from the need to adapt fundamental elements of the Marxist legacy to the new historical and ideological conditions of that present, in which capitalism's undoubted victories seemed ever more capable of self-perpetuation through *cultural/ideological* operations and domains. Thus the sphere of the ideological production of meanings and, classically, subjects for those ideological positionings emerged into theoretical analysis not as a deviation from the political but as a deep political necessity.

Following on from the discovery of Marx's newly translated *Grundrisse*, in which Marx himself poses the problem of disjunctiveness of the historically determined relations between the terms of analysis and that which analysis tries to comprehend, thinkers like Stuart Hall (this can be tracked in the CCCS *Working Papers* that show what they were reading and working through) returned to new texts by Marx to understand the 'relative autonomy' of the ideological and cultural sphere. Visible in Althusser's very influential work, as well as many of new readings of Marx's *18th Brumaire* and *Grundrisse*, was the search for a more nuanced way of thinking the articulation of the elements of the social totality, not as the organic totality of Lukàcs and Co., and not as the unidirectional model of economic base absolutely determining ideological and political superstructure. Instead there was the idea of a complex totality of 'many determinations and relations' in which while there was a totality, each part both was acted upon and acted itself upon the various elements in historically unpredictable relations.

Thus cultural studies could emerge as a new conceptualisation of where social and political struggle was taking place; but equally, this sphere of culture and meaning would be defined as ideology, as institutions, as practices, and as subjectivities interpellated by these practices and their institutional formations. The effect has been a radically expanded understanding of where the forces and plays of power take place that resume threads of Marx's thinking while liberating that tradition from the straitjacket of pure economism and the limited vision of politics that arose from it.

The second redefinition of politics arose from the interventions of a newly remobilised women's movement and the feminist intellectual revolution that attended and outlived it. From an utterly different angle, the expansion of the domain of the political from formal state politics or formal working-class organisational politics was a radical move. I do not think that the phrase 'the personal is political' has ever been given its full acknowledgement because so few people still read the vitally important books that track the development of European socialist feminist thinking in conjunction with, and *difference* from, the largely American liberal impetus to place sexuality, the domestic sphere, the division of labour, the body and related rights of sexual self-determination on the political agenda. Although the women's movement conceived itself as an innovative but still formally political project built around semi-autonomous cells, annual conferences, and agreed demands, its own political forms generated a radical change: a politicisation of social and cultural theory and history. As such it embodied a new mode of democratisation that depended upon the still huge victory of women's emancipation, universal suffrage, whose achievements are always undervalued, but that extended the project to what I call the unfinished business of modernity: the modernisation of sexual difference.

Thus the family, falling traditionally below the threshold of Marxist politics, emerged as a key institution with its biopolitics and cultural politics of gender and sexuality, parent/child power and social/private interfaces. The interface of feminist cultural and theoretical work with cultural studies has not yet been fully acknowledged. They sit side by side, sharing many common theoretical resources and only recently have I noticed publications that address feminist cultural studies. But clearly feminist theory is responsible for and participates in the creation of new arrays of politics: the politics of the institution, of education, of democracy, the politics of sexuality, the politics of the body, health, age, medical care, the politics of writing, reading and of course teaching.

This brings me to the third aspect, relating to the final part of the question. What is the political destination of my take on cultural studies? Well, I do think that cultural studies participates centrally in a politics of education which is intimately linked to continuing questions of democracy and hence of socialist feminist practice and theory.

Cultural studies challenges the politics of the institutions of education in distinct ways: challenging the formalised divisions of intellectual labour called the disciplines, challenging the models of objective detachment and historical distantiation from the subject. Cultural studies takes us as cultural agents and attends to the very practices that constitute us as subjects within social formations. It defines interdisciplinary modes of analysis that contravene the bourgeois university's division of economics from politics, from social theory, from literature, from art, from artistic practice, so that students can begin to understand both a social synthesis, a sense of the totality that constitutes our worlds, and can begin to understand it for themselves, as a singular but socially formed subject in and of it. It can produce the kind of informed, historically situated reflexivity that is necessary to maintain the possibility of democratic citizenship that is the condition of political change so different from what passes for politics both at the formal level and at the level of alternative groupings.

What are the institutions of cultural studies? That is, what works, methods, orientations, etc., have become instituted as the repositories of 'knowledge', methodology, and ways of going about doing things? This is as much as to say, what do these institutions (or the institution of these authoritative guarantors as 'the proper' or 'the best') forbid, censure/censor, limit and enable? What factors determined or overdetermined their institution?

I don't think there are institutions of cultural studies yet. I can only speak from the position of having had to work with a group of people in setting up firstly an MA in cultural studies and more recently a BA in cultural studies. In both instances, we have been dead against the models we found in some other institutions, where the field is defined by 'the big boy syndrome': Marx, Freud and Derrida get their own modules and other things like sexuality and post-coloniality are represented as issues or themes without defining master discourses and Authors. Instead, at Leeds, we selected (and it is a selection, not a canonising move) three paradigms: commodity, language and subjectivity, around which we feel the innovative and transformative work of cultural studies has focused.

Culture can be theorised in relation to the social relations of production within a capitalist field. In this paradigm a range of texts, writings, theorisations, can be considered in both the historical framing and genealogical tracking of a diversity of articulations of the commodity as the defining form of cultural production and experience. Secondly, culture can be theorised in relation to signification and textuality, and a major shift has occurred at this intersection of semiotics, deconstruction and discourse analysis. Thirdly, the agent displaced from the traditional bourgeois idealisations of culture as expressive and possessive individualism can be retraced as 'subject/subjectivity' in the third paradigm that addresses the conflicting theorisations of subjectification (Foucault) and subjectivity (psychoanalysis). The former usefully defines the institutions, practices and discourses through which social positions are produced and enmeshed in strategic power relations. The latter defines both the formation of subjectivities in an economy not consistent with, yet intertwined with, the social production of subject-positions. Subjectivity is both the apparatus for creating subjects and dialectically always in excess of that will to identity. Subjectivity deals with the conditions of failure of the subject within class, sexual, gender, ethnic, etc., formations of identity. It is thus, at its interface with the semiotic, a force that destabilises the will to order and to knowledge/power.

In our recent development of an undergraduate course in cultural studies, we retained a second dimension of the MA. We frame cultural studies through the double vision of cultural theory and cultural history. One of the greatest dangers – enabling the commodification and assimilation of cultural studies as the academic apologist for capitalist media and communications industries, rendering students merely better-adjusted consumers of their cultural products, as intellectually titillated fans – lies in the abandonment of a historical perspective. This sense of the historical framing of cultural practices within and beyond modernity in which the cultural developed its own singularity as a field links back to the political character of the project. Historical knowledges that are not conceived as traditional narratives but as identifications of critical points of rupture, change, discontinuity, and as the scene of the encounter with difference, must play a vital role in cultural studies. Its institutions might then be a very elaborated range of theoretical traditions and projects combined with a critical sense of historicity.

We have also identified the domain of difference as central to the project: difference as history, difference as sexual difference, difference as the necessity for a radically non-Eurocentric and internationalist perspective on the differentiated and differenced centres of experience and practice, difference as – critically – the challenge to phallocentric and heterosexist normalisations of bodies, minds, meanings, institutions and social spaces. The ambition is to make lives more liveable in the creation of knowledges, discourses and practices concomitant with the social subjectivities and collectivities that hegemonic institutions, practices and discourses disown. Thus, any institutionalisation of cultural studies must constantly reflect, in its own forms and methods, pedagogies and social relations, the politics of real resistance. Social theory cannot only be presented as thought by straight, white men. The practice must decentre that hegemony as much as the content. Thus, institutionalising it as 'the big boys' thinking the defining thoughts will not do. Students must encounter the new thinking in the polyvocal, polyaccented, diversely embodied and desiring subjects to which the field aims to offer intellectual and cultural hospitality. Only when students learn their world through these altered prisms and dehierarchised models will cultural studies work.

How does the institutionalisation of cultural studies affect, support or undermine it?

Inevitably, cultural studies must find a home and establish a curriculum. This is immensely enabling, as institutionalisation as a recognised area of academic development, research and teaching enables students to find new ways of thinking the questions that press upon us and those that until now did not have a shape, or the means to be considered researchable. Constantly presenting the history of cultural studies as a *historical* rather than an *author-based* formation that has a longer and wider history ensures that the area does not just become a rather wishy-washy catch-all for anyone wanting to make a new theoretical soup seasoned with a range of fashionable flavours. Institutionalisation means reflecting on how we train cultural studies scholars at doctoral level: at Leeds this has meant attempting to ensure awareness of the longer histories and deeper roots of many of the key theoretical projects that must be encountered vertically as well as in their horizontal interdisciplinarity.

The key question facing cultural studies is the sustainability of interdisciplinarity so that it does not become superficial, deracinated and derivative: a patchwork of citations rather than an intellectual formation of critical self-judgement and political self-understanding. As I said in answer to a previous question, my greatest concern is that feminist and other counter-hegemonic class and sexual politics will not be allowed to impinge enough. The formation of a canon of great scholars will make cultural studies a star system. But as I have found through working with a lot of African-American feminist thinkers, with the works of Friere and Boal, if we take each cell of a society to be already a microcosm of its entire social and political structure, the politics of the classroom and the curriculum, what and how we teach becomes a vital concern. How we institutionalise and how we counter-institutionalise is well developed in feminist theory and practice and cultural studies can benefit from serious engagement with these other examples of differencing the academy/canon.

Does cultural studies have any significance outside of the university at all? If so, what forms does this take?

In everything that I have done I have worked with the notion of the interconnecting cells of social formations, so the notion that there is an 'outside' to the university with an 'inside' is not a model that I favour. The university is a linked site of the social. Linked to education as a whole, we are also linked today to what we did in the 1970s, and to what the schools took on in the 1990s: media studies, semiotics, film studies, feminist theory, expanded reading lists for English, and so forth. The people who study cultural studies find themselves in many kinds of works, linking cultural studies with other cultural institutions and sites of practice. So there is a positive side through curriculum remodelling and through personnel. But there is a blockage on the entry of cultural studies into other privileged and opinion-forming sites such as the media and journalism. Part of this is the class system in this country which still produces a very exclusive bunch of people in charge of these important institutions. There are still gatekeepers who reflect the deep philistinism and anti-intellectualism of English (and I stress *English*) cultural elites. Whenever key events occur, intellectuals are rarely summonsed for discussion. Some political academics have become media personalities and in that role they comfort the media by knowing how to talk. Until we can really challenge this notion that nothing difficult must ever be said on TV or radio, we will have no effect at all. Until we can present to the world the case for what I call cultural analysis, following Mieke Bal, we find that the world beyond the university is imaginatively mapped in utterly conventional ways: experts are called on for the technical fix on a problem and any commentators are drawn from traditional disciplines: politics, or history. Sociology is never permitted and, along with sociologists, cultural studies analysts are consistently delegitimised in the media as lunatics who talk an unnecessarily jargon-ridden and foreign language.

This is a site of important cultural struggle, a politics of the representation of the intellectual which takes us back to the second question. Certainly I think that there is a political agenda for cultural studies. The agenda concerns change through analysis of the conditions of the social and historical formations which shape and situate current possibilities and limitations. Its political address is not to traditional political movements or objectives. Its political potential as a force of destabilising and radical change is in some ways reflected by the total hostility of our cultures to the value of intellectual endeavour itself unless it has a commodifiable and utilitarian outcome in the interests of the capitalist order. Marginalised we may be tolerated, but our voices are then not heard or rendered ridiculous. Successfully acknowledged by the media and society, the challenge cultural studies potentially contains as the historically informed and theoretically resourced analyst of the present might then produce a more serious backlash.

What is, has been, might be, or might have been, the 'significance' of cultural studies within the university?

Cultural studies opens the university to *interdisciplinary* studies in the arts and the humanities. It belongs with a series of moves that bridged philosophy, social theory, the language/culture departments and, at Leeds, what has always been special, art, art history and musicology. Cultural studies, therefore allows students to encounter ranges of thinking and texts, practices and ideas that are normally carved up into discrete sections. Where else would a student in three years encounter Marx and Freud, Derrida and Spivak, Adorno and Kristeva, Foucault and Haraway, and in those encounters with post-colonial, psychoanalytical Marxist, semiotic, philosophical, aesthetic, feminist, queer thinkers and their projects, begin to see the world in its inter-connections, relays, overdeterminations and strategic linkages?

What cultural studies does to the university is to offer an image of the field of knowledge that is not partitioned, that is not kept, as Gunnar Myrdal usefully put it, locked in separate rooms whose dividing walls are the sustaining walls of power. Cultural Studies – like its recently reclaimed predecessor *Kulturwissenschaft*, conceived by Aby Warburg – imagines a library in the round, where strange encounters can take place and hidden connections become visible so that the formal appearances of disjunctive segments reappear as Marx imagined them in complex totalities of many relations and determinations. The second thing cultural studies does is to place culture on the academic agenda not as that capital-c-Culture maintained traditionally through English Literature or the Classics departments. The realm of meanings, the institutions through which they are produced and circulated and the subjects formed for and by them become sites of recognised study. The way of life, the way of struggle, and of course the configuration of the present become sus-ceptible to critical and reflexive study and teaching as they are lived, embodied, suffered, thought and practised. I do not think the university as a whole grasps any of this and sees it, and I do not know how many old universities have fully embraced and supported developments of cultural studies programmes or centres. When Leeds started a centre in 1985, we felt both belated vis-à-vis Birmingham and yet strangely out of step, since it was not a widespread movement. Sussex had an MA in Critical Theory; Goldsmiths and Lancaster seem to have their own axis that emerged in the 1990s. Leeds was welcomed at first by those who thought interdisciplinarity was the economic model for the future. When that criterion waned, academics on committees wracked their brains to grasp what 'culture' was as an object and it took several serious presentations to committees before the assembled scientists, social scientists and arts members were prepared to allow a Centre or a degree in *cultural* studies. That hesitancy betokened a real confusion before a new way of conceiving not a subject area but a project, not a discipline but a collaborative intervention. Most universities nowadays consider subjects/centres/projects only on the grounds of their capacity for income generation. While there are students, there will not be much serious examination of cultural studies. If ever it became a minority field, I am not sure of the nature of the support we would find to defend the twin values of interdisciplinarity and the analysis of the present.

Where is cultural studies going? This question is obviously tied to that of where has it been, which is an interesting and important question itself; but we wonder where you think it should go, or what you think it should now do or try to do: in short, what has cultural studies 'achieved', what has it 'failed' to achieve, and to what extent are these 'failures' inevitable, structural, or is it just that their realisation is only a matter of time or strategy?

A problem I have had in answering these questions throughout is the tendency to reify cultural studies in odd ways. It cannot be understood as a homogeneous thing. At one level, if we read the pages under the banner of cultural studies in Routledge's catalogue, cultural studies is just the space where you find the most interesting books that cannot be classified under anything else, although there will always be several cross-references to appease the marketing people. These books must have several purchasing constituencies. If you do a survey of universities and colleges, you will find cultural studies within or having grown out of literature or media studies/communications departments. Often now cultural studies is linked with something else. What we think of and practise as cultural studies is definitely distinct from the media studies and popular culture end of the spectrum that uses the designation. I am not concerned with training a new generation of medianiks, nor am I much interested in the entirely contradictory operation of validating something called popular culture under a rubric that leaves its status as 'popular', as opposed to an undesignated something not-popular, unchallenged. Cultural studies is more comprehensive but also more critical of the industry-led designations of media and communications, and inherently, through Marxist and other historically and philosophically based ways of thinking, challenges the notions on which popular as opposed to high, unpopular, bourgeois, elite culture functions.

Cultural studies is a project, an intervention, an interdisciplinary initiative within the forms of knowledge as well as a necessary extension of engaged critical analysis of the formations of contemporary societies and the conditions of their existence/persistence/transformation. Cultural studies has not been anywhere and is not going anywhere. It is doing a specific job, or set of jobs, that makes possible thinking and doing. It is precisely the relation of the two that seems to lie behind this series of questions. Is thinking a kind of doing? Yes, and a very important one too. Is doing a kind of thinking? Not always and that is why I give priority to thinking strategically about doing. Thinking is a practice and I value intellectual practice not as a removed and socially immune activity but as a practice within the relating fields of practice that constitute the cultural as well as the political and economic zones of the social totality.

It will, therefore, continue to do its thinking, provided that we are able to develop the study area in the university as an interdisciplinary intervention and a historically based theorisation and analysis of the present. Cultural studies can do historically based studies because I define the present very broadly and I also see historical studies as indexed to the present of its interpreters.

I see a need to distinguish the historical project of cultural studies that emerged out of the political awakening in the 1950s and 1960s in response to the need to have theories of the cultural and methods of genuinely democratising education from that which becomes the academic training arm of the ever expanding media and communications industries. I feel we have only just begun our work to create a space within the academy and the institutions of education for the training of critical intellectuals rather than disciplinary scholars. We must ceaselessly resist our own inevitable commodification as a subject area and as administered cultural workers. But we have the advantage. The very materials we study and learn through teaching are those that formulate the critique of administered culture and commodification while pessimistically doubting the long-term possibility of resistance. The worst thing we can do is to preach despondency and pessimism even if we must acknowledge it as a necessary critical position given what we know. If Zygmunt Bauman points to the shift from the intellectual as legislator to the intellectual merely as local interpreter, and David Macey tracks the end of the engaged intellectual in the French tradition, cultural studies can be the institutionalised support for the irrational persistence of what is now a daydream of the political, transformative and democratising value of thought. This is Julia Kristeva's position when she claims that reason has been appropriated for the technological, massified, administered society, but that thought itself is a form of dissidence. But intellectuals since cultural studies emerged are no longer subject to the illusion of disinterested unpositioned universality. We are particularised, localised, marked, positioned, situated, interested, confronted, antagonised, agonised, classed, raced, gendered, sexualised and captured by the dual axes of generation and geography. Situated, particularised thought engaged in the project of communicative – not instrumentalised – reasoning that is reflexive of the worlds we live in is new and is only at the beginning of its effectivity. As Marx argued, no outcome is certain and we cannot delude ourselves that thought is determining in the last instance. But it is certainly, in this instance, a critical factor, and cultural studies should see its project as fostering that necessity to appropriate the concrete world for understanding and change in the only way it can, through thought, while knowing all the while that its methods and manners are not adequate to what needs to be thought. Upon this sobering possibility, I find it necessary, therefore, to conjugate theory, history and analysis with the aesthetic, or the practices of poiesis, the production of meanings and subjectivities attendant to meaning through different modes of thinking and representing, such as art. I find it also necessary to challenge the internal dynamics of cultural studies as an institution liable to mimic the father institutions, liable to replicate phallocentric, heterosexist and racist habits, by occupying simultaneously several institutional, discursive and political sites. For cultural studies as practised, the genuine and auto-transformative embrace of feminist, post-colonial and lesbian and gay questions is still in the stage of becoming.

NOTE

1. Interview conducted by Dr Alison Rowley, University of Leeds.

Part Four:
What Cultural Studies

INTRODUCTION

The question here is no longer the much-exercised question of 'what is cultural studies?', but rather, 'for what?', 'for whom?', 'in the name of what project?', 'what politics?', what properties, orientations and affiliations does cultural studies have, should it have; what methods, aims, intentions; in what context does it see itself; etc.? Jeremy Gilbert thinks through the schema and the question of 'Friends and Enemies: Which Side is Cultural Studies On?', while Julian Wolfreys interrogates the manner in which it is too easy to forget the lessons of deconstruction, and to consider cultural studies 'as if such a thing existed'.

For Gilbert, it is incumbent upon us to interrogate all conceptions about the nature of our, and all, intellectual work, with a view to determining wherein lies political efficacy. In the face of what he sees as the simultaneous or directly proportional expansion and dilution of cultural studies' political force, he reminds us of what you might call the 'incomplete project' of attacking the essentialism of individualism, the essentialism and ideology of individuality, and the notion of the individual's complicity in aiding and abetting the processes of the dissolution of political consciousness. Without renewed vigour in this particular task, he argues (drawing on the work of Laclau and Mouffe), cultural studies remains complicit in the process of the destruction of the very things it would claim to hold dear.

Julian Wolfreys offers a deconstructive dissection of the questions. Focusing on the implications of the concepts or notions entailed, he, in one sense, sticks firmly to 'the very idea', the traffic in concepts, which are often simply assumed to 'be', to signify, or to refer to something that 'is'. Instead of this error or assumption, Wolfreys channels his responses through an attention to the processes of reading, decoding, interpretation, clarifying the sense in which the way one reads, the way one is taught to read, and hence assumes that manner of interpretation to be 'natural' or 'inevitable', conditions so many things. He does not, however, stick to this infamous deconstructive 'quasi-transcendental' mode of analysis (which is often unfairly deemed 'unrelated' or 'de-contextualised'). He also shows how the apparently transcendental is always tied to the concrete or particular contexts of emergence.

Both chapters show something of the force of deconstruction for cultural studies work in its political dimensions. What they show is not the same in each case, but both indicate something unique of the diverse intellectual and political potential of the strategic deployment of the lessons of deconstruction, in and for cultural studies.

9 Friends and Enemies: Which Side is Cultural Studies On?

Jeremy Gilbert

CULTURAL STUDIES AND THE BRITISH LEFT

What is cultural studies for, and what is it against? There can be, of course, no single answer to this question. There is a habit amongst commentators, especially those who, being located outside the UK, are understandably removed from the political contexts which produced British cultural studies, of deploying the term 'cultural studies' as an adjective, using it to describe certain determinate political positions as well as certain specifiable methodologies. Such references to 'cultural studies' positions or approaches effectively conflate cultural studies – an interdisciplinary field of enquiry – with the political tradition which has informed its dominant strand in the UK.

It's important from the outset to clear this up: 'cultural studies' is not, as such, a political position, nor even, in and of itself, a political project. It is a field of practice which can be informed by commitments to, in theory, any number of political projects or ethical orientations. It happens to be the case that a certain political tradition has been particularly influential on the development of that field. This is a tradition which has its roots in the British New Left and in particular in the moment when key figures such as Raymond Williams and Stuart Hall came under the influence of the work of Antonio Gramsci,[1] a tradition which has subsequently been shaped most dramatically by encounters with postmodernism, poststructuralism, the politics of the new social movements and attempts to formulate creative left responses to the emergence of post-Fordism.[2] However, it is important to note that the political tradition of the New Left and its descendants is not the same thing as cultural studies, and never was.[3]

145

I'm not saying this in order to try to minimise the significance of the relationship between the two projects. Quite the reverse: understanding that the two are not identical should help us to put into proper perspective the relationship between them. Seen in this light, the significance of the New Left and its progeny for cultural studies was huge, lending to its mainstream a meaningful political identity which could only ever have been acquired on the basis of a deep affiliation to something bigger than itself. In concrete terms, it meant that people working within cultural studies – as writers, researchers, teachers or students – could with some justification feel themselves to be allied to actually existing political projects. The key reason that Stuart Hall acquired such totemic status as the pivotal figure within British cultural studies, despite the fact that his only single-authored work was a collection of mainly journalistic political commentaries,[4] was precisely his crucial function as mediator between cultural studies as an academic interdiscipline and these wider political tendencies.

Hall was the key theorist of and commentator on British politics on the magazine *Marxism Today*, which was central to the dissemination of Gramscian, postmodernist and post-Marxist ideas within the British left in the 1980s and which popularised the analysis of Thatcherism as a hegemonic project which had successfully demolished post-war social democracy and could only be resisted with a counter-hegemony of equal daring.[5] *Marxism Today* was itself often seen as part of that wider formation which included its publisher, the Communist Party of Great Britain, the New Left tradition and, most importantly, the so-called 'Soft Left' of the Labour Party and its affiliated trade unions. At the end of the 1980s, this was still considered to be very much the mainstream of the party, back in the heady days when people like me considered Roy Hattersley to be the unacceptable face of the Labour right and *Marxism Today* was known to be influential in the private office of Labour leader Neil Kinnock.

FROM *NEW TIMES* TO NEW LABOUR

While critics on the left continue to see a natural continuity between the analyses and arguments of *Marxism Today* and the emergence of New Labour,[6] I would argue that the moment of New Labour's birth (at the latest the moment of Tony Blair's election as Labour leader, in 1994), marked the point at which the project to create an inclusive, pluralistic and democratic version of modernisation with which to counter Thatcherism was defeated in the British Labour movement. This was the moment when, for example, the decline of the left press began to look irreversible and the *New Statesman* – a public place outside the academy where at one time the impact of cultural studies could be discerned clearly and frequently – shifted itself somewhere to the right of the *Financial Times*. It was the moment when the November 1998 publication of a special issue of *Marxism Today*, several years after the magazine's closure, and apparently having no real purpose other than to point out that almost all of the old *Marxism Today* writers considered New Labour to be a disaster, could have been predicted with confidence.

This was also the moment when it became very difficult to say just what side in what political struggles cultural studies was actually on. For the one thing that New Labour and the Blair government have inherited from their more radical antecedents, and the thing which distinguished the form of neo-liberalism implemented by the Blair government, the Clinton administration, and many similar agencies throughout the world from that implemented by the New Right of Thatcher and Reagan, is a commitment to a certain cultural modernisation and a certain social pluralism. This is a government which has, albeit with some reluctance, allowed the concept of institutional racism to become part of official discourse, acknowledged as something which exists and must be stamped out in locations such as London's Metropolitan Police. This is a government which has taken the first steps towards the normalisation of the legal treatment of lesbians and gay men. This is a government whose reforms of the welfare system, as unwelcome as they may often be, do recognise that it is now normal for mothers below retirement age to work. At the same time, we have seen massive shifts in social attitudes towards race and sexuality over the past 15 years, shifts largely driven by the commitment of broadcast media decision-makers to the dissemination of metropolitan liberalism. Many of these phenomena have been reproduced across those parts of the world where cultural studies has had an impact, and in all cases one must ask the same question: in an age when many of the elements of the dominant culture which cultural studies came into existence in order to critique are simply no longer effective and explicit elements of hegemonic discourse, can cultural studies now be *opposed* to anything except the past?

Many self-identified Marxists fear not. It has become a common-place of Marxian attacks on cultural studies to point out that contemporary capitalism does not only not abhor cultural difference, but thrives on and produces it. Critics like the irrepressible Slavoj Žižek see the politics of difference as simply the ideology of neo-liberalism.[7] Calling for a return to dialectics, political economy, class struggle and the critique of commodity culture,[8] they argue in precisely the same terms as those who see *Marxism Today* as responsible for New Labour. In both cases, the Gramscian post-modernists are charged with being, at best, self-deceiving pseudo-radicals, at worst, willing agents of the spread of capitalist social relations.

What such criticism entirely fails to deal with, however, is the set of problems that the analyses of both *Marxism Today* and many cultural studies writers were made in order to address in the first place. The proliferation, penetration and intensification of capitalist social relations has not produced a concomitant upsurge in class consciousness, nor is there any evidence that remaining forms of raced, gendered or sexualised oppression can be any more easily subsumed under the analytical categories of capitalism and class oppression than they ever could. Nonetheless, it is entirely necessary that we take seriously the challenge from these critics. The danger they alert us to is real: that in preaching multiculturalism and social pluralism we may merely coincide with the agenda of that socio-economic system which is in the process of launching the most intense onslaught on the public services which the world has ever seen, from the UK to Asia to South America.[9]

If we want to resist this danger then it is necessary for people working in cultural studies to do at least one thing, and that is to ask ourselves explicitly and rigorously what our own political and ethical assumptions actually are. What, to be exact, *are* we for or against? If, presumably, we are against the depredations which neo-liberalism is wreaking on the world, and if, presumably, we are not *simply* for the proletariat and its struggle against the bourgeoisie, then there must be other answers to this question.

CULTURAL STUDIES VS. BOURGEOIS INDIVIDUALISM

I'd suggest that the most useful answer is, in fact, a rather old one. It is the ideology of individualism which is the key term which organises the field of hegemonic discourse today, the linchpin which holds together the discourses of 'culture' so-called and 'politics' proper. It is individualism which is the common term shared by that pluralistic discourse of cultural modernisation which is actively hostile to explicit racism, sexism, homophobia and xenophobia and the political discourse which seeks to implement market relations and market logics in every possible sphere of life. It is individualism which lies at the heart of those discourses which are right now being mobilised by our enemies in the great concrete political struggle of our time and our situation: the struggle to defend a notion of the public – public space, public service, public interests, public spheres – against the outright attack on all such ideas being made by agencies such as the Blair government and the signatories to the General Agreement on Trade in Services.[10] In the current conjuncture this is the fundamental element which ties together the 'cultural' and the political, and it is the presence of some critique of it which distinguishes radical forms of politics – socialist, feminist, queer, anti-racist, ecological – from their liberal counterparts.

As Chantal Mouffe has recently pointed out, the political culture of neo-liberalism is characterised by the disarticulation of the two components of liberal democracy.[11] The goals of liberalism in the current era – the spread of the free market and the constitution of individuals as economic competitors and ravenous consumers – are not compatible with any form of democracy worth the name. This view chimes with that of Anthony Barnett, who describes the politics of New Labour as exemplary of 'corporate populism',[12] trying to win the support of the populace by offering them the kind of stake in national life that shareholders or customers have in a corporation and its products. In both cases it is clear that the central ideological operation of this politics is the interpellation of citizens as wholly individualised consumers, and that this latest manifestation of the ideology of bourgeois individualism is wholly inimical to the realisation of any democratic, socialistic or communitarian goals. It will be the degree of cultural studies' success at offering critiques of this ideology that will determine how much cultural studies can contribute to the real struggles against the commercialisation of public services, which will characterise global left politics in the coming decade.

This shouldn't be difficult for cultural studies to do. Although, as I have argued, there is no inherent political meaning to cultural studies as such, there is clearly a bias in its history and in its most minimal assumptions towards an understanding of human life as fundamentally social in character. The very concepts of 'culture', 'community' and 'the social' have been intertwined throughout their history, and the work of Raymond Williams is clearly predicated on a common commitment to the significance of culture and the value of community. This is not to deny that those conceptions have always been problematic, and more recent philosophical developments have done much to problematise their terms. The influence of philosophies of difference in the work of thinkers such as Lyotard and Deleuze, the postmodern emphasis on the value of plurality and the dangers of its suppression, and the deconstructive refusal of all essentialism have made it impossible for many of us to sustain a notion of community as a simple commonality of substance or straightforward sharing of identity. However, the risk which Marxist critics rightly discern in such moves is that in embracing some simple ethics of alterity we abandon any notion of community whatsoever: that openness to difference becomes the only basis for any posited ethics, in a manner which offers no basis from which to criticise a system of social relations which thrives on difference – even self-difference – but which nonetheless wrecks human life and the very environmental conditions of its sustained possibility.

It would be tilting at windmills to suggest that anyone has ever really tried to delineate such a 'pure' ethics of alterity. The works of Lévinas, Lyotard, Deleuze and Derrida can all be read as meditations on community itself, on the mechanics of its possibilities and its necessary aporias. The ethics of alterity can only ever be the obverse of a concomitant ethics of community, if it is to have any value at all. In the work of Nancy and Borch-Jacobsen[13] this becomes explicit. Rather than try to set up some sectarian distinction between different schools, or even between cultural studies and its critics, I think it is crucial here to emphasise the extent to which a critique of what we might still call bourgeois individualism is the common point of reference for a radical tradition which can include Nancy, Derrida, Bourdieu, Deleuze, Foucault, Williams, Lacan, Althusser, Habermas, Adorno, Nietzsche, Freud, Marx, possibly Hegel, not to mention several traditions of feminism and anti-racism. It is a point of reference which needs to be explicitly returned to and reactivated by contemporary cultural studies if it is to play a role in the struggle against neo-liberalism.

It might be objected here that what I am saying is merely obvious, that we all know that individualism possesses an account of human experience which is at once materially false and extraordinarily destructive in its effects, and that of course this opinion is shared by everyone from the Buddha to Jesus to Ernesto Laclau. If this shared opinion is a point of view so common to so many, then where can the interest lie in expressing it?

To this understandable objection I would reply that this may be a view common to us, to radical professional intellectuals, but it is clearly not one common to the majority of our students, and that it is primarily as participants in a general pedagogic project that we have to understand the possibilities of our political efficacy. This does not mean at all that everything we write has to be readable by undergraduates, but it does mean that at the end of the day even the most rarefied piece of theorising must come to inform some piece of teaching somewhere if it is to be politically effective. In this context it is absolutely crucial for us to pay attention to the specificity of the culture in which we operate, and to try to encourage students to interrogate the ideological assumptions which constitute their subjectivities. One of the most basic pedagogic operations in cultural studies is to point out to students that, just because they don't know what their implicit ideological assumptions are, does not mean that they don't have any. I can't be the only lecturer who habitually says to students 'everyone has a theory, they just don't always know what it is'. This is clearly one of the founding claims of cultural studies. And yet, how often do we as professionals fully apply its implications to the consideration of our own work, and especially our teaching? Rarely, in my experience.

To me this failure is a fundamental one, as we can hardly ask our students to interrogate their inherited ideological positions if we don't interrogate our own. So of course, we often *don't* ask them to do that at all – we ask them to interrogate those of a now-residual moment, when explicit racism and sexism were clearly identifiable elements of the dominant ideology. The effect, I think, is frequently disastrous. Students enter with their subjectivities constituted by a hegemonic liberal ideology which is hostile to the explicit racism, sexism, homophobia, classism and elitism of that earlier moment, and they leave with that ideology having been reinforced and never challenged: perfect neo-liberal subjects.

But what else can we do? The answer from the orthodox Marxists is 'nothing'. For many of them, the answer seems to be that cultural studies should just get out of the way and make room for real politics, allowing true radicals to focus on the real business of the economy, on issues of material justice, on the class struggle, to which cultural politics can be at best a minor hand-servant, at worst an outright foe. This isn't the course I would recommend. Rather, I'd like to suggest that a radical cultural studies needs to do what it has always done best: rigorously to examine the contours of the current conjuncture, and to deconstruct those elements of contemporary culture which reinforce and reproduce relations of subordination and exploitation, and that in the current conjuncture that is not simply a matter of exposing imbalances of power as they work along the axes of class, race, gender and sexuality.

This is not to say that power has ceased to work along these axes. Nor is it to downplay the importance of that fundamental term which unites critical attitudes to gender, sexuality, race and class in current post-structuralist thought: anti-essentialism. I agree with Laclau and Mouffe that anti-essentialism is the *sine qua non* of an effective radical politics today, but essentialisms, as they would be the first to acknowledge, come in many forms and can only be effective – and effectively deconstructed – in specific contexts. Far too often, students receive the critique of essentialism as nothing more than a re-statement of individualist liberal humanism: 'These cultural differences are not essential, therefore they are superficial to our real individualities.' The only way to overcome this, I would suggest, is to take on the one essentialism which defines all the others in neo-liberal culture, the term that organises the field of hegemonic discourse in the West today: the essentialism of the asocial individual.

In particular, I think that cultural studies needs to continue to pay close attention to the prevalence of consumerist individualism as the key term of neo-liberal culture. This is crucial because it is essential to realise that contemporary forms of individualism are not simply manifestations of the old liberal subjectivities of the past. The old bourgeois subject was a very different being to the new one. Possessive individualism as it was actually lived inherited a great deal from the moment of radical Protestantism and was constituted by the intersection of phallogocentric discourse with the experience of early capitalism.[14] The hegemony of the Puritan subject – the hard-working, undemanding, self-possessed man of reason – has been deeply eroded by the spread of consumer capitalism and its dependence on an ever greater market for the decadent and feminising pleasures of the flesh. In this postmodern context, the configuration of patriarchy, capitalism, racism and logocentrism is very different to what it was even 15 years ago, and only careful attention to the specificities of contemporary culture can enable us to unpick these connections and retain a radical agenda without finding ourselves in complicity with the most destructive forces on the planet. The work of those who studied consumer culture, its conditions and effects, is obviously central to any proper consideration of these issues.[15]

THE POLITICALITY OF CULTURE: A RADICAL DEMOCRATIC PERSPECTIVE

The question this leaves open is: how exactly do we understand contemporary formations from the point of view of such an analysis? How do we take on the forces of liberal individualism without relying on the essentialist and anachronistic models of earlier moments? The solution I would propose is fairly straightforward: to look to a moment of communitarian cultural studies – the work of Raymond Williams – and ask what it can share, and how it must still differ, from a perspective informed by anti-essentialism and the philosophy of difference. The most consistent and significant attempt to reformulate a radical political position on the basis of the latter has been, without question, the work of Laclau and Mouffe, and it is in the name of a politics which is communitarian in its aspirations and assumptions, but is so only in a sense which is fully compatible with the project of radical democracy, through which I believe a radical cultural studies can constitute itself in this new century.

There is only time here to offer the briefest sketch of what such a practice would look like. I'd suggest that it would firstly need, to some extent, to look at Williams' attempts to formulate a vocabulary by which to describe the political status of given formations in terms consistent with a fairly rigorous set of political assumptions, political assumptions which we may want to revise, but with which we cannot hope to operate without some equivalent to. Williams' distinctions between hegemonic, alternative and oppositional formations and between residual, dominant and emergent formations remain a model of a clear and precise set of political classifications for cultural forms, notwithstanding the epistemological and ontological problems inherent in any such framework.[16] It clearly spells out the issues at stake for the cultural critic who is ideologically committed to a programme of revolutionary transformation and who understands social and historical reality in classical Gramscian terms, identifying the most politically desirable projects with those which combine a certain radical newness, a position on the 'leading edge' of historical change, with a direct opposition to the hegemony of the ruling class. It's important to note that his way of looking at things implies a certain set of convictions not just about politics, but about *politicality* itself. According to this model, what actually renders a given formation political and what lends it its political identity is its relationship to bourgeois hegemony and its position in history, conceived more-or-less teleologically in terms of the narrative of successive modes of production and historical change through class struggle. It seems to me that any form of cultural studies which wants to retain any kind of political radicalism must assert a similar – if different – set of assumptions about what it is that actually *renders political* given cultural formations, texts, projects, etc.

I'm not an expert on ethics or on the debate on the relationship between politics and ethics, but it seems to me that this is where the relationship between politics and ethics occurs. It is a certain set of ethical commitments – which may be, following the meditations of Derrida or Kierkegaard on the irreducibility of the decision, at some level untheorisable – that will give rise to a set of assumptions as to what it is that constitutes the *politicality* of given phenomena. In these terms, a possibly pre-theoretical ethical commitment to community-in-difference is the logical concomitant to, and perhaps the basis for, a radically democratic, radically communitarian politico-ethical position, and such an ethics will lead to a set of assumptions as to what actually constitutes the politicality of cultural-political phenomena and what the desirable and undesirable features of such phenomena might be.

So, what would the political parameters of such a radically democratic cultural studies be? There isn't time to go into details here, but I think that it would ask certain key questions of any formation, text, or project. Firstly, it would ask to what extent it facilitates the breaking-down of concentrations of power, and this question would be refined into one around the issue of how far any formation successfully enables or at least allows the unimpeded proliferation of difference. On the other hand, any position informed by the work of Laclau and Mouffe would have to acknowledge the necessary hegemonic dimension of any project *qua* project or, I would suggest, any community *qua* community. From this perspective the politicality of a given formation must also be understood in terms of its capacity to sustain itself as a formation and to widen its boundaries beyond those of a narrow region of the social. This would be the difference between a cultural criticism informed by Laclau and Mouffe Gramscianism and one committed to the implicit anarchism of a Lyotardian ethics of alterity, or to a Deleuzean position as that is widely understood. Rather than simply valorising cultural forms which promote the proliferation of difference, such a position would emphasise the limitations of such a politics in the context of the hegemonic and counter-hegemonic struggles which characterise politics in the real world, recognising that the realisation of greater degrees of autonomy and difference for a range of subjects may at times require those subjects to suppress parts of their difference in the name of a wider hegemonic project.

These two considerations – the degree to which a given formation enables difference and its capacity to sustain and extend itself – will exist on one level of analysis in a kind of paradoxical tension. On another level, however, it is possible to see both of these as aspects of a single question: how far is the formation in question characterised by a certain dynamic openness? Such openness is, arguably, what characterises any social space in which difference is not suppressed; but it is also what characterises the relationships between subjects-in-community and what characterises any community – political, cultural, national – that is vibrant and porous enough to sustain and extend itself in the possibility of its own transformation. This indeed would connect with the final feature which I would posit of any potentially radically democratic cultural formation: its openness to the radically unknowable possibilities of the future (and here we find an echo of Williams' implicit valorisation of the emergent over the residual or the dominant). A radical democratic cultural studies would therefore recognise that it is the dynamic of openness, the problematisation of boundaries – the very mechanism of politics itself – which at once constitutes communities in breaking down the boundaries between subjects and which constitutes the dynamism of communities, *of* breaking down the distinctions between their interiors and exteriors, in realising them not as hypostatic entities but as spaces of shared self-difference. According to this configuration, and following Jean-Luc Nancy, all of these terms might be reduced to a basic opposition between the 'political' and the 'anti-political': '"Political" would mean a community ordering itself to the unworking of its communication, or destined to this unworking: a community consciously undergoing the experience of its sharing.'[17] This is another way of understanding that that problematisation of the boundaries constituting individual *subjects* which makes community itself possible (as something other than a random collection of atoms) must in some sense be maintained at the boundaries of the community itself for it to continue to exist as such.

We can see from this argument that individualism – which in any form is predicated on the insistence that the boundaries around subjects be kept static and stable – is one of the basic obstacles to the realisation of any radically democratic objectives. The logical conclusion of such reflection, it seems to me, must be that an ethical commitment to community-in-difference, such as is shared by thinkers from Marx to Nancy, must lead to a political critique of individualism and vice-versa. At the same time, the concrete struggle of our times, the struggle to defend the public sphere against the market, demands a similar critique. Whatever forms of intervention a radical cultural studies might seek to make in the near future, be it from a perspective such as that recommended here or one committed to classical Marxism or Lacanian Leninism, or Deleuzean anarchism, the critique of individualism must be one of its key points of orientation.

WHAT IS TO BE DONE?

Now, this is all very well. Yet still it leaves open the question of what interventions cultural studies, armed with this knowledge, might actually make. Firstly here, I want to return to the question of the relationship between academics and their audiences. There's a lot of nonsense talked about this, most of which is the result of a failure to grasp the complex ways in which academic knowledge is mediated. The typical complaint that academics spend too much time talking to each other misses the point that the teaching which those academics deliver to students is in large part a result of the talking they do with each other: either literally or via publications. The fact that an article in a refereed journal may only be read by, indeed, may only be comprehensible to, a few hundred specialists, does not mean that those people will be its only effective audience. Presumably it will have some effect on their teaching and their research and the teaching of people who read that research. So its direct audience may be small, but its 'mediated audience', if you like, may be much larger. It's this complex process of mediation which has to be taken into account. On the other hand, by the same token the ideal of maintaining a 'research-based teaching culture' is too often appealed to by academics who don't want to do anything but lecture on their own research. Thinking about what to teach and to whom has to be a process of weighing up the existing knowledges and situations of students and judging what they can make the best use of in a given context. Again, it has to be understood that what students, as students and as members of a wider public, will receive, is largely an effect of the contexts in which it is delivered.

However, despite such qualifications, it seems strange that left academics should experience such a gap between themselves and the broader public at the present time. If it is students who constitute the primary audience for radical intellectual work such as that represented by the dominant strand of cultural studies, and if there are more students in higher education now than ever before, then why do academics working in this field feel an increasing sense of impotence and frustration?

Within this institutional context, the difficulty facing cultural studies as a project for the production and dissemination of radical knowledge via universities is the marketisation, commercialisation and vocationalisation of higher education. The commitment to interdisciplinary revolution which cultural studies has spearheaded in the humanities and social sciences is a major, and welcome, transformation of academic institutions. However, in the absence of any effective critical politics, the results of such a process can be a fragmentary student experience in which an embarrassment of student choice – between institutions, degree programmes and individual courses – undermines the possibilities for sustained intellectual engagement, subjecting teachers and teaching institutions to the same logic of competitive commodification which already affects academics as researchers, encouraged as they are to auction themselves to the highest bidder in the international marketplace.

As Lyotard already saw happening at the end of the 1970s,[18] students and government agencies increasingly judge the success of education purely in terms of measurable outcomes, specifically in terms of the rate at which it delivers graduates with the skills that the commercial sector wants. In this context, any self-consciously radical pedagogic project has a problem. Many students are simply not interested in internalising radical critiques of neo-liberal culture: they want to be turned into marketable commodities in the neo-liberal job market. Worse, those students who *do* maintain an interest in radical ideas have virtually no means of pursuing that interest after graduation.

One of the most direct and effective responses to this problem is that represented by the recent work of Angela McRobbie, which offers an explicit political critique of the conditions and ideologies prevailing in the 'creative industries'.[19] What's missing from such an approach, however, is any real sense of how those conditions might be changed. McRobbie's recent essay on the institutional politics of higher education in the UK merely concludes by appealing to the government to pursue egalitarian and democratic policies for the training of academics, that would not be wholly governed by the imperatives of neo-liberalism.[20] Clearly the chances of this cry being heeded are negligible, and the recognition of this fact raises the question of what might be done about it.

This, in my experience, is the other thing that both students and a wider public demand from radical intellectuals: some sense of where the possible points of agency might lie, not merely a catalogue of existing forms of resistance, but ideas as to how others might be created. It is here that the disconnection of cultural studies and radical academic work in general from actual political struggles is felt most acutely. This in itself is the result of a very specific structural/cultural transformation of recent times. Twelve years ago students with a more than vocational interest in cultural studies could be referred to publications like *Marxism Today* which interpellated them as part of a wider public for new thinking and a larger constituency for progressive movements. It's the decline of a left press receptive to and interested in developments originating in the academy (and I note here the increasing centrism and anti-intellectualism of liberal media outlets such as the *Guardian* and Channel Four) which has created a situation in which any project that has the university as its primary site of effectivity finds itself cut off from wider debates and struggles. The contraction and virtual disappearance of a public sphere in between the academy and the wider political world is certainly a function of the general decline of public institutions, including the parties and organisations which supported the radical press, but this itself is a direct and reversible effect of the political assault on all public space which neo-liberalism undertakes. As long as this assault goes unresisted, the answer to the question 'Does cultural studies have any significance outside of the university?' can only be: 'It did once; it could again; it should, but right now it doesn't.'

This is a problem which 'radical' academics could do something about. Born in the Workers' Education Movement and the extramural programmes, nurtured at the polytechnics and the Open University, cultural studies always inhabited the interstices between academic institutions and more public arenas. A handful of institutions with stronger or weaker links to the mainstream of cultural studies still struggle to constitute something like such public spaces (*Signs of the Times*,[21] *Soundings*,[22] *Red Pepper*,[23] *Open Democracy*[24]). On the whole, however, UK academics, especially the post-Thatcher generation of which I am a member, seem largely resigned to their own marginality and the apathy of whatever audience they might once have aspired to beyond the profession. It is no accident that at just the moment when cultural studies is making inroads into the heart of the establishment – chairs at Harvard, Yale and Manchester; new programmes at the older, richer universities – those very interstitial spaces which gave it birth seem to have vanished almost completely. It is hardly surprising that this newly respectable (in/ter-)discipline should retreat into traditional sites of academic safety and privilege as its former habitats are colonised or destroyed. Nevertheless, this is a move which could spell the end of any cultural studies with meaningful aspirations to political radicalism.

This is a desperately unnecessary situation. The proliferation of the worldwide web and the historic expansion of higher education create a vast range of possibilities for cultural studies to renew its radical project at the interface between academe and the global struggle against neo-liberalism. However, unless more action is taken to reconstitute that project – more work published, events organised, initiatives taken which are aimed at bridging the gap between academe and other cultures – then it seems likely that the situation will only get worse. It will, after all, be the simplicities of orthodox Marxism, adolescent anarchism, communitarian essentialism and ethno-religious fundamentalism which remain the currency of resistance in the 'real world'. Cultural studies will survive only as an agent of neo-liberal culture, transforming the university into a marketplace and our students into just the hyper-reflexive post-subjects which informational capitalism requires. It doesn't have to be this way, but nobody can improve the situation except ourselves.

NOTES

1. See Raymond Williams, *Problems in Materialism and Culture* (London: Verso, 1980); Stuart Hall, 'Introduction', in Roger Simon, *Gramsci's Political Thought* (London: Lawrence and Wishart, 1988).

2. See David Morley and Kuan-Hsing Chen (eds), *Stuart Hall: Critical Dialogues in Cultural Studies* (London: Routledge, 1996).

3. For an interesting history of the very early pre/history of cultural studies and its relationship to the early New Left, see Tom Steele, *The Emergence of Cultural Studies 1945–65* (London: Lawrence and Wishart, 1997); also Michael Kenny, *The First New Left* (London: Lawrence and Wishart, 1995).

4. Stuart Hall, *The Hard Road to Renewal* (London: Verso, 1988).

5. See Stuart Hall and Martin Jacques (eds), *New Times* (London: Lawrence and Wishart, 1990).

6. See Paul Smith, 'Looking Backwards and Forwards at Cultural Studies', in Timothy Bewes and Jeremy Gilbert (eds), *Cultural Capitalism: Politics after New Labour* (London: Lawrence and Wishart, 2001).

7. See, for example, Slavoj Žižek, 'Multiculturalism – A New Racism?', in *New Left Review* 225 (London: Verso, 1997). The argument is obviously related to Fredric Jameson's *Postmodernism: The Cultural Logic of Late Capitalism* (London: Verso, 1991).

8. See Žižek's contributions to Judith Butler, Ernesto Laclau and Slavoj Žižek, *Contingency, Hegemony, Universality* (London: Verso, 2000).

9. See Dexter Whitfield, *Public Services or Corporate Welfare?* (London: Verso, 2000).

10. See the web-site of the World Development Movement: <http://www.wdm.org.uk>.

11. 'Signs of the Times' seminar, London, March 2001.

12. Anthony Barnett, 'Corporate Populism and Partyless Democracy', *New Left Review* 3 (London: Verso, 2000).

13. Jean-Luc Nancy, *The Inoperative Community*, Peter Connor (ed.) (Minneapolis: University of Minnesota Press, 1991); Mikkel Borch-Jacobsen, *The Emotional Tie*, trans. Douglas Brick *et al.* (Stanford: Stanford University Press, 1992).

14. See Daniel Bell, *The Cultural Contradictions of Modernity* (London: Heinemann, 1976); Max Weber, *The Protestant Ethic and the Spirit of Capitalism*, trans. Talcott Parsons (London: Unwin, 1930); Jeremy Gilbert and Ewan Pearson, *Discographies: Dance Music, Culture and the Politics of Sound* (London: Routledge, 1999), pp. 46–62.

15. E.g., Don Slater, *Consumer Culture and Modernity* (Cambridge: Polity, 1997).

16. Raymond Williams, *Marxism and Literature* (Oxford: Oxford University Press, 1977).

17. Nancy, *Inoperative Community*, p. 40.

18. Jean-François Lyotard, *The Postmodern Condition*, trans. Geoffrey Bennington and Brian Massumi (Manchester: Manchester University Press, 1984).

19. See Angela McRobbie, *British Fashion Design: Rag Trade or Image Industry* (London: Routledge, 1999); *In the Culture Society: Art, Fashion and Popular Music* (London: Routledge, 1999); and 'Everyone is Creative: Artists as new Economy Pioneers?': <http://www.openDemocracy.net/forum/DocumentDetails.asp?DocID=594&CatID=18>.

20. Angela McRobbie, 'Stuart Hall: The Universities and the "Hurly Burly"', in Paul Gilroy, Lawrence Grossberg and Angela McRobbie (eds), *Without Guarantees: In Honour of Stuart Hall* (London: Verso, 2000).
21. <http://www.signsofthetimes.org.uk>
22. <http://www.l-w-bks.demon.co.uk/soundings-project.html>
23. <http://www.redpepper.org.uk>
24. <http://www.openDemocracy.net>

10 ... As If Such a Thing Existed ...

Julian Wolfreys

> How do you position yourself and your work in relation to the cultural studies project, whether in the US or the UK? Or, rather, do you see cultural studies *as* a 'project', and is contemporary cultural studies still the 'same' project or discipline as it once was?

Your questioning location of me, across cultures, within and across particular institutional systems which are both similar and dissimilar, anticipates in a coded fashion my initial thoughts on your question apropos the matter of what we call 'culture', 'cultural studies', and so on. Of course, before answering, and this may be somewhat predictable, I'd say that we can't say for sure that we know what we mean when we speak of culture, or cultural studies, nor should we rush to any definition. It is perhaps the very 'lived' condition of a culture, of different cultures and the differences within any given culture, a culture's difference from itself, which most repeatedly becomes simplified in any academic transformation of culture into an area for study.

Perhaps the problem here – and it's very much a problem of institutionalisation which, to some extent, is inescapable – is that, implicitly at least, there is the assumption in general (though not necessarily in your question) of 'culture' and 'cultural studies', in the singular, despite the plural of *studies*; this is what I mean by 'institutionalisation': culture as object has its multiplicities, its heterogeneities, its various signs of otherness within 'itself' (if we can even say this) erased in the process of objectification which study implies. Culture becomes fixed ontologically, the very idea of culture *qua* concept or object to be studied, to be engaged from some vantage point potentially extrinsic, rather than 'lived' or 'experienced' in some phenomenological fashion, even if this is not the intention – and I'd hasten to add that I don't believe this has ever been the intention consciously in the establishment of cultural studies, whether in Britain or North America.

To put this another way, the fixation politically, ideologically, to study culture as other than literature (and in this there's an implicit division between high and popular culture, which extends back at least as far as the work of Richard Hoggart and Raymond Williams in British universities) still has a residual effect of locating culture homogeneously, even if, in specific, numerous cases, this is not in fact the case. Indeed, I'd go further than this, in response to your question of how I locate myself with regard to the project of cultural studies, a cultural studies or different manifestations of cultural studies. Trained as a literary critic whose work is identified as dealing with both 'literary' and 'cultural' studies, as though the one could be separated from the other, I would have to say that there is no form of literary study, and there has been no manifestation of literary study, however supposedly formalist in orientation, concern or perception, which is not, or has not been, in some sense *also*, *always*, an expression of cultural study.

This can be said to be the case, for example, even if we were to consider the work of F.R. Leavis or Northrop Frye. Certainly, Leavis' criticism – whatever I might think of it politically or personally – however relentlessly interiorised, that is to say, appearing to work only on textual form and content, nonetheless brings to bear certain cultural assumptions concerning value and so forth, and, in this sense at least, is also a manifestation of cultural study. Moreover, given Leavis' insistence on the moral and pedagogical function of literature in British culture, especially in his publications after the Second World War, it is hard, if not impossible, to see how it can be claimed that *even* a Leavisite criticism is not a form of cultural studies, albeit one which is extremely self-circumscribing concerning what is to be considered culture. And, arguably, all criticisms of the politics of Leavis' criticism recognise, in their critiques, at least implicitly, the extent to which Leavis is a cultural, as well as a literary, critic.

So, to go back to my initial response, there's a tension. On the one hand, there is a process of identification which aims however unconsciously to erase difference. On the other hand, there is a conscious sense of wanting to explore through the notion of cultural studies, matters of difference, of hybridity, of aspects of cultural alterity. This is irresolvable to an extent, and this is the experience of cultural studies with which we have to deal, whether in the US or the UK; it is the experience of limits, and of an aporia which opens at the limits of the question of culture and cultures.

Whether therefore there can be said to be a 'project', or whether one even wants to suggest that there is a project, seems to me to highlight both the good and the bad, if I can put it that way, and in so schematic and judgemental a fashion, regarding 'cultural studies'. What is 'good' is that the 'project' as such, if by this term we mean only the most broadly defined interest in all aspects of textual work and the analysis of that work (whether text refers to print, to film or other media, or the interanimating relations of peoples in particular locations, culturally, politically, historically, and so forth), is that the challenge of a possible cultural studies is to incorporate in the acts of analysis, while respecting the difference, diversity and heterogeneity of, cultural forms beyond the high- or middle-brow to which areas of culture literary studies has, in the past, remained focused upon. Thus the 'project', and there are more than one, might be said to be about a certain self-reflexive institutional questioning of the role and function, the scope and interests of an institutional or academic analytics aiming to open itself and its various modalities to the other in cultures, the other of, within any cultural identity (and this is no doubt to risk too hasty a formula), which, in turn transforms the ways in which any professional analytics might proceed. Of course, it also has to be said that such a project, such projects, if indeed they can even be called this, have to be open ended; there cannot be a project which claims to know its goal, its outcome. Were this the case, then the 'bad' aspects of a cultural studies come into focus, inasmuch as there appears to be something of an anthropological turn at work and, furthermore, a return to the sort of disinterestedness of which literary studies was accused by early forms of cultural studies.

The other problem here is of course related to the ways in which a cultural studies proceeds, the ways in which it chooses to read. Whether in the US or in the UK, cultural studies and identity politics appear in some examples to have rejected or abandoned any engagement with or utilisation of what might best be called 'high theory'. This has been commented on at length in recent years, by, for instance, Tom Cohen in North America and Geoffrey Bennington in the UK. Cohen has convincingly announced a return to ways of reading which are more indebted to formalist analyses and to a general humanist ethos (perhaps what is now beginning to be called post-humanism – a spectre is haunting the university, the spectre of humanism) as part of an effort to reject so-called post-structuralism, and this takes place – and I'm in complete agreement with Cohen on this point – in the very name of some form of political urgency and exigency. The argument therefore runs: we have no time to pursue the arcane, elitist, Eurocentric textual dalliance of post-structuralist and postmodernist thinkers because of the demands of political situations, so we need to get on with a certain kind of work. This can be seen some years ago in Benita Parry's rejection of the work of Spivak and Bhabha in the field of post-colonial studies. The problem is that it is the very question of the 'project' which informs the abandonment of theory and thereby brings about what Cohen terms the Schillingerian relapse. Bennington, on the other hand, reading the British situation, has argued that a consensus has arisen concerning sufficient understanding of 'theory' so that there has developed a kind of 'post-theoretical' era of critical (or not-so-critical) engagement reminiscent for Bennington and others of a kind of late-show journalism, to paraphrase his remark. In the very different cases illustrated by Bennington and Cohen, it is precisely, despite the different academic cultures of British and North American universities, that whenever a project has arisen and been mapped out, then reading and thinking are abandoned.

> Cultural studies is said to be a 'political' project. What, to your mind, are the politics of cultural studies? Does it have 'a' politics, or is it, rather, 'political'? Another way to phrase this would be to ask you what are the politics or what is the political significance of your own work? What do you consider to be the 'proper destination' of your work?

I think the relationship between cultural studies and politics, whether a politics or multiple political agendas, itineraries, programmes, and so forth, is on the one hand apparently, absolutely self-evident and, on the other hand, perhaps the most obscure, if not obfuscating aspect of certain manifestations of cultural studies, today. I say this not to position myself in some agonistic relationship to cultural studies *qua* political (and thereby to imply that, in any dialectical fashion, I am in some way 'against' whatever political project cultural studies might be defined as having), but instead to raise the question of whether, despite the necessary urgency of many political projects at the present time, various proponents and practitioners of so-called 'cultural studies' are, in fact, being political at all.

The problem is one identified, to return to the point raised in the previous answer, both in the US and in the UK, as a retreat from, and rejection of, whatever goes under the name 'theory' or its various non-synonymous substitutions, such as 'post-structuralism', 'postmodernism', 'deconstruction', and all other such nebulous terms, which are, in truth, empty signifiers the vacuity of which could not be more self-evident than through the accommodation as ontological fetishes within the academy, comprising as they do, especially for so many of their detractors – as though the detractors knew exactly what they meant every time they wheeled out the terms, along with phrases such as 'post-structuralism is ... X' – a 'spectropoetics' (to borrow a term of Derrida's from *Specters*[1]) of elitist practice, allegedly.

However, to get back to the question of cultural studies and the political: There is a sense in which 'cultural studies' is viewed as political inasmuch as it apparently engaged in the critical analysis of what we call 'the real world', 'reality', and, in being committed to some form of intellectual intervention in the experience of the world, and the everyday encounter with popular culture, there is, in large measure a sense, more or less explicitly stated, that synonymous with the project of cultural studies is a process of political and ideological demystification. The problem with this, if it is indeed a problem, and not simply a misperception on my part, is that the 'revelatory' and 'unveiling' aspect which cultural studies can assume – and I'm not suggesting that all cultural studies practitioners who self-consciously define themselves in so distinct a fashion over and against, let's say, theorists or literary critics – takes on a supposedly self-evident aspect in the very name of politics and so therefore no longer takes the time to examine the ways in which, and the (ideological, epistemological) places from which its founding questions and modalities of investigation are grounded and from which they arise.

Thus the very ground of the politics of a cultural studies is occluded and self-occluding in the name of a politics of demystification, as though politics were reducible to a project or programme for 'enlightenment', 'transformation', and so forth. If there is then a politics to cultural studies, such a politics may not simply be coterminous with the identity of a politics of demystification that cultural studies might think is its mandate. Instead, despite the progressivist political fervour ostensibly and transparently readable in the project or programme of a political studies, it may well be the case that the procedures by which cultural studies 'reads' are informed by the most conservative of epistemological models.

The second part of your question concerns the politics of my own work, and what I view as the political significance of my work or the 'proper destination' of my work. For a start, I think I have to say that I'm not sure what the political significance of my work is; this is not said from any false modesty but a comment which is generated by reflection on the efficacy of that which, in book form at least, sells relatively few copies, and then mostly to libraries, at an often exorbitant price. The 'pragmatics' of academic publishing seems to ensure that the scope and range of any critical work, however political, is always going to be limited, circumscribed. More complexly of course is the question of difficulty. Regardless of which 'school' or 'method', or 'approach' with which my work is associated – and I'm not really interested in such claims, in that they are more or less inaccurate – there is the prevalent sense of critical language being overly specialised or even jargon laden. I've been identified, for example, as being 'wearyingly left-wing' by one reviewer, or, as another put it, 'suffering from wild deconstructive rapture and insane syntax'. Such judgements don't matter, and yet, from the register of both, my work is perceived as, on the one hand, having a Marxist orientation, while on the other, being an example of 'deconstruction' (as though such a methodology existed). It has even been said of my work that I clearly have a post-colonialist agenda and an 'engaging sense of mischief'! (And this about a piece where I thought I was being particularly earnest ...)

What interests and amuses me about such comments, and you see such remarks all the time about countless critics, is the degree to which they operate according to some facile, reductive ontological desire – the need to name, to fix in place, to according the act of reading with a determinate identity and thereby have done with any reading of what is being written. So, if my work has political significance, it is in its ability to provoke and thereby to expose in its reader the ideological, epistemological and, dare I say it, political presuppositions by which their acts of reading proceed and take place.

Regardless of the question of significance – and I *do* think it a mistake to assume for oneself that one's work has significance or is significant; Hardt and Negri's *Empire*[2] has assumed a significance beyond all determination by its author, and the same may be said to be true equally of Karl Marx and James Joyce; one doesn't write, at least I hope one doesn't, with an eye on possible significance, all critical writing being analytical, a response, an engagement with what already exists, what is already written or thought – I think my work *is* political inasmuch as all analytical engagement is political, whether by this one means that work is produced according to the politics of publishing, the politics which inform the concept of professionalism, or the politics of the institution of higher education. I *am* interested in, concerned with, articulating what is silenced, what is marginalised, what remains unsaid, what affirms with respect to difference and heterogeneity in any given textual form, but what these silences, marginalisations, contradictions and affirmations might be are not all of the same order; they belong to or, rather, are in excess of, any textual structure or identity; they are the traces of an irreducible otherness, so many counter-signatures, if I can put it like that, incommensurate with any 'majority' or 'consensus' formation. So, if observing, pursuing, such passing figures belongs to a politics of reading, then yes, my work is political. I would, though, resist according such political activity a single identity, by defining 'it' as an 'it', *a* politics.

As to the question of 'proper destination', given all that I've already said, the answer has to be that there is no proper destination as such but, by the same token, every destination, which cannot be determined ahead of arrival (and in this, as you know there is always the possibility of non-arrival), may be said to be both proper and improper simultaneously. I can neither control nor determine how my work arrives, if it arrives at all, and I can only gauge something akin to destination, when I receive a response. All destinations are legitimate and illegitimate but these cannot be programmed, and no destination is the final destination, only a moment of coming to rest, before being propelled elsewhere.

> Does cultural studies have any significance outside of the university at all? If so, what forms does this take?

I think this question has most forcefully and personally come into focus for me in a graduate seminar I taught in spring 2001, on the subject of urban identity. A student presented the problem of the determination of the 'academic' as opposed to the 'general' reader (supposing we could make such neat distinctions). The problem involved speculation around the reception of a text – Peter Ackroyd's *London: The Biography*[3] – and whether the 'general reader' would comprehend the formal radicality (a radicality which we, as scholars, were debating in relation to the genre of the biography or a historical survey of a city) of Ackroyd's project and thereby fully come to terms with its political import.

The problem here, aside from the assumption that readerships can be so easily identified and delineated, or, indeed, that 'a readership' is so unequivocally homogeneous, is not so much in the text, if in the text at all, as it is in the act of reading the text according to particular paradigms which are themselves produced according to the interaction of various discursive practices which only come together, or which, at least, only come together in so focused a fashion, within the university. This is not to say that the university is the privileged locus for 'specialised' or 'specialist' forms of discourse – though of course it can be, or can at least be perceived as being this, especially when the word 'specialisation' is prefaced by a phrase such as 'there's too much ...', you know the kind of thing, whether we're speaking of editorials in the *New York Review of Books*, some piece in the 'culture' section of the *Guardian*, or in books such as *The Closing of the American Mind*[4] – but, rather, that the ways in which such discourse comes to be translated and transformed 'beyond' or 'outside' the university (supposing for the moment that we can, again, identify the inside and outside so easily), require careful and highly attentive, 'specialised' analyses in their own right, regardless of subject.

But it is perhaps a sign of the porousness of the limits of the university, that the very question of 'culture' and the idea of culture have transformed various disciplines, opened them to themselves, perhaps transforming them in the process. This is of course not peculiar to 'cultural studies' as an institutional disciplinary phenomenon belonging to the culture of higher education in the latter part of the twentieth century. Equally such a commentary can, and has, been applied to the advent of the study of literature, of English literature, of literatures in English at least since the end of the nineteenth century. What this appears to highlight and draw to our attention is that various cultural forms, concepts and political interests will find ways of transforming the university, and much more visibly and markedly than the other way around. So, perhaps cultural studies has little significance beyond the university, except in the most limited and superficial ways, as for example, in a journalist's acknowledgement of a proper name or signature, such as 'Jean Baudrillard' or 'postmodernist', for example, as though the whole textual network summoned by such traces were in some manner self-evident (or otherwise that the readership or audience for that journalist, that magazine, that TV show, were itself homogenous and had had privileged access to all the works that are signed by a particular name). But cultures, culturally specific phenomena, have a great significance for the university, for the vitality of study in all aspects of what we call the humanities.

> Where is cultural studies *going*? This question is obviously tied to that of 'where has it *been*?', which is an interesting and important question itself; but I wonder 'where' you think it *should* go, or what you think it should now do or try to do: in short, what has cultural studies 'achieved', what has it 'failed' to achieve, and to what extent are these 'failures' inevitable, structural, or is it just that their realisation is only a matter of time or strategy?

Nothing could be more difficult than proleptic speculation. It's rather like seeking to expect the unexpected, to anticipate and thereby programme, in however provisional a fashion, the arrival of the other. The problem with such acts is that, at one and the same time, they are both manifestations of fortune telling and conjuration. Each prediction involves a performative element: in saying 'this is what I believe will happen, this is where I imagine cultural studies to be going', there is the ghost of another reply operative within the structure and logic of such a statement which whispers 'this is where I wish it would go, this is where I hope it will or will not go'.

Of course, given the domestication and institutionalisation of cultural studies, an institutionalisation which is, perhaps uniquely amongst academic subjects, also the founding of cultural studies – to put this another way, albeit somewhat contentiously, there is no cultural studies self-reflectively known as such without the institutional manifestation, there is no cultural studies which precedes the university – perhaps it's the case that cultural studies isn't going anywhere, unless of course because of budgetary constraints, cuts in departmental funding, reduction in faculty numbers through redundancies and forced retirements, cultural studies is *going away*, that is disappearing from the buildings, the catalogues, the various structures, discursive and architectural, of the university. Perhaps this is the greatest fear, but also perhaps it is cultural studies' greatest opportunity: that cultural studies, in 'going away', in disappearing or otherwise becoming merely the somewhat ghostly trace of its institutional manifestations, might stand a greater chance of political efficacy, of getting on with some kind of truly radical work, than in its being maintained in a departmental holding pattern, where, in anticipation of the next quality assessment exercise, it isn't going anywhere at all.

NOTES

1. Jacques Derrida, *Specters of Marx: The State of the Debt, the Work of Mourning, and the New International*, trans. Peggy Kamuf (London: Routledge, 1994).
2. M. Hardt and A. Negri, *Empire* (Cambridge, MA: Harvard University Press, 2001).
3. Peter Ackroyd, *London: The Biography* (London: Vintage, 2000).
4. Allan Bloom, *The Closing of the American Mind* (New York: Simon and Schuster, 1987).

Part Five:
Positioning Cultural Studies

INTRODUCTION

What is the position of cultural studies? What does the concept of 'position' entail or mean, itself; or indeed, how might it, paradoxically, position us, in ways that we cannot see – is our viewpoint positioned by our conception of what *position itself* is, and of what *our* position is? Both John Mowitt and Jeremy Valentine are explicitly attentive to this, and trace many ramifications of the problems and possibilities of 'position', an attentiveness that leads to highly circumspect analyses of the agency/structure conundrum, or that is, to the relationship between 'action' and what makes it possible. Steven Connor, too, explores the possibilities of cultural studies in relation to, and through, its positions or notions about what culture and/or society are thought to be, and the way these conceptions can colour our notions of everything. Valentine's analysis of position, for instance, leads him to propose that there has been a unique mutation away from the initial Althusserian conception of interpellation, one that he argues is more appropriate to our times.

The questions of position are cortical to both Mowitt's and Valentine's chapters, and implicit in Connor's, and each in its own way leads into far-reaching reflections on cultural studies in relation to its traditional appeals to 'resistance', or to the question of Connor's title, 'What Can Cultural Studies Do?' Mowitt suggests that 'resistance' could be considered to be a 'fetish concept', a myth, that makes cultural studies no more radical an activity than that of marketing brand-name jeans – an equivalence that may suggest its complicity in functioning to 'promulgate a global vulgate that is about nothing if not US economic and cultural hegemony'. However, one need not be pessimistic, for there is much attendant to the very conceptualisation and positioning of cultural studies which contains reserves of potential for political leverage or agency;

not least being, for example, the insights of 1970s feminism, the relations between culture and politics that they suggest, the limits of disciplinarity that cultural studies makes one of its objects, the paradoxes and conflictual character of the (impossible) currency of 'interdisciplinarity', the deconstructive effects of cultural studies having made 'studying' and 'studying culture' part of its object of study, and so on.

These and many other themes overlap across both chapters, and they also have in common the extent to which 'position' massively problematises ideas of 'possession': the idea that we 'possess' our identity, for instance, once position and relationality are taken on board, becomes disrupted and disruptive. As Mowitt argues, all ways of study which insist or assume that everyone possesses a culture, makes everyone therefore amenable to anthropological knowledge and, ultimately, disciplinary power – which, in a certain sense, is precisely one of the things, one of the forms of domination, that cultural studies always said it did not want to be complicit with. Connor, on the other hand, reminds us of the (Derridean) theme of the unpredictability of destination – the way in which we do not possess our work, cannot control its effects (which may well be nil), and which, perhaps, we should therefore not fret about. For Connor, then, the uniqueness of the position of cultural studies is what it enables you to study – *anything* – which is stimulating and valuable enough, without fretting about that which, by definition and always, is out of your control.

Of course, to conflate the three in this way is highly reductive and simplifying in the face of their manifest complexity and differences. But nevertheless they all engage with what, as Valentine says, 'Although it's not much … will at least help us to know how cultural studies positions itself, its point of view, in order to find out what it does.' They each convey something of the stakes attendant to the effort to know – or at least to theorise, which is perhaps as close as one can ever really come to 'knowing' – the nature of one's practice; because, as each in its own way makes clear, one's conscious or unconscious theory about what one is doing and why, has an orienting and determining effect on what one will do and why. Perhaps how one theorises one's position, and what one believes one is positioned in relation to, determines everything.

11   Cultural Studies, in Theory

John Mowitt

How do you position yourself and your work in relation to the cultural studies project? Or, rather, do you see cultural studies *as* a 'project', and is contemporary cultural studies still the 'same' project or discipline it once was?

I should begin by emphasising that the concept of position is one that has interested me for quite some time. I have written about it both in relation to Fanon and the critique of Eurocentrism, and also in relation to trauma studies. For this reason I fear that I may, almost without thinking, make more of this question, its terms, than might otherwise be necessary. Let's hope that this helps to answer rather than avoid the question.

What strikes me about the concept of position is that it effortlessly calls up both tendency and location, or put differently, it directly exposes the catachrestic relation between the physical and the psychical. In the current debate about 'globalisation', position has assumed all the structural complexity of the rhetoric of relationality. In other words, just as it was once crucial to think about being against sexism but for feminism, it is now equally crucial to think about doing so while working for the local in the global and vice versa.

Thus, when you ask me to position myself in relation to cultural studies, please understand that I feel compelled to respond with precisely these enigmatic demands in mind. My own doctoral degree, just to start somewhere, is in Comparative Literature and, though I work in a department called Cultural Studies and Comparative Literature, I come to the academic project of cultural studies from a position outside the field. Within our department – itself populated by disciplinary nomads – a division is maintained, at both curricular levels, between cultural studies and Comparative Literature. Some might find this odd, perhaps even unworkable, but the fact of belonging to a division, of sharing a separation, actually strikes me as quite productive. It might even be characterised as a symptom of the field itself, for while I have indeed been stressing the local, one could say much the same sort of thing about the emergence of cultural studies at Birmingham after the Second World War. It was about, among other things, the literary in the social and the social in the literary.

To this extent, then, I would position myself both inside and outside the field of cultural studies, and go on to stress that this is disciplinary rather than autobiographical. But you ask also after the 'project' of cultural studies. For me, this is a term freighted with the rhetoric of existentialism where it referred, at a certain point, to the means by which the struggle against immanence, the sense of being reduced to one's 'situation', was waged. For Sartre, who prior to *The Critique of Dialectical Reason* regarded the subject as condemned to freedom, one's project was barely a choice, although it was a political act for which one could be held responsible. It is hard, given this, to think about cultural studies as a project. It overemphasises, in my mind, the analogy between a field and a subject, indeed it invites the reduction of agency to the agent. Nevertheless, there is some sense in which we at Minnesota saw ourselves as aligned with what we imagined Williams, Hoggart, Hall and Johnson to have been doing at Birmingham, although we were never reconciled to the term 'contemporary'. Thus, one might reiterate that our position (and here I am identifying with my department) was both for cultural studies, but against Birmingham (at the time that we – as members of a soon to be closed Humanities Department – formed our graduate programme in Comparative Studies in Discourse and Society we were unaware, perhaps blissfully, of other examples).

> Cultural studies is said to be a 'political' project. What, to your mind, are the politics of cultural studies? Does it have 'a' politics, or is it, rather, political in some other way? Another way to phrase this would be to ask you what are the politics or what is the political significance or your own work? What do you consider to the 'proper destination' of your work?

The terms of your question call to mind (and the imp in me wants to interrupt and ask, is anything ever called to the body?) the distinction, much remarked, in French between *la politique* and *le politique*. When, in the closing sentence you invoke the Derridean formulation, 'proper destination', the French subtext is clear. The intricacies of this debate, captured I should add in the pages of *Rejouer le politique* from 1981, cannot be efficiently summarised in this format. But suffice it to say that the concerns animated by this debate belong to our exchange.

Let us remember that cultural studies is called 'political' on both sides of the Schmittean divide, that is, by friends and enemies alike. For conservatives, cultural studies is political, not because it exhibits a coherent tendency, but because it blows their cover. In other words, to the extent that cultural studies insists upon situating the culture consumed and patronised by elites, it becomes political, and if the left has learned anything from the so-called cultural wars it was that recognising itself in this version of the political was a recipe for a disaster. Why? Because it imputed to the left both a force neutralised in advance (let's call it a force that was 'merely academic') and a coherence, or organisation, that actually needed to be forged, not consumed. Unfortunately, the academic left in the US has both a short memory and a debilitating critique of education, two qualities that converge in its own account of the political character of cultural studies. Too often this account merely mirrors the right's reflections. As you probably know there has been much discussion of this dilemma in both the US and French media.

Indulge me as I elaborate this discussion at some length. In the end it will help frame the terms of my reply. In a recent issue of Thomas Frank's puckish new magazine of cultural criticism, *The Baffler*, in fact, in an issue devoted to a bracing critique of cultural studies, there appeared a piece co-authored by Pierre Bourdieu and Loïc Wacquant. Need I observe that it can hardly be construed as a good sign when a field is essentially disowned by a figure largely revered within it. Of course, in many respects Bourdieu has been preparing 'us' for this since much of what he and Wacquant say repeats the arguments of *Acts of Resistance: Against the New Myths of Our Times*.[1]

On the face of it, their essay is a rehash of arguments made elsewhere about the delusions of globalism. What is new however is the authors' characterisation of 'globalisation' as part of a new 'vulgate', a popularisation of an essentially US corporate doctrine whose other keywords include: multiculturalism, identity, hybridity, and, singled out for special approbation, the underclass. It is no accident that virtually all of these terms are buzzwords in cultural studies. In fact, Bourdieu and Wacquant characterise cultural studies

– once a 'mongrel domain' confined to the UK – as now a 'discipline' fabricated by publishers only too keen to tailor their intellectual decisions to considerations of international marketing. Whence the tie-in with globalisation. In this respect, the entire field is a 'new myth', and very much part of what they call an academically based 'cultural imperialism', stressing that, and the nationalist pose is unmistakable, cultural studies does not, thankfully, exist in French intellectual life. Comparing the nevertheless international appeal of this mythic discipline to the appeal of jeans – both are marketed as reflections of a subversive or besieged opposition – the authors propose that cultural studies, contrary to the way its partisans see themselves, actually functions to promulgate a global vulgate that is about nothing if not US economic and cultural hegemony. If true, and Bourdieu and Wacquant have little doubt, then the very animating problematic of cultural studies derives from a corporate vulgate, which means that the field cannot grasp its own condition of possibility. Why? Because the concepts at its disposal – including, as Frank properly notes, the fetish concept of resistance – are forged out of a structural mis-recognition of their corporate and ultimately US corporate derivation. For the authors this explains why, contrary to what one might expect, cultural studies scholars are so sensitive, indeed obsessed with their complicit relation to the context in which they work. In some sense they realise that the very concepts that enable their entire enterprise are the ones least capable of grasping its enabling conditions.

As with the critique of globalisation, this repudiation of cultural studies sounds vaguely familiar. In particular, it resonates with aspects of Bill Readings' discussion of the problem in *The University in Ruins*,[2] where he had argued that cultural studies had become possible precisely because its object – culture – had been abandoned by transnational, or what we would now call global, capitalism. In other words, once there was nothing at stake for the transnational state in the domain of national culture, this domain could readily be ceded to academic intellectuals, especially those desperate to see themselves in the heroic trenches of the contemporary *Kulturkampf*. Although the explicit emphasis of Bourdieu and Wacquant on the theme of cultural imperialism puts them at odds with Readings, both analyses insist upon an essential depoliticisation of cultural studies, a depoliticisation necessitated by the foundational concepts of the field and rooted in its consequent sacrifice to the very hegemony cultural studies assumed it had discovered the proper name for. Not surprisingly this very dilemma has spurred Henry Giroux, among others, (see his recent *Impure Acts*[3]) to address the 'politics' of cultural studies.

Reduced, abusively, this take on the politics of cultural studies deprives it of a politics, but in the name of a rather under-examined notion of the political. Or, put differently, it argues that the field exhibits a conservative politics. At stake in all of this for me is the question of cultural politics. Is this a rethinking of the political, or is it merely a way of 'modifying' (in the grammatical sense) politics, that is, of thinking about how culture serves both as a means and as an object of political reflection? It may be old fashioned to say this, but I'm not convinced that we have followed through on the insights of 1970s feminism, insights elaborated by Luce Irigaray but also Colette Guillaumin and Gayle Rubin, that linked culture (in spite of their disagreements) to the kinship exchange of women and the workings of *sexage*, thereby constituting this very exchange and the circulation of value it supports as the proper object of a politics of culture. The point is not that feminism belongs on the political agenda, but that it has posed a question about the relation between culture and politics that ought to matter deeply to cultural studies. In this sense I would argue that if cultural studies is not always already depoliticised, it is because it serves as a site wherein a certain re-elaboration of cultural politics is underway, one that in refusing a certain political fundamentalism, nevertheless strives to be for, among other things, an end to *sexage*, and against capitalism both here and elsewhere.

> What are the *institutions* of cultural studies? That is, what works, methods, orientations, etc., have become instituted as the repositories of 'knowledge', methodology, and ways of going about doing things? This is as much to say, what do these institutions (or the institution of these authoritative guarantors as the 'proper' or 'the best') forbid, censure/censor, limit or enable? What factors determined or overdetermined their institution?

The question of the institution is enormous and vexed even if restricted to the educational domain, a domain whose institutional borders are no longer simply the state and the church, but – certainly since the late nineteenth century – also the corporation. In light of this, it seems wise to begin with some general, if flip, formulations.

The intellectual history of the last half of the twentieth century in the West is often, though perhaps oddly, represented as a vehicle. During the 1950s and 1960s we took what has since been called 'the linguistic turn', and now, or at least throughout the last decade of the twentieth century, we have been attempting to execute 'the cultural turn'. Significantly, both turns have resulted in collisions between the humanities and the social sciences. Though both fields have survived, they have not gone unscathed, and I would argue that cultural studies is the scholarly and pedagogical formation that has arisen in the wake of these collisions. It (but also, in some sense, 'they') represents a radicalisation of trends in the qualitative social sciences, reaching beyond a recognition of the decisive importance of meaning to an insistence on the cultural politics (there's that phrase) of meaning production, while also embodying a profound rethinking of the humanities, indeed a rethinking which links 'the cultural' (as in 'cultural tradition') to the socio-historical dynamics of everyday life. Cultural studies as 'body shop'? Something like that.

Here at Minnesota, as elsewhere in the US (and here it is important to acknowledge that the first cultural studies programme in North America was actually established in Canada at Trent University in southern Ontario), cultural studies is located within the Liberal Arts, a fact which underscores an important feature of its distinctively interdisciplinary character. In spite of academia's oft-repeated commitment to 'interdisciplinary' work, disciplines retain strong feelings about how such work is to be done. Although there are other ways to state how disciplinarity remains active, perhaps even determinant, within interdisciplinary scholarship, this captures how such a dynamic asserts itself within the realm of scholarly evaluation and publication. Cultural studies (largely, though by no means exclusively, an academic beast) has become the institutional place where the quarrels that have arisen around the limits of disciplinarity have become the explicit object of reflection, not as concerns ancillary to the interdisciplinary study of cultural practices, but as dimensions of those very practices. In a sense, the paradox of the name 'cultural studies' is serendipitous: we are indeed talking about the study of things cultural, but we are also talking about the cultural character of the act of studying. Because humanistic disciplines have long numbered among what belong within the Liberal Arts, and because in certain cases distinct departments of the humanities have provided the interdisciplinary framework within which such disciplines are allowed to converge, it is within the Liberal Arts that cultural studies has taken hold. It is in this sense the contemporary avatar of what were formerly humanities departments. To use Hegel's vocabulary, cultural studies is the sublation (the completing and superseding) of the humanities.

Which means what? It means that, contrary to received opinion, cultural studies, at least here, is where DWGs ('dead white guys') still matter, not as objects of reverence, not as embodiments of 'our' ultimate conceptual horizons, but as figures of study, figures whose belonging to a history that is, alas, still 'ours' stirs without guiding contemporary reflection. By the same token, cultural studies, precisely to the extent that it insists upon this historical belonging, concerns itself with the experiences and practices marginalised by the passing cavalcade of DWGs. This does not mean, again contrary to received opinion, that the marginalised are simply moved to the centre of cultural studies and made objects of reverence. While it is true, as Bourdieu and others argue, that 'resistance' constitutes a keyword in cultural studies, it is inflected so as to compare different engagements with power, engagements undertaken both within and without power. The point is that even if, even if, one seeks to study the West, 'our' heritage, this can only be responsibly done by situating the West within the full geopolitical and transcultural context of its emergence. Anything short of this not only falls prey to a complacent Eurocentrism, but it provides those inclined to persist in marginalising certain experiences and practices – indeed, those very things which so palpably define our moment – with what, in the end, is a self-defeating alibi. To summarise in a more technical vocabulary: the inversion of a hierarchy (the West versus the Rest) is only half the battle; to complete and supersede something also requires that the hierarchy be displaced, that is, shifted into a wider field of questions and answers.

For cultural studies this 'wider field' includes cultural studies. In other words, cultural studies is not only the institutional place where quarrels among disciplines are made to belong to the study of culture, it is also the place where education, where the institutional precipitates of disciplinary power (universities, colleges, institutes, departments, programs etc.), are made subject to reflection. This is why cultural studies has been the persistent object of systematic doubt. Although perhaps less true of post-war Britain (or true in different ways) cultural studies in the US has been dogged from its inception with both internal and external criticism. Due to the perceived link between cultural studies and the political left, the external criticism has taken predictable forms. For example, Alain Finkelkraut (to take another French example) has recently argued that it is responsible for the decline of Thought. However, what is distinctive, indeed indispensable, about the internal criticism (another example would be the recent issue of *Parallax*[4]) is that it is actually fundamental to the very character of the field. Like the many 'studies' before it – area studies, women's studies, African American studies, etc. – cultural studies worries about its relation to knowledge. However, beyond puzzling over the political cost of institutional legitimacy (the question that haunts Women's Studies programmes nation-wide), cultural studies asks both whether it exists, and whether it should exist, questions which reach beyond cultural studies to the university itself. In this sense it is fully in step with the emerging debate over higher education (whether public or not), but unlike other marchers cultural studies is seeking to cast this debate in intellectual terms rather than in the strictly economic or corporatist ones favoured by the current regime in Washington. Perhaps it is this insistence upon institutionally engaged yet general knowledge that has prompted so many fields in the humanities and social sciences – and one thinks here of such phenomena as English Studies, French Studies, Cinema Studies, etc. – to situate their own vanguards, their own 'cutting edge' scholarship, in relation to the cultural studies initiative.

Now, is any of this 'proper?' I hope not. But I also hope that cultural studies does not settle for a displacement of the humanities that simply replaces an object (the Occidental masterpieces) with a method (the means by which to demonstrate that they are, as Artaud put it, pig-shit). This is why in *Text* I insisted upon the relation between reading and its conditions.

> How does the institutionalisation of cultural studies affect, support or undermine it?

In some respects I have already addressed this, but let me expand on another aspect of what has been said. I would say that in important respects the field of cultural studies is in trouble. This trouble is at once institutional and theoretical. It is also, therefore, political, but let's not turn back there immediately. In its institutional guise, this trouble has been succinctly characterised in an editorial written by the editor in chief at Duke University Press, Ken Wissoker. This may seem like an unlikely object of sustained scrutiny, but because of who this editorial was written by (Duke has long stood at the forefront of academic publishing in the field of cultural studies), and because of where it was published (Wissoker's essay appeared last spring on the pages of *The Chronicle of Higher Education*) this piece – in so deftly crystallising key structural aspects of the US literary institution – may in fact represent an object whose appropriateness is, as is said, overdetermined.

Wissoker situates cultural studies in relation to the task of implementing the broad academic affirmation of interdisciplinarity within the institutions of post-secondary education. This perhaps obvious move is an important one because too often cultural studies is simply treated as an idea from the UK that somehow overrode whatever defence mechanism is currently protecting North America from mad cow disease. Wissoker is acutely aware that publishing is one of the means by which intellectual 'trends' acquire the force to set. Doubtless because he has spent long hours anguishing with tenured and untenured radicals alike, he recognises that even among its devotees cultural studies is regarded with, if not contempt, then suspicion. And it is precisely this that motivates his appeal to the concept of interdisciplinarity. Beginning with an observation that perhaps only an editor might be privy to, Wissoker draws attention to the fact that readers' reports are filled with often vehement denunciations of a given project's interdisciplinary pretensions. From this he concludes that debilitating cross-currents are at work within the academy's embrace of interdisciplinarity, cross-currents that reveal, as I mentioned before, a deep investment in disciplinarity active within the ideologies of even those most passionately committed to interdisciplinary scholarship. For Wissoker this manifests itself in the way scholars attack interdisciplinary pretensions in the work of others, as if *only their disciplines* truly comprehend what is at stake in a serious commitment to interdisciplinarity. Obviously, he is struggling with a particular inflection of the dialectics of innovation – can the present truly authorise the future – and one is heartened to find such intelligence brought to bear on what for him embodies the very facticity of everyday life.

Cultural studies, on this account, thus comes to embody the institutional space where disciplines have projected their own particular interdisciplinary fantasies. Needless to say, like all fantasies, this space is to some degree impossible. On the one hand, the very existence of cultural studies testifies to an institutional affirmation of an interdisciplinary project within and between the humanities and the social sciences. On the other hand, due precisely to the kernel of disciplinarity at work within this affirmation, cultural studies can only succeed by failing, that is, it exists as the space where the disciplines investing in it (both intellectually and economically) come face to face with the profound inadequacy of interdisciplinarity. In effect, cultural studies is institutionally impossible because – at the end of the day – no one, especially those authorised to do so, can really do interdisciplinary work the way we think it *ought* to be done. Although Wissoker does not make this point, the current trend – especially within the modern languages – to put 'studies' after virtually any noun, would seem to confirm his analysis by suggesting that precisely because it is always already being done everywhere, cultural studies lacks whatever specificity might be required to locate it somewhere in particular. In this sense there may well be as many instantiations of the field as there are disciplines.

While this might be taken to mean that the future of cultural studies is wide open (a good thing, one might suppose), it also means that the future is open wide. In other words, cultural studies is profoundly troubled by the fact that just as it has established itself as something like a new paradigm, it has begun to vanish into the very effects this paradigm is generating in cognate fields within the humanities and social sciences. Even though I am not convinced that Wissoker has understood the intricate tenacity of the legacy of disciplinary power, I do think he's on to something crucial about the institutional dilemma of cultural studies. Moreover, in saying this as an editor and in saying it to post-secondary educators at large he is more than just on to something. In effect, he is putting the trouble he has so astutely diagnosed into circulation.

In more strictly theoretical terms the institutionalisation of cultural studies has confronted it with the problem of its disciplinary object. Can it be something called 'culture'? Wissoker's reservation about the practice of interdisciplinary research notwithstanding, any contemporary effort to rehabilitate the concept of culture (whether 'national' or not) must come to terms with the trenchant problematisation of it that has occurred within the discipline of anthropology beginning with Boaz's repudiation of Malinowski, and culminating now in the work being done under the banner of postcolonialism. Even if we grant that Raymond Williams and Richard Hoggart were on to something important when they recast Arnoldian 'culture' as something more like the distinctive way of life of a particular social group, the interaction between such an innovation and the national re-articulation of late imperial Britain cannot be passed over in silence. The problem is not simply that of the geopolitical conditions of anthropology (about which contemporary anthropology has been reasonably frank), it is also, and more importantly, the very concept of culture itself. Relativism, contrary to the claims of devotees and detractors alike, does not so much legitimate cultural differences as it projects an ecumenical yet ultimately national articulation of 'culture' everywhere. Not coincidentally, once all peoples have been granted a culture, all peoples are available for anthropological study, if not in fact, then certainly in principle. Even those who decry the tendency of cultural studies scholars to turn their attentions – wantonly – to virtually everything, are not typically contesting this rather dubious imperial inheritance from anthropology. Were they to do so I would be more comfortable with what is otherwise often little more than a mis-recognised expression of disciplinary envy.

The deeper problem here, however, is philosophical. Buried in the notion that every people has a distinctive way of life, a culture, is more than a particular inflection of difference; there is as well the assumption that culture is a possession, a thing – however dynamic – that belongs to a particular group. The world's various heritage movements openly cast this very matter in the rhetoric of treasure. The issue here is not that this 'objectifies' culture (either one's own or that of another). Rather the issue is that this construal obscures the existence and operation of what I have been calling a disciplinary object. Once culture belongs to groups, it is 'out there' with them, and the task of recognising how this very location is produced and reproduced as part of the labour of study – whether 'here' or 'there' – becomes all but impossible. Methodologically, this requires the now compulsory gesture of 'contextualisation', that is, the intellectual labour of placing – more often than not something resistant to such placement, say, a work of art or science – within its proper cultural context. Although much of cultural studies scholarship is involved in this gesture, very little of it seems inclined to examine what is being done, both theoretically and politically, through it. Culture, perhaps even more so than 'history' or 'society' (two other oft-appealed-to 'contexts'), serves to designate an 'out there', a site different but knowable from 'here', within which a context can gather. And, though some cultural studies scholarship verges on the ethnographic in its capacity to estrange the familiar, it is the investment in contextualisation – indeed, in a contextualisation that, as Wissoker, Bourdieu and Wacquant might have predicted, cannot contextualise itself – that threatens to surrender cultural studies to the very anthropology the discipline's most progressive voices are seeking to abandon. Under circumstances such as this, the anti-theoreticism of much US cultural studies merely complicates things by adding insult to injury. We need to produce a new object, but when theory is regarded as a betrayal of cultural studies even promising alternatives like 'everyday life', cannot rise above the empiricism that has, in fact, imperilled the field.

> Does cultural studies have any significance outside of the university at all? If so, what forms does this take?

Having gone on at such length before let me try to be more concise here, and conclude on a note of modest good cheer. Like 'political', 'significance' admits of various readings. When considering such a question it is important to recall, for example, that the essays that came together to form Barthes' *Mythologies* originally appeared as columns in a French magazine edited by a man who, impressed with their semiological dexterity and insight, insisted upon studying with Barthes at EHESS. In other words, a text which has come to have extraordinary significance within cultural studies is one that has worked the border between the university and 'the real world' in a way that should remind us – not just that Barthes' struggle with complicity is one he comes by honestly – but that the theory and practice of cultural criticism is centrally involved in a struggle over significance that belongs exclusively within the university only if we act accordingly. If, as in Barthes case (surely only an avatar of what is now the common practice of academically trained semioticians going to work for Madison Avenue), the inside of the university comes from the outside, then we need to think carefully about what limit we are seeking to overcome when we broach the theme of significance. Unfortunately, the link now forged between bohemia and difficulty or critique, has made the temptation to act as though cultural studies can only matter to misunderstood specialists virtually irresistible. When these very specialists (let's call them, whether faculty or students, academic intellectuals) are advocating a post-theoretical return to 'the real world', the resulting paradox is stunning (in both senses). But is there an alternative, or at least another way of looking at things?

If we agree that even the American version of globalisation promises to produce a radically enhanced public sphere, that is, a site where individuals and groups gather to form 'public opinion', then cultural studies matters to people outside the academy because it is preparing students/citizens to participate in that enhanced public sphere equipped with an understanding of how differences – ethnic, racial, sexual, etc. – inflect cultural experience, and the expressive resources (in languages, in socio-cultural rhetorics, in audio-visual semiotics) necessary for engaging others. Even here in Minnesota citizens are encountering cultures, languages, traditions that place the state in a radically new global context (in recent years, for example, we have seen a huge influx of mostly Islamic Somalis). If we are prepared to live up to the demand for respect that the US imposes on others, then we will have to move well beyond the arrogance of toleration and come to be, if not fluent, at least conversant in the different cultural literacies active in the new global public sphere. International business, which claims to value such literacies, does virtually nothing to cultivate them and one might well conclude that this has to do, not with hypocrisy, but with the degree to which wealth-based arrogance is one of the kinship structures of business culture, especially in its international incarnation. These are the kinds of issues that have made the current conversations about global citizenship, migrancy and cosmopolitanism so pressing.

One often hears that democracy rests upon an informed citizenry capable of critical thinking. Perhaps foolishly, cultural studies has taken this maxim to heart, only by 'critical thinking' it does not typically understand innovative problem solving. Instead, in its best incarnations it strives for the standpoint from which problem solving might itself be the problem most in need of, if not 'solution', then certainly attention. The intelligence necessary to radicalise democracy, to push it past its republican compromises, is not about speed, is not about applicability, is not about the memorised contents of almanacs, is not about being or becoming a millionaire, but it is about the interests and skills cultural studies can seek to foster in its faculty and in its students. In this, of course, it is far from unique. Nevertheless, its very existence, troubled though it may be, does represent the fact that there are some who feel that there is another future for us, one not defined by the rush to find the medical, technological, martial and juridical means to endure, indeed to outlast, a systematic and federally legitimated refusal to radicalise democracy. If such a future has significance outside the academy (and there are clear signs that it does), then cultural studies might well have a claim to make, not simply on the significance of that future, but on its own.

NOTES

1. Pierre Bourdieu, *Acts of Resistance: Against the New Myths of Our Times*, trans. Richard Nice (Cambridge: Polity, 1998).
2. Bill Readings, *The University in Ruins* (London: Harvard University Press, 1996).
3. Henry Giroux, *Impure Acts: The Practical Politics of Cultural Studies* (London: Routledge, 2000).
4. *Parallax* 11: 'Polemics: Against Cultural Studies', eds Paul Bowman, Joanne Crawford, Alison Rowley, April–June 1999, Taylor and Francis, London.

12 The Subject Position of Cultural Studies: Is There a Problem?

Jeremy Valentine

These questions insist on answers in the first person singular and there's a lot of virement between them. So I will try to answer all the questions but not necessarily in the right order and the right place to make allowances for a fair bit of grammatical and conceptual drift.

So to begin with the first question, I must confess that I barely manage to position myself at all with respect to anything. My overwhelming experience is one of being positioned. So I am not very comfortable with my existence in a culture that can be characterised by the prevalence of the opposite view. I can only assume that this condition is an expression of the fact that it confirms an experience that is universally shared, otherwise someone would have challenged its accuracy, which is something that never happens. Everyone everywhere is doing what they want to do, and everyone everywhere wants to do it. Even those who can't do what they want to do want to do what they want to do and so they are in fact doing what they want to do, they're just not doing it as well as everyone else. So I have no reason to believe that this state of affairs is anything other than perfectly consensual. I am wrong and everybody else is right. You can't argue with that.

Of course, as any psychologist will tell you, my sarcasm is nothing other than a tool with which to mark myself out as different in order to maximise the advantages which I believe this special need is entitled to. In doing so I am manipulating the generosity of society, from which I do not deserve to benefit, and also confirming what I set out to deny. I am doing something very rational, even if I am failing. No one made me do it. 'It's your decision.' I'm out for all I can get. And I am intelligent enough to know that what I like to imagine as unique to me is in no way singular or original but is in fact commonplace. In fact, in setting yourself up in the manner of the traditional vagabond artist one's action is most likely explained as an effect of an identification with its image that circulates freely in our culture, from Nietzsche – or 'Nitch', as Anthony Soprano Jr (and everybody else) pronounces it – to Eminem. The idea that one can be the centre of attention just by whining and making out that you know the truth and common people are stupid is very familiar. Mike Leigh's film *Naked* is a brilliant essay on this type of person and I can't deny that I identify with the central character. Thus I can, as a matter of modernist right, simply ignore or evade moral therapies or, more aggressively, deflect them back on their sources in the spirit of the immortal line from *Withnail and I*: 'shove it up your arse and fuck off while you're doing it'. Because it's what I'm doing, and doing is what I and everyone else wants to do.

And as any dialectician will tell you, by carrying on like this one soon enters into a pathological dialectic of dependency, and one does so in an equally familiar and rehearsed manner in which the universal injunction to 'be yourself' is verified. In doing so I risk nothing and achieve everything by participation in the universal affirmation of individual agency in the same moment that I attempt to establish my *difference*. You must hate me in order for me to be me. In order for me to be me I must hate you. I am everything, you are nothing. Look at you. Look at me. I am Art. You are parody. So when Artaud once announced the intention 'to have done with the judgement of God' this was simply a report on or verification of something that had already happened, in the same way as Nietzsche's 'God is dead, and so is his murderer.' It may have been news to poets and philosophers but to everyone else it was just common sense. Thus what might be taken as a celebration of the total denunciation of the present is really a denunciation of the absence of the resources or force, including upper case Reason, with which to denounce the totality of the present, or the absence of the totality of the present as such. I think that Martin Amis hit the nail on the head recently when he observed that the problem with the death of God is not that people stop believing. Rather, people will believe in anything at all. As Boyzone put it: 'No matter what they tell you, what you believe is true.' It's an empowering message.

But that's enough about me and my problems for the time being. Behind my bourgeois psychosis lies the old theological distinction between agency and structure, or the not quite so old sociological distinction between action and its condition. The distinction is relevant because the specificity of cultural studies can be determined with reference to its use in the constitution of its object; namely, the relation between culture and politics. Culture refers quite simply to the sphere of meaning and sense, and politics refers to the production and distribution of power. Both these spheres are necessarily structured, and both allow for and require agency. The issue that concerns cultural studies revolves around the extent to which the relation between these spheres can be characterised in terms of agency or structure.

Unfortunately I do not possess the competence to construct the sort of complicated diagrams that would illustrate this issue and thus make it easier to grasp. However, for cultural studies the arrows go in the direction of the following syllogism. Because cultural studies maintains that action is meaningful, and is thus not simply behaviour, and that power is structured, and is thus not simply random, political action necessarily entails a cultural dimension. By the same token, because the referent of culture is by its nature limitless the relation between culture and politics extends beyond the restricted domain of politics understood as the mechanics of a formal system so that culture entails a political dimension. One might say that cultural studies reaches the areas of politics that Political Science does not, and succeeds in this ambition to the extent to which a relation between meaning and power can be shown. I think that Stuart Hall and those influenced by his work have incontrovertibly established the necessity of this perspective – it certainly convinced me.

Hence everything depends on the nature of this relation and the extent to which it can be characterised in terms of agency or structure. Indeed, this question is the proper object of cultural studies. On this basis the relation between meaning and power can appear across a spectrum from, at one end, an absolute coincidence between meaning and power in which the two terms are indistinguishable, and at the other, an infinite chasm between meaning and power in which the two terms are radically distinct. Again, I do not have the software to represent this spectrum. But at least it should be clear that the first extreme designates the determinacy of structure and the second designates the indeterminacy of agency. So at one end of the spectrum the relation between structure and agency is a logical and conceptual distinction, at the other it is a relation of radical exteriority in which logic and concepts determine antagonisms.

These extremes constitute two types of cultural-political relation. The first is coded in terms of power and domination, the second in terms of meaning and resistance. The first type is culture as cultural reproduction, which is seen as assisting social reproduction and its material basis. Cultural reproduction is therefore a matter of the status quo and the power relations through which it is maintained. In this case culture is reduced to structure. The second type is culture as cultural dislocation, which is seen as disrupting social reproduction and its material basis. Cultural dislocation is therefore a matter of the avant-garde and the power relations that are challenged by it. In this case culture is reduced to agency. If you like the society the chances are that you like the culture that goes with it. If, like me, you don't like the society the chances are that you like the culture that goes against it.

This choice is not novel as it is internal to culture. It originates with modernism and follows the ways that its shock has cascaded down to the general level of culture. In terms of straightforward intellectual history it can probably be traced to a synthesis of Durkheimian social theory and the Marxist critique of ideology.[1] So to cut a long story short, and if you don't mind doing the working out yourself, cultural studies is what happens when a statement like 'Social life, in all its aspects and in every period of its history, is made possible only by a vast symbolism'[2] meets a statement like:

> The ideological would consist of those discursive forms through which a society tries to institute itself as such on the basis of closure, of the fixation of meaning, of the non-recognition of the infinite play of differences. The ideological would be the will to 'totality' of any totalizing discourse. And insofar as the social is impossible without some fixation of meaning, without the discourse of closure, the ideological must be seen as constitutive of the social. The social only exists as the vain attempt to institute that impossible object: society. Utopia is the essence of any communication and social practice.[3]

So on the one hand culture conditions society. On the other culture makes society impossible. Hegemony is the concept that is used to describe the normal state of affairs when this paradox is balanced. However, cultural studies is distinguished by the fact that it is not indifferent about this paradox and in general declines the option of reducing impossibility to a positive function. This disposition is the basis of what could be called an ethical dimension of cultural studies which is manifested as a responsibility to politicise culture and to uncover hitherto overlooked or newly emerging relations of culture and power. From this ethical dimension it is a short step to the idea that cultural studies is a project that seeks to transform both culture and politics itself, and almost everyone who does cultural studies is happy to endorse this proposal. So cultural studies' transformative project succeeds to the extent to which it destabilises the categories of culture and politics, and which is a function of the relation between culture and politics that cultural studies establishes. Generally, the aim, objective and outcome of this project is to tip the balance of the agency–structure distinction in favour of culture as dislocation. This is usually understood in terms of an excess of meaning over structure in which 'the impossibility of society' is verified.

Obviously this makes things difficult because it raises the issue of the agency of cultural studies itself, and because it raises the issue of the effects of this agency. These issues are condensed in the question of the performance of cultural studies. Although this is not the place to begin a full audit of the performance of cultural studies we can at least evaluate it. To do so a good deal of methodological caution is required. After all, it does not follow that the project of cultural studies is transformative just because it wants to be. At best we could find evidence for the intention – probably quite a lot. But this would only show that its success is its intention to succeed, which is self-serving and far from satisfactory. Similarly, although we could find evidence that would demonstrate that the relation between culture and politics is transformed it would be difficult to establish a metric that would measure the extent to which this can be attributed to the intention of cultural studies to do so. So to simplify matters the methodology of the evaluation will examine the constitution of the agency of cultural studies. Although it's not much it will at least help us to know how cultural studies positions itself, its point of view, in order to find out what it does.

The agency of cultural studies derives from the fact that like any discourse it is concerned with an object, the relation between culture and politics, and the manner in which this object is determined or verified. Yet in determining this relation cultural studies also seeks to transform it. Following the theory of structural linguistics we can refer to this relation between an object and its determination as the subject of cultural studies. In grammatical terms the subject is the referent of an enunciation, or what the enunciation is about. However, structural linguistics refers us to an interesting case when the subject is also the act of its enunciation. This case is the use of the word 'I', or any case of the first person singular and its grammatical extensions.[4] Hence when cultural studies determines the relation between culture and politics it also refers to itself as the transformation of this relation. So the relation between culture and politics is both enunciation and referent of cultural studies. This coincidence is the subject of cultural studies. In this coincidence cultural studies achieves agency.

To understand the constitution of the subject of cultural studies we can recall a classic encounter between Durkheimian social theory and Marxist critique of ideology. Here I refer to the terms of Kristeva's celebration of the heterogeneity of the 'subject in process' radically opposed to the ultra-conformist 'homosexual tendency to identification'.[5] Through the hetero–homo opposition, which is a synonym for the dislocation–reproduction distinction established above, Kristeva determines what has become the enunciative position of cultural studies by establishing the terms by which 'the impossibility of society' can be known. Just listen to this:

> But since it is itself a metalanguage, semiotics can do no more than postulate this heterogeneity: as soon as it speaks about it, it homogenises the phenomenon, links it with a system, loses hold of it. Its specificity can be preserved only in the signifying practices which set off the heterogeneity at issue: thus poetic language making free with the language code; music, dancing, painting, re-ordering the psychic drives which have not been harnessed by the dominant symbolization systems and thus renewing their own tradition; and (in a different mode) experiences with drugs – all seek out and make use of this heterogeneity and the ensuing fracture of a symbolic code which can no longer 'hold' its (speaking) subjects.[6]

Rave on Julia. The 'impossibility of society' is 'set off' by a practice that dislocates the 'dominant symbolization system' by virtue of an effect of absolute heterogeneity. Yet for heterogeneity to be nothing must be said about it. Heterogeneity is consumed by the force of its own enunciative moment. To speak of heterogeneity would entail its symbolisation and thus the corruption of its alterity and so to judge that such and such a practice is radically heterogeneous is the verification that it is not. As heterogeneity is the referent Kristeva's enunciation must transgress the rule that she wishes to institute by which the 'speaking subject' may be known in order to institute it and thus risk the collapse of the sense of the enunciation itself. But as the enunciation makes sense we must ask whether, within the terms that it establishes, this is because it gravitates towards 'the dominant symbolization system' like the example Kristeva makes of semiotics, or because Kristeva's enunciation is an instance in which heterogeneity is 'set off' like the exemplary practices to which the enunciation refers. Of course, the answer is both, which describes perfectly the subject position of cultural studies. Cultural studies decides this question by inscribing the moment of speaking within the enunciation in which it is spoken. Thus referent and enunciation coincide. The antagonism which is its object is inscribed within the enunciation through which it is determined. Yet this clarity of position comes at the price of a structural deficiency. The subject of cultural studies lives vicariously because it desires to do so.

The significance of this passage is that it provides a template for the agency of cultural studies. This is the case whether the emphasis is on the affirmation of practices, and the development of criteria through which the desired qualities of such practices can be identified, or on the negation of the system to which such practices are supposed to be opposed. Thus the flexibility of Kristeva's template could be demonstrated by tracing the different ways in which it has been applied within cultural studies – from ethnographies of skinhead ritual violence to programmatic affirmations of the cyborg sublime. It has acquired this subterranean longevity by virtue of the adaptability built into the antagonism that it constitutes – any content can fill the positions that it structures, and any content can fail to meet the criteria that it upholds, stimulating greater efforts to discover the example of a practice that by definition cannot be identified.

I cannot be bothered to prove any of this, so you'll just have to trust me and take my word for it. However, recently evidence has accumulated that suggests that the conditions in which the aims of the template are intelligible have begun to wither away, and which thus highlight the importance of a hitherto overlooked temporal dimension. That is, the antagonism between 'dominant system of symbolization' and 'speaking subject', or structure and agency. Hence the desire to contain and restrict the remarkable flexibility of the system in the name of that which by right should be exterior to it which is proposed in the following example:

> To understand the Other is no more than a stratagem for the containment, mastery and exploitation of cultural difference. Contemporary Western liberal culture, exemplified by the relations of power-knowledge in the academy, has turned to migrant culture as a tactic for accommodating and pacifying the threat of difference. The threat to the legitimacy of narratives of dominant white masculine bourgeois Western culture that difference may engender has been assuaged by the denial of difference and by the violent exclusion of the Other as racially subaltern. However, in postmodernity, ethnic difference as the master trope of politics has been inscribed into the workings of the heterogeneous fields of power-knowledge that circulate in the new world order.[7]

I agree with everything in this diagnosis, but not at the same time. The diagnosis traces a movement which cannot be contained by the opposition that conditions it such that the transformation that it seeks would eliminate the movement that it describes. As this movement is a transformation that has already taken place, the agency of the enunciation is best described in terms of reproduction. Hence the agency–structure antagonism has shifted, which is visible in the epistemology of the diagnosis. The Other has been understood by something that is itself in turn other or Other to it, and that therefore the Other is no longer known as what it was. In which case this mutual relation of alterity collapses. The accommodation and pacification to which the enunciation refers evidence this fact. Difference and heterogeneity is now the property of power. But it is also evidenced within the enunciation itself as the knowledge which it communicates. In describing the properties of the Other as 'threat' it becomes known and thus the enunciation reiterates the state of affairs which it denounces despite its obvious intention to the contrary.

Consequently, the enunciation is subjected to an ethical oscillation between the production of a true knowledge of the Other, in which case the falsity or inaccuracy of the knowledge of the Other which the enunciation refers to would have to be demonstrated, and the effects of this misrepresentation would have to made apparent, and a withdrawal made from the field of knowledge altogether in order to prevent the Other's symbolisation that would serve to verify the correctness of the knowledge of the Other that is otherwise denounced. After all, to contest a representation is immediately to provide a truer one. One could, as a last resort, insist that representation is unethical in order to preserve the properties of the Other in the name of the right of the Other to be Other. But this would be self-defeating as the Other would be represented in doing so, and the ethical injunction would only affect those who know what the Other is and thus recognise its right not to be known, like a secret or something. In any case, what would be the point if power is now heterogeneous?

Given this undecidability the vicarious desire of the subject of cultural studies remains within the enunciation as the melancholic tone of the claim, as if it witnesses but does not mourn the passing of a state of affairs that is no longer real. Cultural difference, whether conceived as a relation between discrete entities or as a contingent event that disrupts the sense of the terms through which they are located, has become a memory of a thought of the future that is different from the future which is the present in which the thought is remembered. If difference 'may engender' a threat it is a possibility that belongs to a state of affairs that is no longer, a possibility that might have been. And as we know, what is remembered need not necessarily have taken place but can take place in the present event of memory. Yet all that is remembered is the static terms of a relation of dependence in the sense that to threaten something is immediately to affirm its existence, and even if its existence is only a property of an enunciation of the threat and not its referent. That dialectic is absent from the future in which the memory occurs, the referent of the enunciation.

So the task posed for the subject of cultural studies is to determine the extent to which the distinction between agency and structure can be located as an opposition in the different future which is its present. Yet, as this relation has failed to be static, the subject of cultural studies must make an ethical choice between maintaining the prior position of the elements of the relation according to the testimony of memory, or of reconstituting itself in relation to the different future which is its present. The first would derive a culture from a politics, the second would derive a politics from a culture. As the relation between agency and structure which constitutes the referent of cultural studies has changed, the stakes of this decision turn on the position from which the referent is enunciated. These stakes can be summarised as the question of the extent to which the subject of cultural studies is where it thought it was. It is the question of the constitution of this position that I will now discuss.

That cultural studies has always enjoyed a proximity to heterogeneity, difference, alterity, etc., is not surprising given the exceptional value that modernism attributed to these terms. Both aesthetic and political economies confirm this, but also, and interestingly, within the administrative and organisational economies through which the aesthetic and political economies were determined and regulated. The affirmation of this status can be traced back to Adorno who tended to understand structure as the totalising administrative framework of modernity diagnosed by Weber, but who, despite the endless demonstration of the impossibility of escape from this structure, also reserved a privileged exceptional status for the authority of the 'expert' within it who, opposed to the instrumentalism of the 'specialist', is spontaneously disposed to the 'planning of the non-planned'. Thus:

> The minimal differences from the ever-constant which are open to him define for him – no matter how hopelessly – the difference concerning the totality; it is, however, in the difference itself – in divergence – that hope is concentrated.[8]

All the humiliations of administrative existence are transcended in the minimal divergences that administration does not have time or resource to totalise. Doubtless we have all experienced 'experts' who claim this right to administrative transcendence in order to impose humiliations of their own design. Be that as it may, the point is that Adorno's exception provides the position with which the subject of cultural studies negotiates its relation to structure and preserves its honour.

This claim can be confirmed by examining a recent justification of the institutional value of cultural studies as a pedagogic practice. For example, Giroux[9] makes a distinction between authority and 'dominant authority' in order to extenuate the hope that cultural studies 'might be used to undermine the social and cultural reproduction of the dominant ideologies and practices' and thus 'might construct and mediate pedagogical authority as a form of auto-critique'.[10] The problem with this is not simply that the distinction between authority and dominant authority can only ever be an empirical quantitative issue. Nor is it that the condition of the pragmatic matter of 'using the very authority vested in institutions such as schools to work against the grain of such authority'[11] is a possibility provided by a rather convenient 'major paradox in capitalist societies'. After all, what Giroux proposes has been a respectable aim of Enlightenment from Kant to Foucault. Neither is the problem of the same order of the structural determination of Althusser's Ideological State Apparatuses. The problem is the exact opposite of all these and stems from the fact that a position of authority, dominant or otherwise, has to be recognised, and, as Hegel argued, the best proof of its recognition is resistance to it. Indeed, authority can only really be said to exist once a challenge to it has been defeated, although this probably never happens. Hence what Giroux refers to as 'dominant authority' is only recognised in cultural studies' resistance to it, on which the authority of cultural studies depends. The problem is that this 'dominant authority' is not there to resist.

The assumption that links Adorno and Giroux is that as a structure of power the authority of a political regime necessarily has the function of a 'steering mechanism' that can be directed to achieve the aims of a political project. This macrostructure is reproduced in all the microstructures that are subsumed within it. Habermas, one of the most nuanced advocates of this structure, inadvertently demonstrated that this was no longer the case when he admitted that 'Modern societies no longer have at their disposal an authoritative center for self reflection and steering.'[12] In Habermas' functionalist terms, the explanation is that society has fragmented into a series of subsystems without the guarantee of an overarching system to hold it together. Yet despite a default to the hope that the mechanics of the social system will self-correct this complex state of affairs, Habermas could hardly have been surprised at this situation. The interpretation of society as a structure steered by authority depends on its reproduction of the pre-modern condition such that one subsystem 'could occupy the top of a hierarchy and represent the whole the way the emperor could once do for the empire in stratified societies'.[13]

Hence authority existed in modern societies as a nostalgia for a form of pre-modern society, imagined as much as real, that would control the anti-authoritarian logic of modernity itself. That is to say, the structure of political modernity is constituted in order to reproduce a structure that does not exist within its terms except as a memory. Doubtless this structure was always symbolic, and thus

cultural. The situation was always absurd such that his contem-
poraries could regard a political theorist like Hobbes, who is generally
regarded as the theorist of modern authority, as a subversive
precisely because he attempted a justification or legitimation of
authority. The emperor needs no justification. That is why he is the
emperor. Hence to justify authority is immediately to destroy it, or
to reveal that authority is not.[14]

The dissolution of authority is not the secret cynical knowledge of
the hermeneutics of suspicion. It is right before everyone's eyes in
everyday life. It is particularly visible within the administrative
structure that Giroux must defend as the condition of possibility of
the cultural authority of cultural studies. That is, the university or,
more accurately, the higher education sector, or more simply, post-
compulsory education or even education as such. The issue for
cultural authority has been made explicit in Readings' description
of 'the university in ruins'.[15] Thus:

> A generalized bureaucracy no longer needs its state apparati to
> function *ideologically*. The 'culture wars' thus arise between those
> who hold cultural power yet fear that it no longer matters and
> those whose exclusion from that power allows them to believe
> that it would matter, if only they held it.[16]

In fact, Readings attributes this development to the success of
cultural studies in its critique of the cultural authority embodied by
the university, although this probably overstates the case on
numerous counts. Nevertheless there are two major symptoms of
this situation. On the one hand, within cultural studies the
emergence of a 'left-wing fogeyism', of which Terry Eagleton is the
most amusing example (come back F.R. Leavis, all is forgiven, we
love you really!). On the other hand, and as predicted by Lyotard
who Readings acknowledges in many respects, the emergence of a
'generalised bureaucracy' in the form of a discourse of managerialism that functions as a principle of intelligibility precisely because it
is empty of semantic or referential content. Thus the advantage of
managerialist discourse is that it is commensurate with absolutely
everything. If it can be understood as a strategy of power this would
be on the condition that managerialist discourse is a code that can
be attached to any discourse whatsoever, like a file transfer protocol,
in order for discourse to circulate. Because excellence, quality, vision,
etc., are self-verifying, any discourse can meet these criteria simply

by representing itself in these terms. The point is that no one has to believe them or understand them for managerialist discourse to be effective. It just has to be articulated.

Crucially, the defining characteristic of managerialist discourse is the dissolution of authority itself. Again, Hardt and Negri's analysis is instructive, where this process is understood in terms of the dissolution of state sovereignty insofar as the legitimacy of rule was established as a series of contractual relations between citizens and power codified in liberal political thought. Hence modern politics was less a matter of maintaining the mystique of authority through the paradox of the social contract than distributing this mystique through the administrative processes of society.[17] For Hardt and Negri administration no longer has the default of the transcendent position from which these relations could be mediated and regulated at its disposal. Hence all formal or implicit contractual relations have become purely performative, self-validating and contingent. There is no longer authority as such, simply the changing procedures for calculating whether and on what occasions power may be exercised, and how much, as there is no position from which life could be subsumed. Consequently it is no surprise to find that:

> Postmodernist organizations are thus imagined either as located on the boundaries between different systems and cultures or as internally hybrid. What is essential for postmodern management is that organizations be mobile, flexible, and able to deal with difference.[18]

In this respect, cultural studies and its institutional location is subordinate to wider societal processes that have displaced the culmination of modernity in the Keynesian state. Indeed, in a manner similar to Readings, Hardt and Negri suggest that the emphasis on difference, hybridity and the deconstruction of binary oppositions that characterises cultural studies may well have contributed to this state of affairs, although this would only be the case if cultural studies is a positivist science – which may well be true. It is certainly confirmed by the briefest acquaintance with the institutional location of cultural studies, where the aims of the higher education sector constantly shift from, for example, producing graduates who will be able to do the jobs that the economy requires, to, for example, producing graduates who will create the jobs that the economy will require, and always, to greater or lesser degrees, producing graduates who will have the specialist skills 'to meet the challenges of the knowledge economy', which translates into a passing familiarity with a recent Microsoft database programme. The aims change as the failure of one becomes embarrassingly visible. The point is that the higher education sector has aims, which is all that counts. It is no different from the unemployed who have to invent their own personal statement of 'aims, objectives and outcomes' in order to receive benefits. We are all managers now.

One of the sources of Hardt and Negri's position is Deleuze's observation that the content of the Foucauldian notion of governmentality has shifted from discipline to control.[19] This shift has emerged as a consequence of 'the omni-crisis of the institutions' and with it the disciplinary enclosures through which subjectivity was produced.[20] And for those who would insist, against the historicists, that subjectivity is bound up with the transcendental grammatical structure of language, one need only mention the vague and approximate status that language has in contemporary society and the negotiated relation that speakers have to it. Indeed the work of Lacan is very much a symptom of the desire to invest in the reassuring stability's of pre-modern grammar in response to a traumatic encounter with the modern world expressed as

> the increasing absence of all those saturations of the superego and ego ideal that are realized in all kinds of organic forms in traditional societies, forms that extend from the rituals of everyday intimacy to the periodical festivals in which the community manifests itself.[21]

So much for the rustic charms of psychoanalysis and its theory of the essentially pastoral constitution of the subject, like in *The Wicker Man*. It may have managed to get some purchase on the *Wizard of Oz* style illusions indulged by modernity but it's been left for dead by the speed of change. The point is that a whole regime of enunciation has been displaced:

> The institutions work even though they are breaking down – and perhaps they work all the better the more they break down. The indefiniteness of the *place* of the production corresponds to the indeterminacy of the *form* of the subjectivities produced.[22]

This does not describe an antagonism between reproduction and dis-location. Such a distinction is not constitutive but contingent. Neither does it describe a technology of domination in which structure suffocates agency. As the authors of a recent manual for the princes (and princesses) of change advise their readers, 'recognize the hypocrisy, shed the innocence, shed the guilt, play the turf game, play to win on one's own terms – and enjoy'.[23] This activity is not the proof that a regime or discourse has been implemented in dominance. Indeed, implementation is a constant that defines this activity. Arguably it defines the comedy of our culture, from *The Office* to *The Sopranos*. Under these circumstances we could say that the phrase 'Hey, you there' that Althusser used to explain the mechanism of ideological interpellation has been replaced by the question 'Is there a problem?' Instead of the determinate relation between a subject and authority that Althusser's example mediated, this question has the effect of constituting a relation of power in the very moment of its enunciation, and within and outside of any insti-tutional space. In Althusser's example the relative power of the interlocutors is confirmed by the enunciation. In my example the question constructs a relation of power. The former reminds you who you are. The latter reminds you that you don't know. That is why it's safest to answer 'No'. After all, if every problem must have a solution, you might be it.

Given these conditions, what are the chances of the transforma-tive ethos of cultural studies? On this issue we should consider the mechanics of the political system itself. Like Habermas, some people continue to insist on the necessity of emptying the pre-modern structure of authority of its historically specific content such that it would serve as the rational basis of legitimate authority. This proposal is particularly popular with those who are concerned with constraining the evolving political economy of the media in the name of a Public Culture. Unfortunately it's an attempt to lock the stable door after the horse has bolted.[24] This conclusion is not the savage speculation of clued-up cultural theory but the consequence of the current condition of the political system as described by political science itself, and is condensed in the observation that government has been replaced by 'governance'.[25] Governance is characterised by heterogeneity, contingency, and the displacement of hierarchy. These developments confirm that after its crises of the 1970s condensed in the spectacle of punk the state has not sought a new or renewed basis of legitimation. Under these conditions: 'To govern, one could say, is to be condemned to seek an authority for one's authority.'[26] Such an activity is a cost that provides little prospect of a return on one's investment. After all, who would pay for it?

Perhaps this is why recent proposals to incorporate the transformative ethos of cultural studies into the deductions of deliberative political theory are bound to fail. For example, in order to balance the material – money – and cultural inequalities – status – of power in the name of fairness, Fraser has suggested that:

> For both gender and 'race', the scenario that best finesses the distribution-recognition dilemma is socialism in the economy plus deconstruction in the culture. But for this scenario to be psychologically and politically feasible requires that people be weaned from their attachment to current cultural constructions of their interests and identities.[27]

On this basis, the absolute coincidence of the enunciation and referent that constitutes the subject of cultural studies would regulate the 'veil of ignorance' of a deontological jurisprudence that would produce and distribute power. Which is all very well except for the fact that there is no place from which such reforms could be implemented. The principle would suffer the same fate as common or garden corporate visions. At the same time, people are being disattached from their identities although it is unlikely that deconstruction has anything to do with it. Money does. Hence it is almost certainly to be resisted – unless a procedure could be figured out for redistributing deconstruction. For some this scenario is seen as an opportunity to reaffirm the subject of cultural studies as the opposition between agency and structure. Hence in Britain there has been a concerted effort to identify something called Blairism that would function as an enemy in the manner that Thatcherism once did, except that this time cultural studies would have all the advantages of the lessons learnt from hegemony. The results have been disappointing in that the worst crime Blairism is accused of is banality and lack of intellectual rigour – as if it had a mandate to being anything else. If there is an opposition that constitutes an antagonism then it probably resembles the scenario that Laclau has described in terms of the emergence of a 'mythical space' as the condition for a new logic of order:

If the mythical space was opposed to a full 'logical form' of the dominant structural space, then we would indeed be faced with an inverted image. But it is not the 'structurality' of the dominant structure to which the mythical space is opposed, but its *de*-structuring effects. The mythical space is constituted as a critique of the lack of structuration accompanying the dominant order.[28]

Which means that structure and its equation with domination is a property of myth – a discourse of what was and what will be – that is opposed to its absence within what is. The opposition merely seeks to make order and in doing so simply escalates its experience of de-structuration, thus verifying its myth and renewing its desire for order.

We know that most of the consequences of this dialectic of buffoonery are horrific. Hardt and Negri have recently described these movements in terms of 'the boomerang of alterity'[29] and propose a different position through which the subject of cultural studies might be constituted. One of their key messages is: 'We should be done once and for all with the search for an outside, a standpoint that imagines a purity for our politics.'[30]

I want to end on this suggestion without exploring it further, and thus without confronting the contradictions and fallacies that inevitably constitute it. After all, it's only discourse. My relation to it and the text from which it is taken may be explained by nothing else than the trivial fact that it makes me feel positive about being negative. But I would like to speculate that one of its implications is that the appropriate response to the contingency of the question 'Is there a problem?' is the question 'What do you mean?' At least this would dislocate the myth that every problem has a solution.

NOTES

1. See C. Jenks, 'Introduction: The Analytic Bases of Cultural Reproduction Theory', in C. Jenks (ed.), *Cultural Reproduction* (London: Routledge, 1993).
2. E. Durkheim, *The Elementary Forms of the Religious Life* (London: George Allen and Unwin, 1976), p. 231.
3. E. Laclau, 'The Impossibility of Society', in E. Laclau (ed.), *New Reflections on the Revolution of Our Time* (London: Verso, 1990), p. 92.
4. See E. Benveniste, *Problems in General Linguistics* (Coral Gable: University of Miami Press, 1971), pp. 220–6.
5. J. Kristeva, 'The Subject in Process', in P. French and R.F. Lack (eds), *The Tel Quel Reader* (London: Routledge, 1998 [1968]).

6. J. Kristeva, 'The System and the Speaking Subject', in T.A. Sebeok (ed.), *The Tell-Tale Sign: A Survey of Semiotics* (Lisse: The Peter de Ridder Press, 1975 [1973]), p. 52.
7. S. Sharma, 'Sounds Oriental: The (Im)possibility of Theorizing Asian Musical Cultures', in S. Sharma, J. Hutnyk and A. Sharma (eds), *Dis-Orienting Rhythms: The Politics of the New Asian Dance Music* (London: Zed Books, 1996), p. 19.
8. T. Adorno, *The Culture Industry: Selected Essays on Mass Culture* (London: Routledge, 1991), p. 113.
9. H.A. Giroux, 'Public Pedagogy as Cultural Studies: Stuart Hall and the "Crisis" of Culture', *Cultural Studies*, 14, 2 (2000), pp. 341–60.
10. Ibid., p. 350.
11. Ibid., p. 356.
12. J. Habermas, *The Philosophical Discourse of Modernity* (Cambridge: Polity Press, 1987), p. 358.
13. Ibid., p. 358.
14. See Z. Bauman, 'Modernity and Ambivalence', *Theory, Culture and Society*, 7, 3 (1989), pp. 141–69; J. Valentine, 'Governance and Cultural Authority', *Cultural Values*, 6, 1&2 (2002), pp. 47–62.
15. B. Readings, *The University in Ruins* (Cambridge, MA and London: Harvard University Press, 1996).
16. B. Readings, 'For a Heteronomous Cultural Politics: The University, Culture and the State', *Oxford Literary Review*, 15 (1993), p. 166, original emphasis.
17. M. Hardt and A. Negri, *Empire* (Cambridge, MA: Harvard University Press, 2001), p. 99.
18. Ibid., p. 153.
19. G. Deleuze, 'Postscript on the Societies of Control', *Negotiations* (New York: Columbia University Press, 1995).
20. Hardt and Negri, *Empire*, pp. 196–7.
21. J. Lacan, *Écrits: A Selection* (London: Routledge, 1977), p. 26.
22. Hardt and Negri, *Empire*, p. 197, original emphasis.
23. D. Buchanan and R. Badham, *Power, Politics and Organizational Change: Winning the Turf Game* (London: Sage, 1999), p. 231.
24. For a more realistic approach to this issue, see L. Grossberg, E. Wartella and C.D. Whitney, *Mediamaking: Mass Media in Popular Culture* (London: Sage, 1998); and S. Hall, 'The Centrality of Culture: Notes on the Cultural Revolutions of Our Times', in K. Thompson (ed.), *Media and Cultural Regulation* (London: Sage, 1997).
25. R. Rhodes, 'The New Governance: Governing Without Government', *Political Studies*, XLIV (1996), pp. 652–67.
26. N. Rose, *Powers of Freedom: Reframing Political Thought* (Cambridge: Cambridge University Press, 1999), p. 27.
27. N. Fraser, 'From Redistribution to Recognition? Dilemmas of Justice in a "Post-Socialist" Age', *New Left Review*, 212 (1995), p. 25.
28. Laclau, *New Reflections*, p. 62.
29. Hardt and Negri, *Empire*, pp. 130–2.
30. Ibid., p. 46.

13 What Can Cultural Studi Do?

Steven Connor

How do you position yourself and your work in relation to the cultural studies project?

For some time, I have found or at least taken myself to be at odds with what seem to have become the norms and assumptions of cultural studies, as opposed to cultural study. Since I have never been employed in a Department of Cultural Studies, nor had responsibility for sustaining collective belief on a large scale that cultural studies was what I was primarily engaged with, it has been easy for me to maintain a very loose and irresponsible relation with cultural studies. This can be a pleasant and invigorating sensation. Cultural studies seems to me to have produced its most exciting work when it was unsure of its proper sphere of operations, its operating system and its archive of guiding precepts – the period during the 1970s when it was laying in intellectual capital and trying out possibilities.

What are the politics of cultural studies? What is the political significance of your own work? What do you consider to be the 'proper destination' of your work?

Perhaps one should divide 'politics' into political motivation and political effect, for they are not the same thing. The political affiliations of those who do work associated with cultural studies and the political satisfactions to which the practice of cultural studies are held to lead are obviously, as a matter of observable sociological fact, overwhelmingly and definitionally left-liberal. Most of those involved with cultural studies believe that the academic work they do in this area makes a decisive contribution to progressive political thinking, political culture and even political change, or should do. So much, for the moment, for motivation.

What about political effect, though? Like a lot of those involved with cultural studies, I used to have the grandiose delusion that my work was actually a way of doing politics. I now think it absurd to believe that thinking and speaking and writing about cultural forms and processes in the ways and in the contexts in which I am ever likely to be able to do it can serve my political beliefs and commitments, or for that matter anyone else's, in any useful way. It's not that cultural studies has no political dimensions; everything, as we so uselessly know, is indeed political. It is just that cultural studies is such an extremely slow and ineffective way to bail the boat. People in academic life who think they are making important political differences for the most part fail to recognise that they are just marching in step with much more powerful forces that are making the real differences. The legacy of the 1970s was to suggest that politics ought to be natural, organic, expressive, fulfilling, therapeutic, sensuous, stylish, fun: that it should not only be the politics of culture, but *cultural* politics. I have come to think that the work of politics is vastly necessary and for the most part tedious; the study of culture is endlessly fascinating and pretty much gratuitous.

So I find I cannot speak interestingly of the political significance or destination of my own work. I have grown so used to quoting the following sentence from Michel Foucault that I have forgotten where (or if) it can actually be found, but still, here goes again: 'We know what we do and we know, up to a point, why we do it: what we don't know is what what we do *does*.' I've always assumed that Foucault thought there was something wrong with this. We don't know what cultural studies will end up having done, nor is there much point in trying to second-guess it. The significance of what we do is none of our concern, because it depends upon what is done by others with us, and others who will almost certainly have something to gain from misconstruing or outdoing us.

What for example is the significance of phrenology? In its own time, phrenology seemed highly significant, a new way of integrating mind, body and culture. Then it became a laughing stock. But becoming a laughing stock is not to be dreaded or sneezed at, as it prolongs survival, like a process of mummification, in a way that being gently, politely superseded, does not. Now the laughter has died down, and with the conspicuous successes being achieved in neurological investigation, the localisation of cognitive function dreamed of in phrenology starts to seem like a sum done wrong rather than something that does not even belong to mathematics. There is only one *final* destination for phrenology, as there is for any movement of thought, namely oblivion. But until that final destination is reached, until it is forgotten with no possibility of revival, it is always still possible for *anything* to happen to phrenology, for it to come to have any significance, political, cultural, scientific, religious. Thus neither I nor you are in any position to decide the political significance or destination of my or your work. It's hard enough doing the work without being expected to legislate on what is to be done with what you have done.

And yet, of course, academic and political life is more and more driven by this proleptic demand, which strikes me as a gruesome parody of Lyotard's principle of the future anterior: where he said it was the postmodernist work that looked for the rules that it will have followed, in our era of abstracts, outlines, articulated aims, strategies, projections and research proposals, institutions and avant-garde artists both operate equally on the need to know the score in advance of the game. Look away now is my advice.

All this is more or less the opposite of what many or most practitioners of cultural studies seem to think, namely, that cultural studies can and should make the workings of culture transparent to itself.

What are the institutions of cultural studies?

I'd like to try to come at this question, as well as to pursue the point I have just made about making culture transparent to itself, by saying something about the idea of institutions in general. The word 'institution' has come to suggest something fixed, though there is something provisional and voluntaristic in the idea of the institution as something solid or visible. An institution is first of all an established habit or custom (this is the sense in which it is commonly used by nineteenth-century anthropologists): like the institution of Christmas or the habit of monogamy. It then passes across to our modern sense of an organisation, like the police, the army or the medical profession – making possible a phrase like 'institutional racism'. It then becomes increasingly hard not to think of institutions as constituted by their material embodiments: their buildings, their publications, their uniformed officials.

At the bottom of thinking about the idea of social or cultural institutions is a sense of bodies which slow, capture and constrain. Slow, capture and constrain what? Life, that's what: free association, creativity, invention, subversion, multiplicity, heterogeneity, 'the event' (though I can honestly say that, as austerely defined by Lyotard, Badiou, and other enthusiasts of this fugitive *numen*, not a single 'event' has ever taken place in my life), leaping, exuberant difference. The Romantic distinction between binding institutions and organic freely self-defining processes is fundamental in the very beginning of the systematic study of culture. I mean, for example, in the work of Georg Simmel, who, writing at the inception of modern cultural studies, saw everywhere a dialectic between objective social forms, which defined things from the outside, and subjective social energies, which emerged spontaneously and self-definingly against the background of objective forms. Cultural studies preserves this distinction, even though it might now shy away from the word 'subjective'. It sees institutions relating to social processes as finite forms relate to unharnessable forces. Whatever the form of its vitalism, Nietzschean, Bakhtinian, Derridean, Foucauldian, Kristevan, Deleuzean, Lyotardian or Serresian, cultural studies is on the side of the life force, and remains driven by the vitalism that was everywhere to be seen at its moment of inception, in the sociology that formed itself in the long, multicoloured moment of early modernism, at the intersection of Nietzsche, Bergson and Freud.

Modern cultural studies came into being during the 1960s out of the uneasy convergence of, on the one hand, a strongly functionalist kind of sociology that was strong on measurement and description, but weak on critique or evaluation, and, on the other, a form of literary study that had almost no language at all with which to describe its object of study, nor yet ways of checking its observations, but was almost pathologically saturated with value and positively addicted to orgies of discrimination and judgement. This uneasy conjuncture finds expression in the contrasting definitions of 'culture' to be found in the work of Raymond Williams, when he was still in his left-Leavisite phase: culture as anthropological 'whole way of life' (rituals, structures and habits), and culture as expressive form (statues, poems and novels), or the distinction between what collections of people characteristically do and what said collections produce and leave behind them in the way of art and monuments. This distinction in turn codes a distinction between cultural forms as involuntarily expressive (visible to the analyst-anthropologist) and voluntarily expressive (acts of purposive distinctive self-expression). Cultural studies grew partly out of the intuition that it might be possible to bring to bear the forms of understanding designed for looking at and affirming the expressive value of works of art on apparently less self-conscious expressive activities like those being analysed by Roland Barthes in *Mythologies*: striptease, wrestling and so on.

Why has the word 'culture' driven out its competitors, especially that great, booming nineteenth-century word 'society'? One reason may be that the word *culture*, with its well-documented origins in the idea of *Bildung*, or the cultivation and care of self, preserves the idea of the analogy between the individual and the mass self. In making cultures known and transparent to themselves, cultural studies has had as its aim the making good of the analogy between social and subjective process. The assumption in modern societies has always been that the way to understand and therefore be able to direct a society is to accord it a self-understanding – to grow it a mind and a voice. This is perhaps the kind of growth principally signified in the word *culture*. A culture has institutions as a way of making itself known to itself, a way of acting itself out. Cultural studies is actually one of these institutions, which is to say, one of these anthropomorphisms.

What cultures most seem to want – although this way of speaking is precisely the thing I would like to see become dubious – is to stay on the side of life rather than petrifying into institutions. This is the reason why cultural studies is so uneasy about becoming institutionalised. Cultural studies aims to restore or preserve the life of what it describes. Cultural studies has been driven by various models, but it seems to me that the psychoanalytic one remains dominant, even among non-psychoanalytic critics and in work where psychoanalytic language is not apparently in evidence. This may be because the psychoanalytic model of culture allows us to clump together social processes as the expression of collective wishes, anxieties and strategies of self-deception, just as creation myths see in natural formations like hills and reefs the stretched-out bodies of primeval giants. In cultural studies, as in psychoanalysis, the governing principle is Freud's 'wo es war soll ich werden': where there was it, let there be I. This is the difference between a culture (*Gemeinschaft*) and a mere association (*Gesellschaft*), in Tönnies' famous formulation. A culture is association become conscious of itself. There is no doubt that collective self-representation is one of the things that societies characteristically and constitutively do. But these collective self-representations are the outcomes of what a culture is and does, not autonomous sources or principles of social functioning; they are part of what cultures do rather than what they are.

What if we take seriously the analogy between a culture and a consciousness? Consciousness arises in the brain as a result of the interactions of millions of neurones. This does not justify the view that each of these individual neurones, or each one of its transactions with its neighbours, need itself be conscious, or possess a little portion of the consciousness of the whole. Consciousness is, as they say, an emergent phenomenon, that is more than the sum of its parts. Social life, by contrast, is composed of many actions, reactions, interactions, projects, conflicts, convergences, all of them embodying human will, or interest, or appetency. But it does not continue to consist of the forms of intentional behaviour that form its units all the way up to the top layer. In this sense, it is less than the sum of its parts. In the case of a human brain, mere mechanism seems to lift into consciousness; in the case of a society, or collective, acts of individual will produce effects that cannot necessarily be thought of as the expression of collective will. In the first case, consciousness does not have to go all the way down; in the second, it need not go all the way up. Does this mean that there is no such thing as society? No. But it does mean that a society or a culture is a pattern of behaviour, a set of ways of doing things, not states of living awareness.

I have become tired of this anthropomorphism. I don't think cultures can or need to be brought to life, nor am I anyway on life's side (it always turns out to be such murder).

Cultures and collectivities in general do not mean anything, not in the sense that they have no significance but in the sense that they do not in any very intelligible sense mean to do what they do and are. Of course governments, political parties, unions, churches, learned societies and boards of governors do mean to do things, indeed exist in order to do them and seem to mean them. But it is the doing that extrudes the collective will, not the other way round. Of course, societies and cultures do have mechanisms which are aimed at drawing them together into collective purpose; indeed, a large part of what we mean when we speak of a culture, is the effect of such drawings together, as well as the ascription of a common purpose to them. By willing ourselves into action that bears the impress of willed action, we invent ourselves tautologically as a 'we'.

Explanations of cultural or social phenomena in these terms, as the expressions of mood, the shiverings of collective anxiety, the eruptions of mass desire or discontent, the heroic cleavage to principle or following-through of programmes, are as mythological as explanations of weather in terms of the whims of the rain-god. On my reading, the replacement of the idea of society by the idea of a culture is the expression of a desire (here we go again) to give coherence, interiority and self-conscious purpose to the phenomena of social life. Now, given its origin as the offspring of sociology and literary criticism, cultural studies ought to be in a good position to perform this act of bringing to life. Cultural studies inherited from various directions, including the Romantic rejection of industrial modernity by Arnold, Ruskin and Morris, and the Marxist social theory of the Frankfurt School, a tradition of social critique, prompted largely by a growing sense of the mysterious, unregulated and irrational powers of mass social formations. These forms of mass life seemed to resemble terrible machines, which were lifelike, but terrifyingly lifeless, or lacking in interiority. The point of critique was to put life, which was thought of as unbounded, spontaneous, self-forming and generative, in place of the machines of social living. And because the life in question was identified with self-conscious as well as generative life, then the best way to change society is to describe it, to make its workings visible and knowable to itself. Once the workings of the machine were made clear, it would be obvious how to escape them. Once a society became self-consciously aware of its mechanisms, it could be ensouled, as a 'culture'.

The problem with cultural critique, which was already the sorest of possible sore thumbs when it was inherited by modern cultural studies, was that both culture and critique had already been taken up into the workings of the rationalising social machine. Mass culture – the 'culture industry' – and the generation of social descriptions and modellings could be seen increasingly like centralised functions exercised by the state and its institutions. Cultural studies inherited the idea that making cultural forms and practices visible to themselves and others was a good way of bringing about desirable social change, but it also inherited the disabling suspicion that the mere mapping of social life and its functions might resemble the orderings of social life too closely to contribute to the liberation of new, freer, less describable forms. But this suspicion was not disabling enough, and cultural studies actually ended up taking its characteristic form from the problem that might have stymied it at the outset. Hence the strange but wholly characteristic mixture in cultural studies of a neo-functionalism, carried to its most parched and masochistically passionless extreme, in its talk of formations, levels, grids, apparatuses, territories, spaces, margins and lines of force, with the wildest and most untutored sorts of exoticism and libidinality. It is as though August Comte had set up house with Walter Pater. The mechanism and the vitalism of cultural studies actually seem to depend one on the other. One needs to think only of the uses in cultural studies of Bakhtin, in which the grinding apparatus of social linguistics is solemnly deployed to yield bizarre and unlikely celebrations of carnival, pleasure, heteroglossia and 'the body'. Cultural studies has sought to solve the problem of the mal-adjustment of analysis and affirmation by forcing its affirmations more and more through the mill of its analyses, to make the former seem as though they arose naturally and inevitably from the latter. But there is nothing in the description – apart from the preference for life over structure – that makes heteroglossia more desirable than monologism.

The most important move made in this process is the idea of the politics of cultural identity, the idea that describing what groups of people characteristically do will be sufficient to build in them an 'empowering' sense of who they are. This in turn will assist the process of making a culture in general, a culture that, because it knows itself inside-out, because it can reach unimpeded into every corner of its multifarious self, without exclusions or blindnesses, can fully be itself. Cultural studies trades on this ancient ideal of the knowable social totality, on the Delphic maxim 'know thyself' raised to the level of social and even global life. It comes centuries too late.

Nowadays, I actually feel it both more plausible and infinitely more soothing to think of a culture as a meteorological phenomenon. Almost immeasurably complex interactions of a small number of determinate variables – wind speed and direction, pressure, temperature – produce determinate weather effects. There is no difficulty in establishing whether it is or is not, at any particular place and time, raining. But what is the 'it' that is raining, and that, so to speak, wills or *weathers* the weather? And where, or what is this it, before it becomes available to be presupposed as the action of an intending awareness? I hope we will want, or mean to learn to want, not to think of society as having self-consciousness and actively self-directing purpose on the analogy of an individual will. A cloud forms, a waterfall plunges and seethes; but not as an expression of desire or the unease of the cloud or the waterfall.

Our mass mediated culture involves ever more rapid exchanges, encounters and transactions, of money, information, desire, and so on, through ever larger and therefore less self-aware and self-directing masses of people, hooked up in more pervasive but also more various ways. I don't see it happening any time soon, but the idea of the institution, as that which channels or fixes the forms of otherwise unconstrained human encounter, may give way to something much more localised and temporary. The hydraulic metaphors which have governed our way of thinking of complex structures like economies and societies, metaphors which allow us to think in terms of flows evenly and regularly channelled along pipes and regulated through valves, or the even more static topography of centres, margins and levels, mechanical images that belonged to the age of the spinning jenny rather than our own, ought to give way to something more labile and indeterminate, without necessarily becoming in the process more like ourselves.

Rather than hoping to see cultural studies become less mechanistic, I would like to see it become properly and thoroughly so, which would mean developing a much more complex notion of what a machine is, and a correspondingly richer and less fixated language for grasping the soft machinery of cultural life. I would prefer to see the development of ways of studying culture that were much less programmatic, and much less determined to generate value out of the description of how things are. I would be interested to see the effects of a real cultural materialism, therefore, one that does not assume that culture is made up indifferently from top to bottom of broadly analogical acts of mind.

It is certainly true that cultural studies has also given me the desire to find ways of writing about a hundred and one different topics that do not show up on the radar of most academic disciplines, cultural studies included. But this is not because I have a project, to illuminate and enliven and give significance to such unmarked or disregarded areas. I fear that recent developments like the interest in 'the everyday' make me shudder, despite the fact that by writing about mundane things like bags, sweets, wires, clapping, cleaning, itch, unction and skirts, rather than about ideology, or gender identity or counter-hegemonic formations, I might seem to be giving succour to it. But I think there is no culture of the everyday, no 'the' or definite article involved in everydayness, and therefore no easily

...l output from studies of the everyday. I want to write
things for the same reason that corresponding members
...yal Society in the seventeenth century wanted to write
...the phenomena of spontaneous human combustion or phos-
...rescent fish; because they are there, or seem to be.

How does the institutionalisation of cultural studies affect,
support, or undermine it? Does cultural studies have any significance outside the university at all? What is, has been, might be,
or might have been, the 'significance' of cultural studies within
the university? Where is cultural studies going?

I feel as though I should try to answer all these questions together,
under the general heading, 'What can cultural studies do?'

Cultural studies has both won and lost. It has won because it has
changed, or been part of a change in the landscape, everywhere; in
history, art history, anthropology, literature, legal studies, women's
and gender studies. It has lost because it is no longer directing that
change, is no longer credibly even the name of that change.
Everything now, as Fredric Jameson observed years ago, is culture;
and everything we do with it is a kind of cultural studies. Everywhere
we see the signs of pop versions of cultural studies, in the snapshot
analyses of social dynamics and motivations offered by columnists
and commentators. Everywhere we forgo the opportunity to describe
the complex mechanisms of mass mediated existence in favour of
trying to give its lived reality.

Cultural studies has now settled down into a familiar and predictable set of routines, having colonised a cosy precinct of what
Michel Foucault sourly calls 'the true'. So there will probably still be
'cultural studies' going on for some time yet. It was always dangerous
for cultural studies to canvas itself as some variety of the unthinkable
or outlandish or unformalisable, since the effort to maintain such a
self-image is always likely to involve the maintenance of a level of
religious zeal that easily reverts to the conservative urge to bind
oneself to recognisable procedures and outcomes.

Cultural studies will inevitably continue along this line for a considerable while. It is likely to institutionalise itself more and more, up
to a certain point where boredom, generational antagonism or com-
petition diffuse its energy. There will be more journals, more readers
and anthologies, and more courses. There will also be mutations,

accidents and freaks: almost every time they will have no effect, and we will continue to think as though society and culture were personality merely scaled up. But just once, which may be the first time or the hundredth time it happens, there will be the flicker of a new understanding of how one might go about describing the phenomena of mediated collective life and, depending on surrounding circumstances, that once may be enough to unleash an epidemic.

Cultural studies believes it needs to sustain itself in the ecological niche it has scooped out, and needs to think how to sustain itself in order to do it. I can't decide whether it would be better for the prospects of its survival for cultural studies to return to its barefoot, Franciscan moment, living off berries and radishes, or better for it to be solid and secure enough to create dissatisfaction and disaffection, but not big enough to neutralise them. I think I lean to the latter. The best way for cultural studies to be renewed or productively transformed would probably be for it to continue in its dutiful, wearisome way, identifying anxiety, affirming identity, celebrating plurality, seizing on contradictions, squeezing out subversions; showing that there is nothing that one cannot do these dear, tired old tricks on. This is more likely to stir irritable invention and dissent among those interested in working with the phenomena of culture than programmes of outreach, renewal, or conscientiously pondered self-transformation.

Part Six:
Against Cultural Studies

INTRODUCTION

Here we see the two most critical contributions, but critical in an immensely valuable way. The criticism is far from unjustified. Thomas Docherty's 'Responses', and Lynette Hunter's 'Unruly Fugues', strenuously interrogate what might be termed dimensions of cultural studies that have been overlooked, downplayed, or otherwise neglected. If cultural studies is to continue to be – or, indeed, if it is ever to become – a vital and valuable academic, intellectual, cultural and political force, then one must never be complacent or self-congratulatory. The charges levelled against cultural studies here are potentially quite devastating. But, again, to the extent that they may be correct diagnoses, then the onus is on cultural studies to take them on board, and, if necessary, strenuously revise itself in response. The cultural and political consequences of the alternative could perhaps be far more devastating.

Docherty sees cultural studies, perversely, as complicit in the process of the *reduction* of culture. In more or less entirely disagreeing with the general cultural studies consensus about the truth of Raymond Williams' famous maxim that 'culture is ordinary', Docherty challenges the entire orientation of it. For Docherty, culture is far from 'ordinary'. Rather, it should properly be treated as something *extraordinary* – something that always might not happen, might not happen again, and might *cease* to happen. The 'everyday' is, for him, something mediocre, repetitive, almost machine-like. In treating culture as ordinary, and celebrating this mediocrity, cultural studies is complicit both in culture's denudation, and in making the university and academia become this 'everydayness' continued by other means – hence, also, a denudation and degradation of the vitality and potential of the role of the university in *making culture happen*. This critique he combines with that of Bill Readings' famous arguments about the deleterious and insidious intrusion of professionalisation and managerialism into academia, and from it he provides a compelling argument as to why studying culture *should* be difficult. Bioscience is 'difficult', but it is a sign of its worth. Cultural studies' simplification is a kind of patronisation that reduces the ability of the university to enable culture to 'happen' – it makes university life the continuation of (a virtually cultureless) everyday life by other means.

Lynette Hunter, on the other hand, argues that cultural studies has no position, no text and no history; that it is banal, cynical, with no content; narcissistic, melancholic and bitter; without rhetorical understanding; about endless deferral: 'the place where people go when they get frightened of moral labour, ethical commitment and of things they can't articulate'. Damning indeed! The gauntlet is thrown. How shall we proceed?

14   Responses

Thomas Docherty

(1) How do you position yourself and your work in relation to the cultural studies project? Or, rather, do you see cultural studies *as* a 'project', and is contemporary cultural studies still the 'same' project or discipline as it once was?

(2) Cultural studies is said to be a political project. What, to your mind, are the politics of cultural studies? Does it have 'a' politics, or is it, rather, political in some other way? Another way to phrase this would be to ask you what are the politics or what is the political significance of your own work? What do you consider to be the 'proper destination' of your work?

(3) What are the *institutions* of cultural studies? That is, what works, methods, orientations, etc., have become instituted as the repositories of 'knowledge', methodology, and ways of going about doing things? This is as much as to say, what do these institutions (or the institution of these authoritative guarantors as 'the proper' or 'the best') forbid, censure/censor, limit and enable? What factors determined or overdetermined their institution?

(4) How does the institutionalisation of cultural studies affect, support or undermine it?

In all that follows, I shall make a distinction between 'cultural studies' on the one hand, and 'the study of culture' on the other. In making such a distinction, I aim to distance myself and my work, such as it has been, from 'cultural studies' while at the same time identifying myself as one who studies not merely or not only literature but also what used to be called the 'histories of ideas', philosophy, the histories of everyday conditions of living, the other arts, and so on.

It might be wise, at the outset, for me to outline what has been my particular take on the meaning of the word 'culture'. When I hear the word 'culture', I reach for my dictionary. There, I find that it has something to do with growth and with an improving kind of development. Yet one of the illustrative uses of the word that is cited is from the title of C.P. Snow's 1959 Rede lecture, which he called 'The Two Cultures and the Scientific Revolution'. That usage allows for the slippage of the semantics of 'culture' into something slightly different: it can also come to mean something like a 'mentality', a 'way of conceptualising things', a 'mode of life' shared by a group or identifiable collectivity. This latter usage is one that I am extremely unhappy with; yet it is true that this is the dominant sense that the word now has, at least in the humanities disciplines. Snow's lecture characterised knowledge as something contested between two disparate cultures, one associated with the literary intellectuals, the other with the hard or natural sciences. In this particular usage of the term, we find that cultures multiply inexorably. Participants within the ambit of 'cultural studies' are able to understand and to sit comfortably with, as *relatively* unproblematic terms of their discipline, notions of 'women's culture' or 'Black culture', or 'Irish culture' or 'working-class culture' or 'popular culture' (the list could be extended almost indefinitely). Such colleagues might be less happy with – though I believe that their theoretical stance requires that they would have to accept the viability of – 'gun culture', 'drug culture', 'Mafia culture', 'paedophile culture', 'serial-murderer culture' (again, the list could be extended almost indefinitely). Once one accepts the weaker sense of culture as meaning something like the general description of a very vague way of life or set of beliefs or everyday practices with their attendant value-systems, then, I believe, the term has begun to lose its purchase. Worse, I believe that the culture in whose history I am interested – the culture that is marked by what I think of as edifying growth – is itself endangered, threatened, derided.

How might I understand the term, then? Culture, I believe, is not a state of affairs, and therefore not a way of life or set of values that can be 'identified' or associated with a more or less stable collectivity that gains its identity through its sharing of those values as normative. Culture, I contend, is something that 'happens', something in the nature of an 'event'. It is episodic and rare; but it is recognised in terms of its capacity for edification, growth, *Bildung*. Insofar as it is concerned with growth or development, especially improving development, it involves not the identity of the self, but its transformation and thus its difference from itself. Given that it *enacts* the self in the form of an *undecidability* of identity, it is therefore opposed to any form of 'identity-politics' that would allow me to associate myself, however willingly, with, say, 'working-class culture', 'Glasgow culture', 'Irish culture', 'academic culture', 'boringly straight and white bourgeois British culture', or whatever other terms might properly be used to describe aspects of my biography.

In one way, then, neither I nor my works, such as they may be, have any relation at all with cultural studies; or, at best, the relation would be one of profound opposition. However, I and my works have (I think) consistently been interested in the episodic occurrences of culture, the 'events' that constitute the possibility of difference, the potential to be otherwise than one is. Here, it is important to make clear that an 'event', in these terms, is the something that happens when happening itself is entirely unpreprogrammed and unpredictable. An event, we might say, is what happens when we know that something is happening but we do not know what it is that is happening. The 'outcome' of the event is entirely unforeseeable, unpredictable. It is therefore not amenable to a categorisation or understanding that is available to us prior to the event.

An analogy might explain this further. Those of us involved in university education are by now tiresomely aware of the notion of the 'outcomes' of our teaching. It is part of the triumph of the managerialist ideology damaging education at the present time that we must be able, whenever we propose a new course of instruction, to predict with total certainty its 'outcomes': what the student who follows the course will be able to do after she has followed it. This, as we know – and as the managerialists (who are, of course, anything but managers, for they depend on supposedly 'neutral' systems to make decisions, afraid of making decisions themselves) will never concede – is anathema to education as such. An education that is worthy of the name cannot predict outcomes: it is part of the point of education that we do not know what will eventuate in our processes of thinking and working and experimenting. In this sense, education should be of the nature of the event: the Docherty who is there after reading and thinking about Joyce or Proust or Rilke or Woolf is different from the Docherty who was there before that activity; but the earlier Docherty could never have predicted what the later one might think – that was the point of the exercise of reading in the first place: to think things that were previously undreamt of in my philosophy. My contention is that the study of culture is open – historical – in this kind of way; but that cultural studies is too often complicit with the managerialist ethos that is afraid of history, afraid, fundamentally, of freedom.

Thus, more precisely still, culture would be an instance of growth in the sense of edifying improvement; but in a situation when we do not yet know what would constitute 'improvement' or betterment or edification. Culture is shocking, extraordinary, in that it calls to us to be other than we are. More, it calls us to be better than we are, in a situation where we do not yet know what would constitute the good, the better, the best: those are precisely the values that are being sought in and through the event that is cultural. It is like the shift in Kant between a reasoning that is grounded in determining judgement and a reasoning that is ungroundable, unfoundable, because it is actioned on reflective judgement. It is, to put this simply, what happens when I stand before a painting and feel translated, feel that the painting is not there for me, that it is from a world that is in a profound sense *inhuman*, beyond that which the human can presently comprehend. This culture takes the ordinary – looking at an image – and makes it extraordinary. For this, we need a certain receptiveness or humility: a belief that it might just be possible that we are not at the centre of the world, not at the centre indeed of *any* world, that the world is foreign to us and may not even be interested in us. It is that world into which culture calls to us to grow.

Against all this, cultural studies comes to me as a world with which I am all too familiar, a world that is human, all too human. In an obvious historical sense, there was indeed a project called cultural studies; and, in most official histories of the project, the origins lay in the work of Hoggart or Williams, came through Birmingham, and is carried on now not only in the line of direct descent (through to Stuart Hall, say), but also in the scattering far and wide of these seeds into the burgeoning development of departments of cultural studies in many leading universities worldwide. The influence of this project has been massive, pervasive. Indeed, it has led to the establishment of a whole new discipline. There was, very clearly, a political dimension to this project in its aim of dignifying the work and the thought of a class whose modes and mores seemed to be systematically excluded from the determinations of social value. This, essentially drawing attention to the profound strengths and extremely worthy values of a working class, was and remains admirable. It was and is a work of 'recovery': a making visible again that which has been systematically occluded and derided by a rival set of values or mores.

Yet there was also, I suggest, a reason for this development of the discipline that was less eminently ideological and more pressingly due to the happenstances of historical chance. It is a historical fact that not all university libraries are the same. Not all libraries can hold the same 'special collections'; and not all of them are copyright libraries. Those that are copyright libraries, or that have a lengthy history of collecting documents, are often the repositories of texts that require a certain kind of scholarly work. Thus, for instance, it used to be the case that many of the new PhDs in English during the middle part of the twentieth century would have been gained by the scholarly editing and preparation of a text that had not previously been widely available, or that had been available only in suspect editions. That kind of work would typically have been carried on in, say, Oxford's Bodleian library, where the history of the text and its variant corrupt editions could be worked on quite simply because the relevant documents were to hand. During the period of expansion, after the Robbins report, other universities offered the possibility of doing research; but their libraries were different in terms of the archives that they held from Bodley or other ancient copyright libraries. The work that could be done in Sussex or Essex or York or Warwick, say, was not primarily concerned with textual commentary (or 'scholarship'), but rather with textual *interpretation*. It is no real surprise, then, that the kinds of study that developed in such libraries would take a different turn; and that turn was the turn that led not just into interpretation and theory, but also the turn that led into more 'contemporary' studies in and through which a certain attitude to history itself began to prevail. This attitude ran counter to the 'antiquarian' and old historicist view associated with 'scholarship', and attended more firmly to making links between the past and the contemporary moment: it is in this context that the aesthetically inclined left (the left intellectuals) began to rest assured in the phrase, 'History tells us that …' as a means of analysing contemporary predicaments. At this point, one is not far removed from the presiding questions that governed cultural studies, with its attempts to recover a history that had been silenced, a 'history from below', a history as seen from the point of view of history's victims.

The influence of the project of cultural studies has been influential beyond the academy as well. The project is one that we can now all recognise very firmly: 'inclusion', one of the catchwords of the British 'New' Labour Party in its second term of office (2001–). The belief or governing assumption has been that there is something happening somewhere from which numbers of people have been excluded. That something might be literature, art; in a larger scale of things, it might be freedom and autonomy. In any case, it is ostensibly undemocratic if this is not shared. Leavis, who was Snow's adversary in the 1960s and since, and who himself had some influence on cultural studies (though often not explicitly acknowledged), had something to say on this. He repeatedly attacked what he saw as a bogus version of democracy, one based on 'the axiom that it is an offence against democracy to advocate for anybody anything that everybody can't have'.[1] Interestingly, Leavis identified this bogus notion of democracy as specifically 'American'; and one can surely see its presence still within the so-called 'politically correct' movement. It is precisely this bogus democracy that has shaped current British political 'thinking' (the term is rather too dignified, especially if applied to successive British ministers for education such as David Blunkett or Estelle Morris or Margaret Hodge) regarding 'social inclusion'.

In his analysis of the rise of cultural studies within the university-as-institution, Bill Readings offers a useful gloss on this. He alludes to the kind of move made by Antony Easthope when Easthope advocated the supposed 'paradigm-shift' from literary into cultural studies: and such a move was indeed one of the most frequent determinants of the shape of cultural studies, emerging as it did from disciplines such as 'English'. For Easthope, the world was best construed as the scene of a series of 'signifying practices'; and 'culture' was, effectively, everything and anything *so long as it was construed as signifying practice*. Thus *the signs of* everything and anything become grist to the mill of cultural studies. However, when culture becomes everything and anything in this way, it starts to lose any positive *content*, and becomes rather simply the *form* – the 'signature', if you will – in which we understand things. The shocking corollary, as Readings argues, is that cultural studies rises (gets its content, its classes, modules, presiding questions and research) in a kind of inverse proportion with culture itself (which is increasingly voided of specific material content, becoming reduced to what I have called the 'signatures' of culture). More important for present purposes, however, once cultural studies commits to this generalised notion of 'signifying practice' (a notion that effectively 'standardises' and homogenises the very difference that cultural studies is supposed to explore – and that 'standardises' it in ways that are perfectly consistent with the bureaucrats of 'quality assurance', itself the single greatest threat to substantive quality of education in recent times), then it 'can only oppose *exclusions* from culture'.[2] At this point, the *only* legitimate speaking position 'within' the culture is that which is located 'outside'. One can speak now *only* from a margin: to everyone her or his own victimisation – but a victimisation that is *purely* formal, and hence, being devoid of content also thereby devoid of politics. (It is interesting, in passing, to note that even the political right now assumes for itself precisely this position of victimhood; for it is only the victim who legitimately speaks in this predicament.)

The categories of these exclusions are now well established in cultural studies; and they are associated with gender, 'race', class, sexuality, and so on. The most important thing to note, however, is that these categories are firmly tied to an identity-politics – in many cases, quite simply to a personal biography – and that the critic who speaks of them assumes a structure of 'inclusion/exclusion' that shapes what will be legitimately and authoritatively sayable, or that shapes the content of what counts as 'knowledge'. Not only, then, is this predictable (and thus, in my terms, precisely anathema to knowledge), it is also complicit with a monumental view of the social, a view that suggests an *abstract* version of 'society' that has little or nothing to do with real historical societies. The latter are full of content and specifics; the former is vacuous and purely formal. And, as Benjamin and others associated with the Frankfurt School (whether on its margins or not) well knew in their historical position in the middle of twentieth-century Europe, the evacuation of content and the corollary prioritisation of form can become complicit with a mentality sympathetic to a certain fascism. I do not myself say precisely this here; but I do say that such a situation is complicit with the fear of thinking, the fear of historical change, the fear of decision-making or judgement, the fear of criticism – indeed, the fear that we might face a cultural event whose outcome would shock our identity or would simply allow us the freedom to be different and to offer the gift of difference that I prefer to call 'freedom' to others.

To reject, or to distance oneself in this way from the 'project' of cultural studies is, at the same time, to endorse the study of cultural events – and with it, I believe, to give a content back to politics.

RESPONSES TO QUESTIONS (5), (6) AND (7)

(5) Does cultural studies have any significance outside of the university at all? If so, what forms does this take?

(6) What is, has been, might be, or might have been, the significance of cultural studies within the university?

(7) Where is cultural studies *going*? This question is obviously tied to that of 'where has it *been*?' which is an interesting and important question itself; but I wonder where you think it *should* go, or what you think it should not try to do: in short, what has cultural studies 'achieved', what has it 'failed' to achieve, and to what extent are these 'failures' inevitable, structural, or is it just that their realisation is only a matter of time or strategy?

In the light of what I have suggested above – where I endorse the view that cultural studies rises at the cost of culture itself – it would follow, I think, that cultural studies could have significance *only* 'outside' the university (in ways that I have identified in relation to British governmental policy, say). The logic of the question is in some ways itself expressive of the limiting strictures of cultural studies in its 'place-logic' of inclusion/exclusion, inside/outside, centre/periphery. In my own thinking, for what it is worth, I don't see that there *is* an 'inside' to a university (even if less than a majority of the population come to classes organised by such institutions). I suspect that what governs this question is, in fact, the predicament facing arts, humanities, and aesthetics more generally in our current social and political environment: the twin demands that we make these disciplines 'available' to all, and that we make them serve certain immediately instrumental financial ends.

It would make less sense to pose the same question to a bioscientist, I think; for the 'cultures' with which she/he works are cultures that very definitely impinge on life outside the walls of the laboratory, even if the technical aspects of her/his work remain specialised, inaccessible or even unavailable to those of us who do not spend much time inside those laboratory walls or inside that realm of work and its attendant vocabularies. I must say that I, for one, prefer my bio-scientists to be extremely specialised, even in ways that might exclude me from any detailed knowledge of what is going on in their treatment of my illnesses, say. I would probably have less trust in those bioscientists who argued that their technical knowledge, gleaned over (let us say) 30 years or more of extremely dedicated work, was immediately accessible to me, decidedly not in possession of such knowledge. To say the least, I would feel patronised; and behind that patronising attitude lurks the very 'elitism' that 'access' to education is supposedly countering; for he who patronises me is reassuring me in my condition of mediocrity with respect to his spe-cialised knowledge. In assimilating 'the everyday' as a means explicitly of bringing 'culture' to all (and everyone has an 'everyday'), cultural studies is complicit with this reassurance of mediocrity. Worse, in reassuring everyone that their 'everyday life' is itself culturally valid and dignified, cultural studies removes the reason for valid and substantive political struggle from those whose everyday life is anything but a fulfilment of their life-possibilities.

The fact that the language of criticism, or the language in which we might properly and sensibly discuss literary history (or the history of other arts), is a specialised language and not *immediately* available to those 'outside' is, of course, a pseudo-problem; and the idea of 'widening participation' in the interests of something called 'access' is a pseudo-reply to this pseudo-problem.

My own stance on this is, effectively, simple. The study of cultural events is, of necessity, difficult; and this is especially so if it is accepted that culture is episodic and rare in the ways I have discussed above. The pretended 'access' to education goes hand in hand with the bogus 'democratisation' of education that happens under the sign of cultural studies, in which everything is grist to the mill of 'study'. Both are complicit with an evasion of the real issue that they fear, which is the question of what we might call 'access to freedom'.

In adopting the view that everything and anything, construed as signifying practice, is amenable to study, we sell the pass to a certain philistinism in which it becomes acceptable to deny people access to, say, the writings of Eliot (T.S. and George) or Beckett, or to the music of Mozart and Beethoven and Stravinsky, or to the painting of Braque or Picasso or Pollock and so on (the examples are all random, and might be infinitely extended) – and all this in a university situation. The consequence is that 'university' becomes a continuation of everyday life by other means; and everyday life is precisely where culture cannot happen – else it would, by my definition, not be 'everyday' or 'ordinary'.

The diagnosis that I advance here, then, suggests that cultural studies has achieved little in the way of emancipation of people; rather, it has fulfilled the desires of the political right that would limit such freedom. This is a dismal diagnosis, especially since (as I have suggested) such a failure is intrinsic or structural to the project itself. It is, in my own view, a fallacy to imagine that a 'radical' or 'critical' teaching 'within' the university has any real political purchase 'outside', even and especially if what is being studied 'inside' is effectively the same kinds of activity that constitute 'everyday life' in a realm 'outside'.

Nor do I expect there to be a seamless continuity between my activities as an academic researcher and teacher and other aspects of my biography. Thus, I believe that it is perfectly possible for me to advocate, let us say, 'tolerance', while at the same time trying to ensure that people do not have to tolerate repressive regimes, such as those established in totalitarian states or in monarchies. I do not ask that my teaching of *King Lear*, say, should mesh into a seamless continuity with whatever letters I might write to the national press lamenting the fact that the British parliament can be recalled from its recess when the Queen's mother dies (what, exactly, was there to debate?) while no debate takes place over the possibility that Britain might slavishly follow the US into a war against Iraq (which at least is a topic worthy of discussion). These are separable realms, even if my goal in both types of engagement (teaching, letter-writing) has the obvious overlap in that both are concerned to validate and to extend freedom and autonomy. In that they are separable, one might talk not so much of the 'inside' of a university, but rather of its special tasks or priorities, tasks that are highly specific to its purpose.

It is in this sense that I want to claim that the study of culture (which, as an event, is more likely to happen when engaging T.S. Eliot or Chinau Achebe, say, than when engaging 'graphic novels' or the lyrics and dance movements of boy/girl bands, say) has a primary place 'within' the activities of a university, even if not actually 'inside' such a space. I have claimed that culture is associated with a kind of edifying growth or with a development of people that is associated with *Bildung*, *formation*, 'education'. It would follow from this that an institution whose primary task is education might have a special role to play in relation to the study of culture.

Universities, I wish to suggest, have a primary responsibility to *make culture happen*. That is, it is the responsibility of the university, as an institution in which research and teaching are properly combined, to be forever ensuring and enabling the freedom of those who engage with its teaching and research. Perhaps needless to say, this is hardly what happens in most contemporary universities. In common with most of the so-called 'developed' or 'advanced' world, we suffer in Britain from a political attitude to education that is structurally opposed to its cultural possibilities or its potential to free people. By this, I do not mean merely to suggest that all political parties are now in agreement ideologically with the Conservatives, or the 'stupid party'; rather, I mean to suggest that the attitude to education that prevails, governed by an instrumental attitude to knowledge and by an ethics of individual greed (you go to university to get a better-paid job and one that serves straightforwardly and immediately the economic end of making money for the sake of making money or for the sake of increasing one's own salary), is one that is, strictly speaking, inimical to education as such – and certainly is structurally opposed to cultural events. As long as the university continues to renege – or be forced to renege – on its task of education, we will continue to lose culture; and British 'education' can effectively be one in which knowledge is reduced to the contents of the game-show or quiz, most especially the game-show driven by the hot pursuit of personal financial gain, or greed. It is not entirely surprising to discover that government money is now being used to sponsor *Who Wants to be a Millionaire?* – and this in the name of education. By no stretch of the imagination might such a programme be called 'culture', in my view.

In such a state of affairs, culture – that unforeseen growth or development of the self, another word for which is simply 'thinking' – is impossible. Insofar as cultural studies sees itself as an 'instrumental' kind of university programme – that is, insofar as it believes that it has a *political purchase* beyond the purpose of education, or insofar as it proceeds on the assumption that it is instrumental in effecting political change – then it, too, is complicit with the demise of culture.

In the light of the foregoing, cultural studies becomes itself part of a more general problem; yet it does not follow that, in preferring the notion of 'the study of cultural events', we should entirely reject all that cultural studies is and has been. It might be useful to consider cultural studies as the site of what Agamben thinks of as a potentiality. Agamben notes that there are two ways of construing potential (and in this he is following Aristotle). One kind of potential is an energy that gets used up or exhausted in realisation, as it were: the potentiality in my boyish body, say, to become manly. If or when it does become manly, it is no longer boyish: the condition of manliness, in realising itself, exhausts the potential that was there in the boyish body. Against this is a more interesting potential, such as the potential of the poet to write poems. In this kind, the potential to write is not exhausted once the poet writes her poem, but remains still as potential. Further, she is still a poet even if, at the moment, she is not writing a poem – not realising the potential in an artefact. It follows from this that, in this kind of potentiality, the potential to be must maintain the potential not-to-be.

Following this, we might say that we have two separate kinds of choice. On one hand, we might advocate a potential that is exhausted in its realisation of itself: this is the description of the instrumental knowledge that shapes not only philistinism, but also cultural studies. On the other, we have the possibility of opening ourselves to culture as potentiality; and in this, we become like poets in the sense that we do not exhaust culture in its realisation, but rather acknowledge that its realisation is grounded in the very possibility that it might not come about at all – that culture faces the great literary question of modernity itself: to be or not to be. If we follow this route, then culture becomes a *poiesis*, a making that is endless, endlessly different, and thus endlessly free.

Finally, this conception of freedom is one that is based less on our power to bring things about and more on our capacity to acknowledge our limitations. For it is only by acknowledging that there are such limitations that we might have the humility required to respond to the event that is culture. Such a response is our responsibility.

NOTES

1. F.R. Leavis, *The Critic as Anti-Philosopher* (London: Chatto and Windus, 1982), p. 160.
2. Bill Readings, *The University in Ruins* (Cambridge, MA and London: Harvard University Press, 1996), p. 102.

15   Unruly Fugues

Lynette Hunter

Legend

c. The written explanatory matter accompanying an illustration, map, etc. Also attrib., as legend-line. (*OED*)

THE MUSEUM

As with other museum pieces, the sections in this commentary are accompanied by a legend, which are as effacing and illuminating as most of those little bits of card placed alongside museum exhibits. They pose seven assumptions about cultural studies in the UK with which I'll try to engage:

1. Cultural studies has a) no position and b) no text [and c) no history].

No position

2. Cultural studies is banal or cynical: a convenient way of finding an institutional name for theory which is a) metadiscursive and therefore without material, and b) interdisciplinary and therefore with no content.

3. Cultural studies is narcissistic: only interested in special interest groups concerned to add to their own 'special rights'.

4. Cultural studies is melancholic and bitter: the acceptable face of a psychologistic understanding that underwrites essential humanism, that desire is *necessary* and that identity *is* difference.

No text

5. Cultural studies is thematic: recognising that social and historical context are missing to many textual analyses, yet adding them without rhetorical understanding or textual work.

6. Cultural studies is either technical or transcendent: the place where people go when they feel guilty about not dealing first hand with people or the natural world.

7. Cultural studies is about endless deferral: the place where people go when they get frightened of moral labour, ethical commitment and of things they can't articulate.

Cultural studies has no position

Cultural studies is banal or cynical: a convenient way of finding an institutional name for theory which is a) metadiscursive and therefore without material, and b) interdisciplinary and therefore with no content.

The assumption derives from the sense that cultural studies has no material social context. Yet historically this is questionable. The scientistic moves by the 'arts' (i.e., critics) to legitimate themselves shortly after universities expanded in the UK at the end of the nineteenth and beginning of the twentieth century, such as definitive bibliography or practical criticism, crumbled by mid-century. They were replaced by philosophical systems such as Leavis', yet the gap was more ardently filled by the theoretical developments of post-war European thinkers such as Lévi-Strauss, Jakobson, Lacan, Foucault, Derrida. We know this history, but it had institutional implications that are less well-worked.

I am not an historian of education, but what I saw was that people in many disciplinary areas became interested in the theoretical developments, attended interdisciplinary discussion groups that in effect threatened their disciplinary base. But the second rapid expansion of universities in the UK in the 1960s–1970s led to massive changes in the use of architectural space separating different areas of thinking from each other, to huge numbers of students that upset the balance of discussion and teaching and research, and to the stringent cutbacks of the 1980s – all of which sent many people scuttling back into their baseline disciplines.

But the experience proved the value of the discourse.

From my own perspective the cultural studies project is to provide an account of the rhetoric of culture, which means that it is entwined with an analysis of current modes of western democracy. This is only one way of looking at cultural studies, but I will argue that using rhetoric as a tool to think about cultural studies allows one to work in other areas than the ideological and hegemonic. Recognising the rhetorical work in cultural studies reminds us not only that culture is rooted in society and history but also that it is messy. It reminds us that discourse is a largely man-made field around which are many other environments. I would like to pursue its effects specifically in the area of situated knowledge and textuality.

The work of cultural studies on the rhetoric of culture is similar to that by other fields in discourse studies such as gender studies, or studies in ethnicity, although to some extent it has come to be the site where coherent theoretical developments in all these areas are explored. Cultural studies arose in its present incarnation as a response to the determinism of New Marxism, especially Althusser. After its elaboration of cultural state apparatuses, its main insight was that not all elements of social relations were interpellated, not all elements of a person were 'called' or hailed. Cultural studies was working from an attempt to account for social change, and its discourse came to offer a rhetoric that promised social change.

Within an Althusserian framework, ideology and the subject engage in a set of relations constrained by representation. There are problems with this that we now see more clearly:

1. subjects are citizens but many people are not full citizens, hence do not stand before the law in the same way

2. subjects are never fully represented by representations, and are therefore always already lacking and in different ways

3. ideology needs stability in order to project representations, stability to maintain society and more importantly markets; such stability is guaranteed in most western nation-states by the family, but this varies from nation to nation with obvious differences challenging stability – although some obvious differences can also maintain stability by becoming the depraved 'other'.

(False) consciousness is the fiction that all this is stable and determined: a Freudian model developed to explain bourgeois necessity/a capitalist model developed to explain psychoanalytic necessity.

Yet although retrospectively problematic, it was an enormously courageous political gesture that was attempting to assault the authoritarian/anarchic divide that characterised much of early twentieth-century political thinking in the West. That divide encouraged the illusion that individuals could operate in isolation, which may have nauseated Sartre but inspired many others. The divide also encouraged the illusion that authority existed independent of the individual. By insisting on a relation between authority and the individual, even the determinist subject–ideology relation of representation, New Marxism was insisting on a different kind of social interaction and responsibility. Indeed it now looks very honest, precisely because we have come to recognise more overtly that it is only applicable to those citizens who already have power.

The heart of this political gesture was to provide a discourse, a vocabulary, grammar and semantics, that insisted on the relation between authority and the individual, the state apparatus and human beings. Yet what I see as the enforced retreat back to disciplinary bases left a sense that this area of discussion was metadiscursive and divorced from practical issues. That metadiscursiveness had made interdisciplinarity possible – taking over from Latin and then science – with 'discourse'. However, if metadiscursiveness is held to be inherently divorced from practical issues, not only does discourse become metadiscourse but interdisciplinarity loses its content: if interdisciplinarity is held to be inherently divorced from practical issues not only does it lose its content, but discourse becomes metadiscourse. The debate, interestingly, had itself provided the vocabulary to describe this event. Cultural studies as it came to be called, or discourse studies more broadly, was a postmodern simulacrum. Cultural studies was 'merely playing games with words'.

Cultural studies follows no different a path than many other institutional disciplines, yet its material reason for practice is to work in an interdisciplinary mode. Hence the apparently inexorable stability it acquires as it becomes part of the nation-state structure of education, demands that it become represented. Once represented it necessarily also puts itself under constraint, because representation makes subjects of us all. Under constraint its political effectiveness may be rendered banal, and may generate Magazine-cultural studies: cultural studies for the cynics, those who have power (or think they should have power) but can't use it (or can't use it effectively).

Nevertheless, cultural studies also acquires a position, the hegemonic power to speak to and have an impact on state power. Some of those unruly people who survived came to offer a rhetoric that promised social change.

Cultural studies is narcissistic: only interested in special interest groups concerned to add to their own 'special rights'.

If cultural studies understands that 1) not all people are subjects/ed in the same way, 2) that the partiality of representation accounted for desire, and 3) that state power is always two-way even if constrained, it deals to a large degree with 'fit'. Fit is what keeps ideology stable, and cultural studies has often worked by turning to specific fields such as race, gender, and sometimes class, which for the moment of the end of the twentieth and the beginning of the twenty-first century at least, present elements which are radically unfit.

As an institutional discipline cultural studies will have no necessary focus of fit to which to turn, yet it has never looked to the hegemonic activity of its own interdisciplinary mode to articulate the fittingness of its studies. For institutional political reasons its ethos echoes that of other disciplines and is self-evident. In effect it has been left to the cultural studies worker to deal with fit, and I am uneasy about the neglect of the rhetorical effect of relation between the 'discipline' and the worker, a neglect which mimics the author-itarian/anarchic divide. In order to recognise the central issues, the individual people working on cultural studies have had to choose to respond to a field of the fit/unfit, often recognising something in their own lives that didn't fit.

Who were these workers? People in positions of some privilege, because integrated into higher education, yet also often people from particular backgrounds with particular issues that didn't fit. Cultural studies is partly a response to democracy in first world western states where economic imperialism has constructed a standard of living high enough to promote class mobility for diverse groups. It is no surprise that in the UK cultural studies becomes instituted after the effects of 1968 became interpreted: that people who had moved into positions of relative power in terms of the vote, of income etc., made apparently little difference. Cultural studies is there partly to work out why this is so, and partly to argue for the right to that effective-ness by valuing the cultures of the newly 'empowered'.

Cultural studies workers were and are partly motivated or impelled by ideologically problematic issues, elements of society that for a wide variety of complex reasons come to the fore and urge their unfittingness on us – and to that extent are assimilated into the ideological process. Stuart Hall, and later Laclau and Mouffe, are good examples of people who shifted the ground for cultural studies and made the interaction with the ideological hegemonic not determinist, in effect replacing 'ideology' with 'discourse'.

Since cultural studies is fundamentally engaged with nation-state politics, wanting to provide the vocabulary that makes possible the representation of those particulars of life that don't fit, to that extent it is not only challenging the ideological status quo, but also constructing it. It is rhetorically agonistic because it is always bound to the grounds it challenges. Yet it carries on the perception of New Marxism that revolution simply perpetuates repression, and develops a politics of the intellectual (highly unconventional in the UK), the licensed challenger of the state, always compromised but also highly effective. We could say that such activity is overdetermined by the ideological issues with which it engages, but this would not account for the change it both describes, un-writes, and in de-scribing affects and effects.

What limits and censors cultural studies is how people deal with the sense of 'fit'. Workers in cultural studies are working from their sense of subjectivity and what has been excluded from it, what cannot be represented, what does not fit. One example might be the bisexual person who in effect lives a life of bisexuality that cannot be represented in current representation. Not that this bisexual life doesn't happen, but that it has no vocabulary of recognition. In cultural studies this seems to pose a splitting of the ways: that nonrepresentation may be thought of as a 'lack' or a 'gap' that fuels empty desire, but it may also be thought of as a lived life with social and political consequences. In either case, to deal with those consequences, the life needs to become visible and audible. With the former, finding vocabulary all too often loses materiality, duplicates the rhetoric of ideology and leaves discourse to be assimilated; while with the latter the situatedness of the life can be more rhetorically effective by building vocabulary that insists that that person becomes integral, necessarily shifting the form of representation itself.

At the same time the process of 'adding to' the special rights of the disempowered does not address the problem of the 'natural rights' of privileged men at the heart of the social contract that binds western nation-states. As Pateman argues, the existence of 'natural rights' makes 'special rights' necessary to deal with exclusion, disempowerment and lack of equity.[1] The weakness of 'special rights' is precisely that they are allocated to a special case. The people with 'special rights' are in fact the privileged, because they have rights not accorded to anyone else. Because of its institutional rhetoric cultural studies may be seen to be narcissistically arguing for the special rights of particular groups already partly assimilated into ideological representation, rather than speaking from a position of partial disempowerment, exercising its democratic right to be heard and thereby inventing an articulacy for hegemonic integration.

My argument would be that hegemonic articulacy deals with the 'unfittingness' of people mainly in terms of desire and is left helpless with the sense of inadequacy, whereas it derives its effectiveness from unacknowledged situated labour on the textuality of the particular lived experience that articulates need.

Laclau and Mouffe's concept of articulacy,[2] which as I indicate here is different from 'articulation', is fundamental to the concept of the individual being unrepresented, to a part of their lives being 'under erasure'. In this, cultural studies adopts the critique from psychoanalysis that as subjects, individuals can never be fully represented and are therefore always already with a loss or gap or absence. Stuart Hall describes the steps taken by Foucault in moving from the 'transparent' or fully represented subject to the individual with an identity 'operating "under erasure"'.[3] He argues that we still have to think in these terms because it allows us to write in agency and politics. For Hall current discussions of identity 'attempt to rearticulate the relationship between subjects and discursive practices'.[4] This is 'the point of *suture*'.[5] At the same time the psychoanalytic artefact of desire skinned over by this suture brings its own problems.

Cultural studies is melancholic and bitter: the acceptable face of a psychologistic understanding that underwrites essential humanism, that desire is necessary and that identity is difference.

Desire is the unrepresentable, the lack. If desire becomes representable, does it become something else? Has the strategy, where successful, of finding vocabulary and acceptance for previously outlawed sexualities made them no longer part of 'desire'? Is the representability of desire a self-conscious choice to defer, to make secret, to maintain individual isolation and guarantee essence? As Catherine Belsey argues in rehearsing Freud's commentary on the death drive: it entices us beyond pleasure yet that movement is in itself pleasurable.[6] Do we in effect desire 'desire'? Do we make it exist to explain change? Is it more fun because it is secret? Does it promise, in its unknowableness, heroism? desire as necessary because it guarantees our identity: an identity that by the presence/absence of a particular desire is different from others, and hence essentialist?

On the other hand do we resist realising desire or, in effect, does deferral have more to do with the frustration of knowing the inadequacy of that realisation? that articulacy is in effect another representation, and by definition inadequate since inadequacy is what makes it a representation? Is it because the articulacy is a social act, and we know that the community to whom the representation becomes available isn't getting the whole story? that articulacy realises only at the cost of constituting a representation, with its own shadows of exclusion? generating melancholy and bitterness?

Another way of looking at this is to remember that very large numbers of people live lives partially if not mainly outwith representation. Does this mean that their whole lives are 'desire'? or are they completely without desire? Can they articulate their lives if representation is wholly inadequate to the realisation? Well, I guess I think they/we/I can, but it's difficult to account for within the predominant model of ideology/hegemony. Cultural studies workers appear to recognise this, and initiated by the spreading democratic franchises of the twentieth century, have built a highly contradictory location for work on identity where people attempt to devise guidelines for thinking about human beings-in-proximity. That contradiction is helpful in addressing state structures of power, but is often at a loss when faced with the messiness of lived lives.

Belsey notes:

> The signifiable, translated to the realm of signification and momentarily, provisionally and ultimately ineffectually 'fixed' as the signified, undergoes the pain of a loss, a kind of death; the experience of the part reappears in the present tense as merely differential and differentiated: Other than it is, no more than the lost cause of its own representation.[7]

Yes, but: another way of looking at this is through the textual labour that has pursued signification, thrown out lines of realisation, worked with others on articulation. Belsey continues saying that this status of the signifier necessitates interpretation, however precarious, uncertain, provisional, and that 'what is lost when a need is formulated as a demand reappears as desire'.[8] Yes, but: what's also there is that if need is formulated through locatedness, a situated textuality, it does not become a loss or a desire. It makes something. Shifts modality.

The status of the signifier in representation is one of inadequacy, necessary failure. This status will ensure its failure and its construction of desire. Yet just as we may choose to understand that the signifier is inadequate, as have many conventions of post-Cartesian language studies, so we may choose to understand that the signifier is instead, as Wittgenstein and others have suggested, limited, not referring to something else but making itself into significance in the engagement with writer and reader.[9] If the signifier is limited, inadequacy is not an issue. Nor is failure. Nor is desire-as-lack.

I remember when I, along with many other people, felt completely overdetermined by ideology. I remember working with such contradiction and stress to understand the processes of discursive interaction that eventually became called hegemony. And I remember the frustration of then feeling overdetermined by hegemonic complicity (see Macdonell). But I also remember when I first had the opportunity of working with others on a particular need, something so urgently pressing that we had to engage with its articulation, and realising that this work, although it didn't get rid of ideology and hegemony, simply happened in a different location and with a different rhetoric (Hunter).

Cultural studies without situatedness becomes cynical, banal, narcissistic, melancholic and bitter. It needs location and partiality. Hall suggests that the critique that describes the cultural studies balancing act between ideology and hegemony, between representation and desire, derives from a combination of location and of psychoanalysis that has turned to deconstruction, Belsey's 'precarious, uncertain, provisional'. He adds that, since

> they have not been superceded dialectically, and there are no other, entirely different concepts with which to replace them, there is nothing to do but to continue to think with them – albeit now in their detotalized or deconstructed forms ...[10]

There are probably no 'entirely different concepts' because concepts are spoken in language, and language is always related. But there is another way of looking at this: from the position of rhetoric and situated textuality.

Cultural studies has no text

Cultural Studies is thematic: recognising that social and historical context are missing to many textual analyses, yet adding them without rhetorical understanding or textual work.

The idea that cultural studies is 'merely playing games with words' largely derives from an understanding that cultural studies is *the* postmodern phenomenon. And postmodernism is a radical challenge to cultural representations, both antagonistic and agonistic, that frequently discards 'history' in order to sever inappropriate referential links. In this it is perceived not to be doing anything different, but merely breaking down what is there. The view is endemic in some political environments where the possibility that the truth of representation is not absolute has led to a tide of absolutist irony: irony that defines all common ground as groundless, all difference as the same. I rarely recognise this kind of postmodernism in the culture of third or fourth world communities. 'Post-colonial' cultures have always lived with a knowledge of the co-existence of different common grounds, difference fostered differently in different places.

If cultural studies is perceived to be merely playing games with words, and not about their incarnation or realisation, then doing cultural studies implies that you are not connected to society, you are just free-floating along the surface. Cultural studies is partly responsible for this because methodologically, just as it has not paid much attention to the relationship between the institution and the cultural studies worker and the resulting implications for ethos/pathos/stance, neither has it paid enough attention to the way it describes texts or textualities. It tends to remain discursive rather than pursue other rhetorical space and stance. I would argue that cultural studies workers recognise precisely that social and historical context are missing from much textual work, but that without an understanding of rhetoric, adding them in leaves them thematic rather than material.

Rhetoric is a word that encompasses all communication in social and historical contexts. Discourse describes part of rhetoric, as does classical political rhetoric to which discourse is intimately related, and as do also Biblical rhetoric, storytelling, poetics and many others. Discursive rhetoric is bound to representation, to shifting it, to altering it, to the agonistic processes of articulacy. It contributes directly to that part of rhetorical study that is concerned with nation-state democracy, and throws into relief the current shift to more democratic rhetorics just as did the civic rhetoric of the sixteenth century. The results of discursive rhetoric are highly effective in immediate political terms because those institutions with effective power can hear what is being said and recognise grounds they understand. They can therefore approach and listen to, if not welcome, the argument. But the discursive is locked into its particular field, the grounds of nation-state ideology. It doesn't look to other modes of rhetoric for help with working outside the double-bind – perhaps because it does not know this is possible, or perhaps because it is simply not aware of them.

Many of the inspirations for cultural studies, such as Michel Foucault or Jacques Derrida, are steeped in rhetoric. Although not interested in using the same elements, they both draw on an extensive methodology. And there are pros and cons: 'rhetoric' as a discipline is heavily influenced by classical rhetoric. For example, Althusserian determinism depends on the classical paradigm of scientific rhetoric for its model of power, and Derrida still has difficulty imagining an individual who is not primarily subjected.[11] On the other hand Foucault's shift of position in the 1970s was a shift made possible by simply stepping sideways out of classical rhetoric. But you can't do that if you don't know it's there.

A distinguishing feature of UK cultural studies, despite Raymond Williams, is that most people make little even implicit reference to rhetoric, classical or not, whereas it pervades European and North American studies. Again this has pros and cons: classical rhetoric was the primary discursive structure in which anyone who held power in western Europe, and then in its colonies, was educated for at least ten years of their life, from the medieval period onward. Knowledge of it can be smothering, suffocating, ideologically binding, and you can never leave it completely behind. But once you recognise that it's there you can begin to see/hear/taste/feel if not smell, its extents, its fallings off, its abrupt cessations.

Belsey describes the effect of discursive rhetoric on 'Traditional cultural history' as 'The more totalizing the narrative, the more readable the history': the more thematic the content, I would add. She argues that for a 'material practice' we need 'history at the level of the signifier',[12] and reading that pays attention to the text:

Culture resides primarily in the representations of the world exchanged, negotiated and, indeed, contested in a society. Some of these representations may coincide with existing practices; they may determine or legitimate them; or alternatively, they may challenge them. Representations are not, however, purely discursive; they also have, in my mind, their own materiality. That is to say, culture is in its way *lived*.[13]

If, as Belsey claims, cultural history acknowledges the gap between the past and the present[14] it is 'not in consequence empty, a blank sheet, or a self-proclaimed fiction, … because we *make* a relation, in both senses of that term, out of *our* reading practices and *their* documents'.[15] This attention to textuality is part of what situates the work socially and historically in a material location. Without it the thematic focus may leave the work banal.

Cultural studies is either technical or transcendent: the place where people go when they feel guilty about not dealing first hand with people or the natural world.

The move to deal with people or the natural world may have a political impetus, which is often misplaced in the sense that work on the material text, whatever it is, is always 'lived' and therefore political. But cultural studies work is also often scientistic in its textuality. Science treats language as if it were necessarily inadequate, which is not surprising since modern science has its roots also in classical political rhetoric. The writer of science usually assumes that words will fail to describe the experience of the experiment, hence the focus on informing the reader of how the experiment can be replicated so that we can experience it for ourselves. The words do not acknowledge the difference between signifier and reality, they are simply there to convey information about how to reproduce that reality. Occasionally the science writer writes in the transcendent mode typical of hegemonic poetics, which recognises the inadequacy of language as only surpassable by some heroic gesture of verbal transcendence: the mainstay of modern aesthetics.

It may be significant that people who have tried to position themselves socially and historically with respect to science are not often thought of as doing cultural studies. Donna Haraway, Sandra Harding, Hilary Rose, are not doing cultural studies but SSST: Social Studies of Science and Technology. There is no cultural studies of 'poverty', as if some conditions implicitly cannot afford irony – a rhetorical stance that maintains what it critiques – as if cultural studies cannot contemplate the possibility that poverty may not go away within the structure of the double-bind.

Furthermore, people who deal with other cultures are anthropologists or ethnologists, not cultural studies workers. Cultural studies workers often position themselves to talk about what they know, and cultural studies is often most satisfying when dealing with its own difference from the representable. Just as it seems less willing to engage with other cultures, it is arguably not as helpful when dealing with the differences we construct in our engagement with others. Belsey indicates her uneasiness with a similar issue but challenges it to engage, saying that cultural historians should be archaeologists, dealing not with synchronicity (ethnology) nor with similarity (anthropology) but with the medium of temporal and spatial difference.

But there is another way of looking at this, for we know that the classical political rhetoric which envelops so many western nation-states does not work in many social and political environments. If we know, not necessarily even as specific knowledge but as tacit knowledge, that the culture and society does not fit, and that rather than having to make it fit there's another place to inhabit, then the work shifts its location. But the rhetorical structures of this kind of work are difficult to pin down. Their usual premise, the value of their own difference, can be similar to that of the cult, but cults assume that once on the inside sameness predominates. Alternatively, the rhetoric can work from the tacit into strategies and a stance close to those enacted by people working on situated knowledge. But no knowledge exists without textuality, and textuality shifts the premise of the work: from the value of its own difference to the recognition that it exists to make difference, both its own and others, and hence must value both.

Cultural studies is about endless deferral: the place where people go when they get frightened of moral labour, ethical commitment and of things they can't articulate.

There is a sense in which deconstruction is sometimes read as 'endless' deferral. Stuart Hall speaks of the need for 'arbitrary closure'[16] in order to make agency possible in these circumstances. Without moments of closure, deferral becomes the 'mise en abyme' necessitated by the tautological structure of ideology, representation and the subject. Deferral makes possible the artefact of desire central to hegemony and discourse. Belsey argues, despite her insistence on the material, the lived, the reading of text and the making of a relation, that we can only analyse the signifier. It is analysis 'in which not only the real, but meaning too, while not simply lost, is forever differed and deferred'.[17] But the real that is made in the process of reading the signifiers, no matter whether these be words or gestures or signs in any other medium, is what I call articulation. With articulation we do not analyse the signifier but articulate our process of the construction of difference. Difference isn't just there, we make it. Difference is not only the gap in representation which a certain kind of difference certainly is, but a particular thing made by us in our negotiations and recognitions of others.

A strategy for deferral is to attain agency by temporarily halting its movement, which is perfectly legitimate and often useful, but doesn't do much to representation. Such transcendence is not necessarily an attempt at transparency, yet neither is it attuned to difference, ambiguity and partiality. If we work instead with an understanding (which we put under the work in order for it to have a ground to stand on) of language as limited like most human things are, rather than inadequate, then articulation *is* action, and different positions of articulation will lead to different kinds of action. If desire becomes the marker of the place where we recognise need, it may also become the place where we meet others and negotiate articulations and make differences. Although poetics is historically the place were people go to articulate something important to them that has as yet no mediation, cultural studies is where people go when they want that articulation to participate in a wider social world. In both cases, unless they are situated the articulation will buy into representation in ways that assimilate the individual.

Nicole Brossard describes the rituals of the process of reading as a) 'trembling' or the recognition of/by the body, b) 'shock' or the consciousness of the suffocating texture of representative words (traditional aesthetics), c) 'sliding' or an intense need to work the skin of the text to a revised ecosystem, what she elsewhere calls the 'holograph', and d) 'breath': the stage for the performance of our reinvention.[18] Reading Brossard's writing is about altering our body memory. We have to learn to breathe with the text, slowly, arresting time, unhinging the representative functions of words, their sounds, their look, their collocations, their syntax and grammar, nudging them into more appropriate articulation. This we do because the writer is also breathing with the text, through that huge second lung: the skin, the texture of syntax, grammar, wordplay, phonics, and embodying it into different extents and shapes so that we together negotiate its language. The process of doing so, this rhetorical work on textuality, responds to present need and makes the intimate and public social relations of our situatedness. It may also, as another effect, distort representation, torsion it at the surface of containment, and make an impact on discursive power.

Brossard for many years has worked with an idea of 'fiction-theory'[19] that does not represent but gives birth to the 'holograph'.[20] It is a holograph because from the discursive position it cannot be translated beyond the frame of hegemony. However if we look at it another way, and think of it in terms of situated textuality, the holograph becomes the structure of another location in which activities happen in a different mode. Discourse does not go away, but its power to define identity, to limit it to agonistic relations with representations, is diminished because we recognise that this is happening in a particular space that does not make up the whole of social rhetoric. The situated becomes a place where what we 'live', the materiality of our relations, articulates the differences we make ourselves into.

The rhetoric of situated textuality suggests not that we are different as a condition of identity, but that we form communities by making the differences between and among ourselves. The former implies that discourse 'does' difference to us, the latter that difference is something we work on in order to communicate and that it affects/effects our culture. Cultural studies could also go in this direction. To do so would add to its capacity for important but short-term effects, an array of long-term strategies, and there are many instances where this would not be appropriate. But there are also many instances where nothing will happen if someone doesn't turn their mind to stepping out of the discursive frame.

THE ARTEFACT

Cultural studies is only valuable insofar as it is positioned and has a text, and therefore engages with history. One way of looking at this activity is to insist on its rhetoricity. By virtue of being instituted it is listened to by institutions and hence by nation-state politics, but it is only effective if it remains an unruly discipline: a) if it is metadiscursive, its helpfulness is only from its material knowledge, and b) if it is interdisciplinary it is currently one of our few ways of understanding the material connections and differences between diverse areas of thought and culture. It derives its strength from individual cultural studies workers speaking from or to some position of exclusion and exercising the democratic right to be heard, hence it has to invent articulacy. In doing so it throws into relief the current shift to more democratic rhetorics, and locates highly contradictory work on identity, initiated by the spreading democratic franchises, where people attempt to devise guidelines for valuing human-beings-in-proximity even for elements in their lives that devalue their citizenship and subjectivity in the eyes of the state. Cultural studies recognises the need to engage with the material field of society and what it makes of history and nature, and the importance of articulating the differences that are made. However, without a sense of the situated labour that goes into articulation and the rhetorical stance of situated textuality, articulacy remains in the double-bind of ideology/hegemony, of representation and desire.

Some cultural studies attempts situated textuality, and some doesn't. Why is a different matter.

A MUSING (ON WHAT HAPPENS TO THINGS BEFORE THEY GET INTO THE MUSEUM)

Three interesting patterns around current cultural studies are: 1) the analysis of the impact of GSAs on ISAs and individuals, and vice versa; 2) the exploration of the mechanisms of hegemonic power and/or the discursive structures of representation in the changing economic situation; and 3) the engagement with practices (our own and/or others') that do not get recognised by representations/subjectivities yet which realise us as human beings.

Cultural studies has not been very keen to look outside the cultural boundaries of its practitioners, possibly because it is not well equipped to do so, but there is no reason why it should not. Cultural studies is exceptionally good at understanding how state power works, and is becoming better at understanding how global economic power works. But just as Marxism had to acquire an understanding of the interconnection of other social, cultural, political structures with the economics of the nation state, so we need to acquire an understanding of the interconnection of these elements with global economics: a theory of the GSAs if you like (I think I would be prepared to argue that global organisation is predicated on state structures). Exploration of the GSAs and their impact on and assimilation into national states and individual life is a logical development, and recent work on communities by Stuart Hall or Priti Ramamurthy, to name but two, are examples.

But we could hope for more. Cultural studies has explored the ISA-subject or Symbolic-subject, and the hegemony-subjectivity axes largely by putting its practitioners in the position of 'subject', investigating their own subjectivities. This has two effects at least. First, it doesn't investigate the impact on those many people (a majority) who do not appear as 'subjects' within the state. Or even those who do so but to such a marginal extent that their concerns never gather enough mass to become focalised as a disciplinary area in cultural studies. An enormous amount of work is done in the name of cultural studies on biological specificity (what would happen if what cultural studies takes as biology were dropped from the equation?), and virtually none, to take just one example among many, on poverty: do we conclude that most cultural studies workers are not poor? Yet how would cultural studies investigate the discursive elements of lives not recognised as subjected without producing problems analogous to those in anthropology or ethnology? problems that arise from the epistemological set of the investigator as someone with privileged knowledge – privileged to the extent of being empowered, of being subjects, but only recognising that privilege to some degree.

That privilege can never be displaced, but it is possible to learn about different epistemic sets, about people living and working with sets of practices that do not get articulated in or by national or global state structures. This is the classic position of situated knowledge articulated by Sandra Harding as 'strong objectivity'.[21] Yet situated knowledge has to be communicated to have any effect on discursive structures, and in that communication, in the textual strategies and techniques, the communicator is realised/made real/engages critically with the reality of another person. The communication, the textuality of the situation, cannot be practised without working with other people, not that they necessarily effect a 'writing down' in whatever medium, but that they are inextricably part of the forming of the text. This is not as easy as it sounds because the rhetorical strategies for texts are ideologically and/or hegemonically bound to the extent that they are 'heard', legitimated and valued. Working with situated textuality means that we are trying to 'hear' things that can be valued, but which haven't been heard as valuable before – so how do we do so? It's vulnerable-making, risky. We may say things no one else recognises as valuable (till later), we may have to speak in ways no one else hears. *But* cultural studies people, precisely because of their privilege, are in a better position to take risks than many others. But also it's time-consuming and requires commitment to other people, and cultural studies people are often institutionalised into producing work in very short timeframes.

Working on situated textuality also changes us. The second effect of the focus of cultural studies on its own practitioners that I briefly want to look at here, is that it doesn't investigate the sources of subjective agency: what gives us the energy to attempt to change representations. Yes, the theoretical structure of hegemony makes it conceptually possible for us to tell ourselves that we are not over-determined by ideology, that 'desire' can be at least partially represented and publicly recognised. But where does the impetus, even the vocabulary, to do so come from? It's not hegemonic or it wouldn't change the representations. Usually it comes from a position or practice that is happening but is not yet recognised, legit-imated or valued, but oppressed, put down, even authoritatively de-legitimised, thus generating a need. This isn't the location of desire: the lack that representation doesn't allow us to pin down, but need: something we practise but which remains unseen and unheard because its articulation upsets or challenges or destabilises the rep-resentations on offer, something that is often perceived to threaten other people's subjectivities. Culture exists because it articulates hegemonic structure. To the extent that it changes it changes hegemonic power. But how does culture begin to happen? what is culture before it becomes legitimated as such? where does culture come from? and how does it change hegemonic power?

To work on this, cultural studies practitioners could call on those parts of their lives which do not appear within subjectivity. Subjec-tivity calls on notions of the 'universal' insofar as it interconnects with the determinations of ideology: representations. Rhetoric tells us we resist representations in different ways. We can recognise that there is something lacking: desire. We can differ from the gener-alised in our own individualised ways: relativism. We can work with others on the articulation of practices that lie outwith representa-tion: situated textuality. The relative, as an individuated take on representation, is bound to the essentialised self (defined as such by representations in the first place) in a necessary relation. It can facilitate the recognition of different practices, but doesn't usually face the issue of the destabilisation of subjectivity needed to accommodate them. But we can also work on material practices which are not individuated perspectives on generalised or universal representations, by working on different epistemological sets with texts, with verbal articulations. But even though investigating personal practices, this kind of engagement necessitates working with other people's texts, either mediated or with the person (who may not use words, or use them infrequently, or use them in ways not recognised as 'use'). This is what situates the work, makes it different from subjectivity.

Working on material practices with others to articulate their needs or our own, which is one way of realising a non-essential self, generates value. If we work with someone else (singular or plural) on the articulation of a different epistemological set, which by definition might threaten our subjectivity, in the process we constitute the difference between us. Yet because we are both working on it we value that difference – not just recognise it, tolerate it, hate it, admire it, but value it. The process of learning how to value it will inevitably affect everything else that we do or think. It's like changing your diet, engaging in a new friendship, negotiating situations of trust and/or betrayal (both can be valuable). It's messy because it's only partly predictable insofar as material practices are inflected by representation, and frequently destabilising.

And it takes a long time.

NOTES

1. See C. Pateman, *Democracy, Freedom and Special Rights* (Swansea: University of Wales, 1995).
2. E. Laclau and C. Mouffe, *Hegemony and Socialist Strategy: Towards a Radical Democratic Politics*, trans. W. Moore and P. Cammack (London: Verso, 1985), p. 94.
3. S. Hall, 'Introduction: Who Needs Identity?', in P. DuGay and S. Hall (eds), *Questions of Cultural Identity* (London: Sage, 1996), p. 2; and also 'Fantasy, Identity, Politics', in E. Carter, J. Donald and J. Squires (eds), *Cultural Remix* (London: Lawrence and Wishart, 1995), p. 13.
4. Hall, 'Introduction: Who Needs Identity' in DuGay and Hall, *Questions of Cultural Identity*, p. 2.
5. Ibid., p. 5.
6. C. Belsey, *Shakespeare and the Loss of Eden: The Construction of Family Values in Early Modern Culture* (London: Macmillan, 1999), pp. 169–70.
7. Ibid., p. 176.

8. Ibid.
9. See L. Wittgenstein, *Philosophical Investigations*, trans. G. Anscombe (Oxford: Blackwell, 1967).
10. Hall, 'Introduction: Who Needs Identity' in DuGay and Hall, *Questions of Cultural Identity*, p. 1.
11. See, for example, J. Derrida, *The Politics of Friendship*, trans. George Collins (London: Verso, 1997).
12. Belsey, *Shakespeare and the Loss of Eden*, p. 5.
13. Ibid., p. 7.
14. Ibid., p. 12.
15. Ibid.
16. S. Hall, 'Cultural Studies and its Theoretical Legacies', in D. Morley and K.-H. Chen (eds), *Stuart Hall: Critical Dialogues in Cultural Studies* (London: Routledge, 1996).
17. Belsey, *Shakespeare and the Loss of Eden*, p. 13.
18. N. Brossard, 'Writing as a Trajectory of Desire and Consciousness', trans. A. Parker, in A. Parker and E. Meese (eds), *Feminist Critical Negotiations*, (Amsterdam: John Benjamin, 1992).
19. N. Brossard, *Picture Theory: théorie/fiction*, pref. L. Forsyth (Montréal: L'Hexagone, 1989).
20. N. Brossard, *The Aerial Letter*, trans. M. Wildeman (Toronto: Women's Press, 1988); and *Baroque at Dawn*, trans. P. Claxton (Toronto: McClelland and Stewart, 1997).
21. See S. Harding, *Whose Science? Whose Knowledge? Thinking from Women's Lives* (Milton Keynes: Open University Press, 1991).

Contributors

Mieke Bal is Professor of Theory of Literature and a founding director of ASCA (Amsterdam School for Cultural Analysis). Her most recent books are *Quoting Caravaggio: Contemporary Art, Preposterous History* (1999), and *Louise Bourgeois' Spider and the Architecture of Artwriting*.

Catherine Belsey is Professor of English at Cardiff University, where she chairs the Centre for Critical and Cultural Theory. Her books include *Critical Practice* (1980), *Desire: Love Stories in Western Culture* (1994), and *Shakespeare and the Loss of Eden* (1999).

Steven Connor is Professor of Modern Literature and Theory at Birkbeck College, London. He is the author of books on Dickens, Beckett, Joyce and the contemporary novel, as well as *Postmodernist Culture* (1989, revised edition 1996), *Theory and Cultural Value* (1992), and, most recently, *Dumbstruck: A Cultural History of Ventriloquism*. His *Skin: An Historical Poetics* will appear in 2003.

Simon Critchley is Professor of Philosophy at the University of Essex and Directeur de Programme at the College International de Philosophie, Paris. He is author of *The Ethics of Deconstruction* (1992), *Very Little ... Almost Nothing* (1997), *Ethics-Politics-Subjectivity* (1999), *Continental Philosophy: A Very Short Introduction* (2001), and *On Humour* (2002).

Thomas Docherty is Professor of English and Director of Research at the University of Kent; and formerly Professor of English at Trinity College Dublin. He is the author of *Reading (Absent) Character* (1983), *John Donne, Undone* (1986), *On Modern Authority* (1987), *After Theory* (1990; revised and expanded 2nd edition 1996), *Postmodernism* (1993), *Alterities* (1996), and *Criticism and Modernity* (1999). Books on Aesthetics and Democracy are forthcoming; and his current research is on English and the University.

Jeremy Gilbert teaches Cultural Studies at the University of East London. With Ewan Pearson, he is the author of *Discographies: Dance Music, Culture and the Politics of Sound* (1999), and with Timothy

Bewes, the editor of *Cultural Capitalism: Politics after New Labour* (2000). He was the last known convenor of the Signs of the Times group <www.signsofthetimes.org.uk>.

Lynette Hunter is Professor of the History of Rhetoric at the University of Leeds. She has worked in several areas in the arts and sciences, and has published on the philosophy of science and computing, the history and bibliography of household practices, literary criticism and theory, and rhetoric, ethics and politics. Her most recent book is *Critiques of Knowing: Situated Textualities in Science, Computing and the Arts* (1999). Her current work is with people developing new democratic rhetorics.

Martin McQuillan is Senior Lecturer in Cultural Theory and Analysis at the University of Leeds. His publications include *Deconstructing Disney* (with Eleanor Byrne); *Paul de Man*; *Deconstruction: A Reader*; *The Narrative Reader*; *Theorising Muriel Spark*; and the co-edited volume *Post-Theory: New Directions in Criticism*.

John Mowitt is Professor of Cultural Studies and Comparative Literature, and English at the University of Minnesota. He is a senior editor of the journal *Cultural Critique* and has published widely on the topics of theory, culture and politics. His most recent book, *Percussion: Drumming, Beating, Striking*, was published in 2002 by Duke University Press.

Christopher Norris is Distinguished Research Professor in Philosophy at the University of Cardiff in Wales. He has published more than 20 books to date on various aspects of critical theory, philosophy of science, and philosophical semantics. They include – most recently – *Quantum Theory and the Flight from Realism*; *Minding the Gap: Philosophy of Science and Epistemology in the Two Traditions*; *Deconstruction and the Unfinished Project of Modernity*; *Truth Matters: Realism, Anti-Realism and Response-Dependence*; and *Hilary Putnam: Realism, Reason, and the Uses of Uncertainty*. His 1982 book, *Deconstruction: Theory and Practice*, will soon be appearing in a revised and expanded edition to mark the twenty-fifth anniversary of the Methuen/Routledge 'New Accents' series.

Griselda Pollock is Professor of Social and Critical Histories of Art at the University of Leeds. Between 1987 and 2000 she was Director of the Centre for Cultural Studies and is now Director of the AHRB Centre for Cultural Analysis, Theory and History at Leeds. Recent publications include *Differencing the Canon: Feminist Desire and the Writing of Art's Histories* (1999), and *Looking Back to the Future: Essays on Art, Life and Death* (2000). She is working on a book *Theatre of Memory: Representation and Trauma in the work of Charlotte Salomon* and a collection of essays called *Towards a Virtual Feminist Museum*. Her current interests include relations between femininity, modernity and representation and representations of trauma and cultural memory.

Adrian Rifkin is Professor of Visual Culture and Media at Middlesex University. He is the author of *Street Noises: Parisian Pleasure 1900–1940* (1993), and *Ingres Then, and Now* (2000). He has researched and written widely in cultural and art history on topics ranging from popular music and opera to Kantian aesthetics and gay subjectivities. He is editor of the journal, *Art History*.

Jeremy Valentine teaches Cultural Studies at Queen Margaret University College, Edinburgh. He is co-author of *Polemicization* (1999), with Benjamin Arditi, and co-editor of the monograph series *Taking On the Political*. He is currently thinking about relations between Culture and Governance.

Julian Wolfreys is Professor of Victorian Literary and Cultural Studies with the Department of English at the University of Florida. Amongst his recent publications are *Victorian Hauntings: Spectrality, the Gothic, the Uncanny, and Literature* (2001), and *Readings: Close Acts of Reading in Literary Theory* (2000).

Index

Sand, Georges, 115
Sartre, Jean Paul, 116, 121, 176,
   236
Saussure, Ferdinand de, 77, 105,
   116
Schmitt, Carl, 177
Schönberg, 88, 114
Schopenhauer, 84
Schubert, 88
Schumann, 88
Schuppers, Martijn, 36
science, 26, 27, 71, 77, 86, 185, 222,
   228–9, 236, 243, 244
Screen, 22, 23, 110
Scruton, Roger, 90, 93, 94
second person narrative, 36
semiotics, 28, 77, 96, 127, 134, 136,
   186, 187, 194, 195
September 11th, 74–5
Serres, 210
Sewell, William, 115
sexism, 1, 141, 149, 151, 175
sex/uality, 23, 107, 127, 128, 129,
   132–6, 141, 147, 148, 152, 179,
   187, 227, 239
Shakespeare, 27
Signs of the Times, 67, 159
Simmel, Georg, 210
The Simpsons, 25
simulacrum, 236
Snow, C.P., 222, 226
social sciences, 33
social studies of science and
   technology, 244
sociology, 22, 28, 45, 76, 81, 86, 97,
   126, 137, 210, 213
Soundings, 159
Spark, Muriel, 44
spectropoetics, 166
Spivak, Gayatri Chakravorty, 45,
   137, 165
Staffordshire University, 44
stakeholder pensions, 110
Stalinism, 102, 130, 131
Steadman, Carolyn, 119
Stedman-Jones, Gareth, 115
Steele, Tom, 125
Stradling, Rob, 87
Stravinsky, 89, 114, 229

structuralism, 93, 116, 117, 126
subject, 60, 103, 106, 119–20, 128,
   129, 131, 133, 134, 141, 151,
   152, 155, 156, 176, 193–5, 202,
   203, 204, 235, 236, 238, 239,
   243, 246, 247, 249, 250, 251
superstructure, 112, 126, 131
The Sopranos, 203
Sussex university, 138
symptom, 8, 14n1, 102, 176, 200,
   202

Tarantino, Quentin, 25
Tavener, John, 91
teleiopoeisis, 50
teleology, 113, 154
Teletubbies, 100, 107–8
Tel Quel, 96, 110, 116
text, 24, 27, 32, 42, 52, 96, 98, 108,
   120, 121, 122, 124, 129, 164,
   169, 233, 249
textuality/intertextuality,10, 37, 80,
   98, 108, 116, 117, 122, 124, 127,
   134, 168, 170, 235, 239, 240–5,
   249
Thatcher/ism, 19, 146, 147, 159,
   204
Thompson, E.P., 21, 23, 25, 29n1,
   102–3, 130
Tillyard, E.M.W., 21
time, 119, 122, 195, 245, 250
The Times, 93
Tintin, 52
Titanic, 65
Tönnies, 211
transcendental aberration, 48
translation, 6–7, 52, 73, 95, 169,
   187, 224, 240, 247
trauma studies, 175
Trent University, 180
Turner Prize, 25

Umbr(a), 120
United States, 67, 75, 125, 129, 132,
   162, 163, 165, 173, 177–8, 180,
   181, 183, 186, 187, 226, 230, 243
university, 7, 13, 21, 25, 46, 48, 49,
   50, 54, 66, 67, 68, 69, 73, 78, 93,